W9-ANB-777

Boys and Foreign Language Learning

Boys and Foreign Language Learning

Real Boys Don't Do Languages

Jo Carr
Queensland University of Technology

and

Anne Pauwels
The University of Western Australia

macmillan

First published 2006 by
PALGRAVE MACMILLAN
Houndmills, Basingstoke, Hampshire RG21 6XS and
175 Fifth Avenue, New York, N. Y. 10010
Companies and representatives throughout the world

PALGRAVE MACMILLAN is the global academic imprint of the Palgrave Macmillan division of St. Martin's Press, LLC and of Palgrave Macmillan Ltd. Macmillan® is a registered trademark in the United States, United Kingdom and other countries. Palgrave is a registered trademark in the European Union and other countries.

ISBN-13: 978–1–4039–3967–8 hardback
ISBN-10: 1–4039–3967–5 hardback

This book is printed on paper suitable for recycling and made from fully managed and sustained forest sources.

A catalogue record for this book is available from the British Library.

Library of Congress Cataloging-in-Publication Data
Carr, Jo, 1943–
    Boys and foreign language learning : real boys don't do languages / Jo Carr, Anne Pauwels.
      p. cm.
    Includes bibliographical references and index.
    ISBN 1–4039–3967–5
      1. Language and languages—Study and teaching. 2. Sex differences in education. 3. Language and languages—Sex differences. 4. Boys––Education. I. Pauwels, Anne. II. Title.

P53.775.C37 2005
418'.0071—dc22

                                      2005051272

10 9 8 7 6 5 4 3 2 1
15 14 13 12 11 10 09 08 07 06

Transferred to digital printing in 2006.

For Kylie and Sasha Carr

Contents

Preface

This book has been a long time in the making. The research project around which it is structured had small beginnings more than a decade ago in North Queensland, Australia; our interest in the issue of gender and foreign language study, however, goes back much further. We thought it worthwhile to briefly summarise our respective routes to this exploration of boys' relationship with languages education.

Jo Carr

My experience of learning a language in school – French – began in an all-girls school in Yorkshire in the late 1950s. The question of boys and language study, therefore, wasn't one we thought about. Boys were occasionally encountered at inter-school language competitions, where they typically did less well than we did, appearing uncomfortable and embarrassed by the whole event; and there was a vague sense that brothers tended not to choose languages as much as we did; but this didn't really add up to any sense of languages being more of a 'female' than a 'male' project. In Yorkshire in the 1950s, gender wasn't an issue. There were no critical analyses of gendered curricula or gendered language practices; no affirmative action for girls in maths and sciences or boys in arts and languages. The one male teacher in our school taught history; and our French teacher, a wonderfully dynamic, very French (to our eyes) woman, was the single reason why many of us went on to study French at university.

It was at university that gender began to appear around the edges of my consciousness; not in any theorised or critical way, more as a realisation that the majority of my fellow languages students were, like me, female. This was more a social realisation than any kind of sociological analysis. Male students studying languages were a minority group; a rather exotic one, not just because they were few in number, but because they tended to come back from the compulsory study-abroad year smoking Gauloises and wearing leather jackets. As an undergraduate, then as a postgraduate student, I accepted as normal the fact that most language students were female (although most senior academic positions were held by men).

Once out in the workforce, teaching high-school French before moving into the allied trades of educational publishing and broadcasting, my sense of the 'gendering' of languages education became further settled into the common sense of 'how things are'. There was a general understanding that languages are, on the whole, what girls do. They are 'good' at them; boys are 'better' at other things. These understandings informed what we did, as language teachers and programme developers, and were continuously reinforced by broader school-based practices. A move to Australia in the 1970s confirmed the truth of this account. Australian boys were even less interested in languages than British boys; probably, I assumed, because they were further removed from the possibility of 'real' encounters with native speakers (in North Queensland in the 1970s the languages offered in schools were still mainly European, with Asian languages only just beginning to be introduced). I taught large cohorts of equal numbers of boys and girls for the first year of compulsory language study at high school; and some of the most enthusiastic and successful learners were boys. I was regularly dismayed when they disappeared en masse at the first post-compulsory moment. This was the beginning of a more focused interest in the 'boys don't do languages' phenomenon. In spite of my best efforts to keep them – in what I now see to be very inequitable affirmative action – they continued to disappear. I dedicated most of our 'culture' time in class to what I believed to be boy-friendly topics: stories of World War 2 French resistance fighters; military manoeuvres; the Tour de France; my own manoeuvres clearly reflecting my understanding at that stage of both 'gender' and foreign language teaching methodology; and they were for the most part unsuccessful. There were some powerful influences in play which I had no way of counteracting – or, at that stage, understanding.

Several years later, after a long absence from both teaching and academic work, I reconnected with both, enrolling in postgraduate study which included language and literacy education, but also gender studies and critical, discourse-oriented studies. Like all gender studies novitiates, I experienced the inevitable 'road to Damascus' gender realisations: seeing gender everywhere, in my own professional and personal relationships; in my children's negotiation of individual and collective identities; in workplace relations and the political world order. And the boys–languages relationship came back for reconsideration.

I moved from postgraduate study to teacher education, where I have worked for the last ten years, finding myself directly reconnected with language classrooms and gender issues. Over all this time, and across these different contexts, there has been little change in the profile of language learners. Language classrooms continue to be peopled mainly by girls and women. The majority of language teachers are women. Boys continue to show massive disinterest in the foreign languages option. As a pre-service language teacher educator, I scan the list of incoming enrolled students each year, hoping to see a more equal balance between male and female contenders; and every year I see the same imbalance: at best 5–10 per cent of incoming pre-service language teachers will be male. I have thought about this issue from many angles now: as a language learner, as a French teacher, as a first-language/literacy educator with an interest in language and gender, as a pre-service language teacher educator of both domestic and international students, as a parent, as an in-service consultant to teachers in the field. My thinking around the issue has shifted significantly in terms of informing frames. Critical cross-disciplinary debates around language, culture, identity and discourse have long since moved me from the 'how things are' frame to a more critical, interrogative, socially and culturally informed position of considering the boys–languages relationship as a 'text' which sits within several constituting contexts. And so I reached a point of feeling confident in terms of theorising the boys–languages relationship: 'recognising' core elements which have sustained its shape over such a long time and through such changing external conditions; and it became time to test these theoretical understandings, to look for confirmation (or reconfiguration) from real data. It was time to go to the source, talk with boys and find out what they had to say about themselves, about foreign languages as a curriculum option, and about their experience in language classrooms.

Anne Pauwels

My experience in the area of languages learning and teaching is rather different from Jo's. I grew up in a country with official bilingualism where the learning of foreign languages was compulsory (at least of the first foreign language). Boys as well as girls engaged in foreign language learning in similar numbers at least up to matriculation. At university the presence of men in foreign language study was also not exceptional: there certainly were fewer men than women engaging in the study of (mainly) European languages but male students were not a 'rarity' in the tertiary language learning environment, making up about 40 per cent of most classes. This changed quite dramatically when I moved to the Australian university environment in the early 1980s. There I taught German and class composition was almost entirely female. In fact it was unusual to have more than five males in a class of 20 students irrespective of the level (beginners, intermediate or advanced levels). Those male students who did participate were usually quite motivated and were very similar to their female counterparts in terms of linguistic/language proficiency. Furthermore my experience did not seem to be unusual, with colleagues teaching other languages at university experiencing similar enrolment patterns. Involved in language contact research, I did not analyse this gendered participation pattern further but assumed it was 'just an Australian thing'.

After some time my research on language maintenance and language shift in Australian immigrant communities brought me back in contact with gender and language. Analyses of language use patterns in several migrant communities revealed that women and men behaved differently in terms of the maintenance of the migrant language and the acquisition of English (Pauwels, 1995). In the early 1990s I also became involved in analysing the attitudes and motivations of Australian students towards the study of foreign languages – known in the Australian context as either Community Languages or Languages other than English – LOTE (Fernandez, Pauwels and Clyne, 1993). The findings of these projects showed again that gender was a significant factor in understanding language learning dynamics in Australia. An analysis of the gender dimension had to wait though until I completed other work which focused on gender and language reform (Pauwels, 1998). A conversation with Jo, during a Modern Language Teachers congress in Canberra where she had presented findings from her research into the boys–languages relationship in North Queensland triggered our collaboration on this larger project.

The research project

As indicated, the project began on a small scale, as a pilot study, funded by a regional university. About 30 boys in one of the largest state high schools in the region were interviewed, some continuing with languages, most having dropped out; and the findings were overwhelmingly discouraging (Carr and Frankom, 1997). From this small sample, the message was loud and clear: languages are not an option taken seriously by the majority of boys. They are seen as irrelevant, uninteresting, and – for many boys – discouragingly difficult. More than anything else, however, they are too closely associated in boys' minds with girls.

When the findings of this pilot study were presented at a national conference in Canberra in 2001, a surprising number of teachers came forward with accounts of their own experience working with boys, requests for support, advice, information, some encouraging success stories, but many more accounts of concern and frustration. Invitations were issued to address professional associations and national conferences, in

New Zealand as well as in Australia; this appeared to be the 'sleeping dog' issue of languages education; and it seemed time to embark on a more substantial exploration of the boys–languages relationship.

It was at that point that Anne Pauwels expressed interest in being involved in a larger project to collect a substantial corpus of data and engage in more theoretically detailed analysis. Her contribution is presented in Chapter 2, where she provides the broader framing of the more locally-situated boys–languages relationship explored in the book, placing it both in historical and cross-communities context. She has also provided helpful feedback at various stages of the project, especially at the final stages, contributing her knowledge and expertise in terms of thinking about the global dimension of the issues and contributing occasional additional data from research which she carried out some years ago.

Acknowledgements

We wish to thank the schools who allowed us access to their students, the teachers who contributed significantly both to the impetus and the implementation of this project, and, most of all, the students who talked with us. Their good will, thoughtfulness, humour and energy made this an enjoyable as well as productive research experience.

We would also like to thank Julia Rothwell for her valuable assistance in collecting and collating enrolment data on language learning around the English-speaking world; and the educational departments who assisted her in this work: the Department of Education and Skills, United Kingdom; the Data Management Unit, New Zealand Ministry of Education; the Scottish Qualifications Authority; the Northern Territory (Australia) Department of Employment, Education and Training; the New South Wales (Australia) Office of the Board of Studies; the South Australian Department of Education and Children's Services; the Victorian Department of Education and Training (Australia); the Queensland (Australia) Studies Authority; the Western Australian Department of Education and Training.

Finally, we thank Mitchell Ryan, a student at Kelvin Grove State College, Brisbane, who provided the cover photo to the book: a much appreciated contribution.

1
Introduction

Contextual frame

From the moment when foreign language study becomes optional, classrooms across the English-dominant communities of the world are inhabited primarily by girls and staffed predominantly by women: boys for the most part disappear. Foreign language classrooms, it would seem, are considered inappropriate or uninteresting places to be. Although this has not always been the case, this gendered shape of foreign language programmes has long since settled into the status of 'how things are'; there is nothing new about the situation, which is only occasionally commented on. What *is* new, however, is the context within which it now sits.

Educational thinking is currently framed by discourses of multiliteracies and global citizenship. The world outside school is recognised as requiring new kinds of competencies and skills, presenting new kinds of opportunities and challenges. Intercultural competence is identified as a core targeted outcome and young speakers of the global language are officially encouraged to join in the global project of increased intercultural communication. Proficiency in additional languages would seem to be an obvious component of this agenda; yet the majority of boys continue to refuse the languages option. And the fact that players in the increasingly imagined global games will consist largely of all-girls teams seems to be of minimal concern to educators, parents or to students themselves.

There is a second context to the boys–languages relationship which also makes the lack of interest in boys' disinterest surprising. Countries such as Canada, Australia, the United States and the United Kingdom are currently collectively reporting themselves as being in 'crisis' in relation to boys and schooling. Recent studies into gender equity, gender disadvantage, that is, gender differences in terms of what happens in

1

classrooms, indicate that the 'gender' which is now the locus of concern is that of boys (for an overview, see Collins, Kenway and McLeod, 2000). Boys are increasingly constructed as a disadvantaged and problematic group in school; underachieving in comparison to girls, particularly in the areas of language and literacy. This concern is translating into initiatives to improve their level of engagement and learning outcomes in these areas; but intervention is directed almost exclusively at first language and literacy. Little attention is accorded to the continuing poor representation of boys in foreign language programmes. While educational planners, teachers, parents and wider communities engage in vigorous debates about boys and literacy, about multiliteracies and boy-friendly pathways to literate futures, there is continuing silence in most quarters about boys and foreign languages. The literate futures are seemingly understood as uniquely English-speaking places.

This book represents a contribution to the empty space in the conversation about boys, education and foreign language learning. It comes out of a determination to find out more about the issue from the perspective of boys themselves; to see how they think about themselves as boys in school, as learners and – most particularly – as foreign language learners. It acknowledges the interconnection between foreign language study and the broader, more foundational relationship between language, culture and socially constituted masculinities; and draws upon theories of discourse, culture and gender constitution, as well as on findings on masculinity, schooling and languages education. In this sense, then, it is an academic, theoretically framed project; but it is a grounded one, built around commentaries collected from conversations with more than 200 boys, aged between 12 and 18, from a variety of school contexts and backgrounds; with commentary, too, from teachers and girls who work alongside boys in language classrooms.

It is important to clarify that the focus is not on *all* boys studying *all* foreign languages. It is on boys in the major Anglophone countries of the world: The United Kingdom, the United States, parts of Canada, New Zealand and Australia – where the project was carried out. These are what Kachru (1996) would refer to as 'inner circle' boys – native speakers of the global language; for the most part, comfortably monolingual boys. As will emerge from both the data and analysis, this first fact is part of the boys–languages 'problem'. Incidental conversations with boys from other language backgrounds not included in this study produce different accounts. Boys from countries such as Japan, Norway, France, Hong Kong or Korea speak differently about foreign language learning. Many, of course, are learning English, which represents access to valued cultural capital, a global commodity; but many are not only bilingual, they are multilingual. They know from lived experience the usefulness of additional language and cultural proficiency; and while many (not all) subscribe to the stereotypical views that come through our data from English-speaking boys – about girls being 'better communicators' – they appear to have no gendered sense of languages being an inappropriate curriculum option for boys. The issue of compulsion is certainly part of the equation. For most of these boys, languages have never been an optional elective, but rather an ongoing, compulsory, core component of their education. This is an important difference. Signals from the wider community that languages are (or are not) important are noted and internalised.

It is also important to clarify that this project itself involves some 'empty spaces' in terms of focus and analysis. The notion that there is no such thing as a 'generic' boy – that gender always intersects with other key informing social variables – is central to the analysis; and the variable which emerged most saliently from the data collected in this project is that of social class. The boys in this study speak from distinctively different social spaces; and this has been selected as the variable which is in this case most helpful in terms of identifying the complexity and variability of the boys–languages relationship. An equally relevant and complex analysis would have been an exploration of the relationship between boys from other-language backgrounds and in-school language programs. This dimension of the boys–languages issue fell outside the parameters of this study, but is clearly an equally important focus waiting to be explored.

The structure of the book

Following this introductory chapter, Chapter 2 sets the scene in broader terms. A short review of the history of the boys–foreign languages relationship, together with an outlining of the participation of boys and girls in foreign language learning in four regions – Australia, England and Wales, New Zealand and Scotland – provide an informing frame to the following chapters. Many of the issues which subsequently emerge from the data can be linked back to the patterns traced here. Chapter 3 provides closer discussion of the key contexts in which the boys–languages relationship is being played out, identifying the discourses, debates and various positions currently framing the 'problem', as well as identifying the points of connection between the boys-schooling-languages discussions and wider cultural conditions. This chapter elaborates the theoretical frame which guides subsequent analysis of the data.

Chapter 4 is the first of the four data chapters. After an introductory account of the circumstances and approaches to data collection, the chapter presents the commentaries collected from boys in state schools, who talk in detail about their sense of themselves as boys, as students in school and as communicators/language learners. They talk about their experience in foreign language classrooms, and about the teachers – and the teaching – which went with this experience. The following chapter, Chapter 5, presents commentaries collected via the same process but from different contexts, from boys enrolled in private/independent schools. The same issues are explored, the same questions asked; and some clear similarities show up in the commentaries collected. But there are also some interesting differences in how these boys talk about the languages option; differences which indicate the significance of the intersection of different social and cultural variables.

Chapter 6, the third of the data chapters, shifts focus from the voices of boys themselves to the voices of teachers who work with these boys. They talk about similar issues, and are seen to share remarkably similar opinions in many respects with boys themselves. Their comments reveal the tensions involved in teaching (boys or girls) when it comes to aligning theory with practice; and gender is seen to be an interesting point of focus in this respect. Their comments indicate the extent to which pedagogy is shaped by teachers' understandings of how boys/girls 'are'. Chapter 7, the final of the four data chapters, provides insight into how girls 'read' the boys they share the language classroom with – from the other side of the divide. This complementary evidence shows how closely differently situated cultural narratives about boys parallel each other, cumulatively constructing a solid binary account of boys/girls as learners and communicators.

Chapter 8 reconnects with the original research questions which framed this project in light of both the evidence presented in the preceding chapters and the conceptual frame outlined in Chapter 3. The final chapter, Chapter 9 – resisting the temptation to offer definitive conclusions or fail-safe solutions – considers the implications of the intersecting frames which impact on the boys–languages relationship and suggests some points of departure for developing dialogue, changing thinking and ultimately transforming practice in ways which might result in more appropriate levels of engagement by young people of both sexes in the project of additional language learning.

2
Setting the Scene

Foreign language learning: the learning of another language

The central focus of this book is the relationship of male students to the learning of a language other than their 'first' or 'native' language. The nomenclature used to describe this *other language* is multifarious, reflecting different attitudes towards such languages as well as the differing status of such languages in a country or community. Examples of naming include *modern language, classical language, community language, heritage language, minority language, language other than English, foreign language*. The term *foreign language* is probably the most widespread, although it is certainly not the most popular, especially in multilingual communities where the *other language* is in fact not *foreign,* but very much part of the everyday linguistic landscape. In fact in countries like Australia there have been significant debates around appropriate nomenclature for languages used in the community and learned in schools (e.g., Lo Bianco, 1987; Clyne, 1982). Our adoption of the term *foreign language* is somewhat reluctant in view of these debates and of the rather loaded meaning associated with the word *foreign*. However, our choice is motivated primarily by convenience: as the terms *foreign language* and *foreign language learning* are well known across the English language world, we use them as umbrella terms for the many terms associated in various communities with the learning of another language. We will minimise its use, however, by often referring to our topic as the *boys–languages relationship*.

Foreign language learning in English language countries: a historically gendered area of study?

In the introduction we mentioned that the incentive for this book came in large part from our personal experiences and observations as language

5

professionals regarding the reluctance of many boys to participate in foreign language learning. In this chapter we explore to what extent our observations – and those of many other language professionals working in English language countries – are backed up by numerical or statistical evidence regarding boys' participation in school-based foreign language learning. Prior to presenting this statistical profile, we address briefly the question of whether foreign language learning has historically been a gendered area of study. It is not our intention to undertake a historical survey of foreign language learning in English language countries, but to highlight some milestones in education and language education which shed light on the question of foreign language learning as a potentially gendered area of study.

Before the introduction of universal access to primary education in England in 1944 (1944 Education Act), education – either school-based or through private (home) tutoring – was a privilege accorded primarily to the sons of the upper and middle classes. These boys had access to education from the thirteenth century, with the introduction of grammar schools, the so-called *libera schola grammaticalis*. Language study, in particular the study of Latin and Ancient Greek, featured prominently in the curriculum of these early grammar schools, with German and French being added in later centuries. Until the daughters of such elites started to receive education, foreign language study was, therefore, an exclusively male domain. Although little is known about boys' attitudes to the study of languages in those times, the continued prominence of foreign language study in the expanding academic curriculum offered to boys in the eighteenth and nineteenth centuries seems to suggest that languages were not considered 'feminine' or inappropriate for a boy's education. Perhaps the only gendering that occurred in those days was linked to the choice of language to be studied. When the daughters of the social elite were given access to education through home tutoring – usually provided by governesses and later through grammar schools – their curriculum often included a foreign language, usually French, but later also Italian and sometimes German. It seldom stretched, however, to the Classical languages – Latin or Ancient Greek. There was no evidence of a dramatic change in foreign language study among the boys when girls started accessing formal education.

Similar observations can be made for other English language countries, especially Australia and New Zealand whose educational systems were heavily based on the English system (e.g., Ozolins, 1993; Pauwels, 2004, 2005). In these countries there was also no evidence that boys shunned this area of study. Perhaps the more telling observation to be made about past participation in foreign language study is one of social class and, indirectly, intellectual privilege. In most English language countries foreign language study was mainly if not solely available in schools preparing the intellectual elite for entry to university study. These schools were heavily skewed towards the children of the middle and upper classes, not least because of the fees attached to schooling. The rigour of learning a foreign language was seen to be a good indicator of intellectual capabilities. Thus the study of a foreign language, preferably a Classical language, was often a prerequisite to university entry irrespective of the course of study to be undertaken. We should note here that this approach to foreign language learning was very different from current models and approaches. Text exegesis was the focus of attention: texts were analysed in terms of linguistic and grammatical structures as well as for their literary qualities. Whilst oral proficiency was not excluded, it did not feature prominently in the teaching or learning of foreign languages.

Changes in enrolment patterns started to occur when foreign language study became more universally accessible across age groups and school types and when the rationale for foreign language learning moved away from a primary focus on text exegesis and acquaintance with 'high' culture, to one which included linguistic and communicative competence as well as exposure to various cultural expressions and practices. In countries like Australia, New Zealand and the United Kingdom this led to more languages being taught in more schools at both primary and secondary level. For example in the mid-twentieth century in Australia, less than a handful of languages were routinely available for study in schools and fewer still were offered to matriculation level. By the early twenty-first century, secondary school students have access to more than 40 languages in which they can take final examinations. Furthermore, almost all secondary schools offer a choice of languages for study, usually including at least one Asian and one European language. The language learning scene in the United Kingdom has also expanded in the past 50 years, students now having opportunities to study up to 20 languages for their GCSE level. Importantly, foreign language study is now also available in vocational education. The increased choice and availability of foreign language study in a broader range of schools have brought about changes in the place and perceived value of languages in education. Whilst many of these changes have been welcomed and have raised the profile of foreign language learning both in educational circles and in the wider community, they do not seem to have dispelled stereotypical views about foreign language learning being difficult and therefore only suitable for the academically 'gifted', or that foreign language learning is a luxury not relevant for most employment areas. Furthermore, the introduction of many new areas of study in the school curriculum has meant that foreign language study now competes against many other subjects, often perceived as more rewarding, more relevant to the workforce and less difficult.

These developments have foregrounded the dynamics between foreign language study and gender. In the following sections we explore this dynamic from a statistical perspective by comparing enrolment patterns of boys and girls in foreign language study in four countries.

Boys and girls participating in school-based foreign language learning: a statistical overview

Although our main purpose in this book is to explore the reasons and motivations for boys (not) participating in school-based foreign language learning, there is value in having some knowledge of the extent of participation of both boys and girls in languages programmes. The exercise of providing accurate figures for their respective participation is, however, fraught with immense difficulties, mainly due to the substantial inter-country differences in educational systems, their data collection and data management procedures. In addition, the place of foreign language learning in the school curriculum varies from country to country, as does the range of languages offered for study. Another difficulty has been the lack of consistency in providing a sex-based breakdown for foreign language study: for example, in Australia some states (which control school-based education) provide the breakdown by sex as a matter of course, whereas others do so only for particular years or levels of study. Also problematic has been the variation in the recency of figures: in most cases we have been able to obtain figures collected in the early 2000s: 2001, 2002 and even 2003; but in some cases the figures date from the late 1990s. These difficulties mean we have had to limit the detail we can provide about boys' and girls' participation in foreign language programmes. We would also like to stress that the contrasts and differences noted at national level do not adequately reflect what happens at local levels – the individual school or a particular classroom. For example our later chapters speak of classrooms in which only one or two boys participate, suggesting a more dramatic dimension to the gendered nature of foreign language learning than that discerned from a national profile. Therefore the statistical picture provided in this chapter should be seen primarily as a means of discerning *trends* about gendered participation rather than as detailed *evidence* of such participation. The information presented in the tables below has been compiled using publicly available data provided by a range of educational authorities in Australia, New Zealand and the United Kingdom, with sub-data for Scotland.

As this book is not intended to be a comparative study of foreign language learning in several countries, we will not analyse or discuss any inter-country differences other than those directly pertaining to the focus of the book – boys' and girls' participation in language programmes. Hence we won't comment on the differential range of languages available for study or on the place and status of foreign language learning in the school curricula across the selected countries.

Overall participation in foreign language study by girls and boys

In Table 1 we present the overall participation rates for boys and girls in the study of foreign languages in three countries: Australia, New Zealand and the United Kingdom, with separate figures for Scotland. Overall participation rates comprise both compulsory (for Australia, United Kingdom, Scotland) and post-compulsory levels for foreign language learning. Inclusion of the compulsory levels clearly tempers the extent of difference. Table 1 reveals remarkably similar trends, however, across the countries. In all cases boys participate less in foreign language learning than do girls, with the most pronounced difference occurring in New Zealand, where there is no compulsory foreign language study. The results from this table point to the fact that gendered participation in foreign language learning is clearly not unique to a particular country or educational system.

Participation rates by boys and girls at different levels of schooling

Of greater interest and relevance to this study is the tracking of participation rates in foreign language study across different levels of schooling. Unfortunately – due to the very substantial differences between the countries in how the curriculum is organised, that is, when the study of a foreign language is introduced, whether there is a compulsory stage and if so, when the transition to optional study sets in – it did not prove possible to provide a cross-country comparison of the breakdown

Table 1 Female and male participation rates in foreign language learning (per cent)

	Country			
	Australia	United Kingdom England/Wales	United Kingdom Scotland	New Zealand
Female	54.5	54	56	59.6
Male	45.5	46	44	40.4

between compulsory and non- or post-compulsory foreign language study. Instead we have attempted to capture for each country the difference at different levels of schooling, which frequently coincide with compulsory or optional stages.

Australia

For Australia we can provide a breakdown for participation rates at primary school level and secondary school level with specification of enrolment in the final year of schooling. The availability of foreign language study at primary school level is neither universal nor compulsory at this stage, although there is an overall positive attitude towards its introduction: depending on the state and school system (public vs private), students between the ages of 6 and 12 may have access to the learning of a foreign language, usually referred to as LOTE – Language other than English. At secondary level there is usually a period of compulsory LOTE study, most notably in the early years of secondary schooling, followed by optional language study until the final year. Most schools, especially those in large urban areas, offer more than one language for compulsory study. The final year figures give the best indication of participation rates at the non-compulsory stage – students who do not plan to sit the final exam in a foreign language will not be undertaking foreign language study at this level. The data in Table 2 are slighter older, dating back to 1999, due to the absence of more recent comprehensive data. Table 2 shows an interesting pattern of gendered participation rate across different levels of schooling: although foreign language study is not a compulsory part of the primary school curriculum, those primary schools that decide to offer it to students do in fact treat the study as compulsory. In other words, if the school offers a foreign language then all students at particular year levels will participate in it. Consequently girls' and boys' participation rates at primary school level are very similar, because all government primary schools and the majority of private primary schools are co-educational (open to boys and girls). The secondary school figures

Table 2   Participation rates for female and male students across different levels of schooling in Australia (per cent)

	Level		
	Primary school	**Secondary school**	**Final year**
Female	49.8	56.4	62
Male	50.2	43.6	38

include around six years of schooling. Usually at least two years of secondary schooling involve the compulsory learning of a foreign language.

Comparing primary, secondary and final year enrolments in LOTE study shows the increasing 'gendering' of foreign language study. By the final year of schooling the contrast is starkest, with girls making up almost two-thirds of final year students of foreign languages.

New Zealand

For New Zealand we can only report on figures pertaining to the secondary level of schooling covering Years 9 to 13. Foreign language learning is available in some primary schools in New Zealand, but statistics do not show a breakdown by sex. Whilst New Zealand does not have compulsory foreign language learning, most schools offer widespread opportunities to study languages in Years 9 and 10. The New Zealand results displayed in Table 3 continue the trend established in relation to Australia: boys participate less than girls at all levels, with their participation decreasing significantly at higher levels. Final year participation levels are very similar to those found in the Australian context.

Table 3 Female and male participation rates at different year levels in New Zealand (per cent)

	Level		
	Year 9–10	**Year 11–13**	**Final year (13)**
Female	57	67	65
Male	43	33	35

United Kingdom

For the United Kingdom – excluding Scotland – we obtained figures for students' participation in language courses at both GCSE and to A level. Until recently (2003), the study of a foreign language was compulsory up to GCSE level, which is reflected in the figures below which date from 2003. Taking a language up to A level is not compulsory. Despite the compulsory nature of language learning at GCSE level, we note in Table 4 some degree of gender-based differentiation with more girls taking a foreign language than boys. The A level figures reveal a much more significant gender difference, with two-thirds of A level enrolments being girls and only one-third boys. These figures are again similar to those found for final year participation rates in both New Zealand and Australia.

Scotland

The Scottish educational system underwent significant changes in 2000 which saw the introduction of the SCQF – Scottish Credit and Qualifications Framework. The SCQF recognises 12 different levels, six of which (Levels 2 to 7) would normally be associated with courses and awards undertaken during primary and secondary schooling. They include courses of Standard Grade, Intermediate Grades and Higher Grades. Table 5 distinguishes participation rates according to these grades. The results emerging from this table are in line with the trends reported for England and Wales as well as for Australia. Boys' participation in foreign language study is lower than that of girls, with the difference increasing across grade levels. The difference between boys and girls' participation rates at advanced levels is even more pronounced than for Australia or the United Kingdom: in the Scottish context fewer than 25 per cent of participants in intermediate and advanced grade foreign language study are boys.

The most interesting observation emerging from these tables is the remarkable similarity across these English-dominant countries in terms of girls' and boys' take-up of foreign language study. The difference hovers around 12 per cent (except for New Zealand where it is 20 per cent) in favour of girls for overall participation rate, but this difference increases markedly at post-compulsory or more advanced stages of study. At these

Table 4   Participation rates for female and male students at GCSE and A level in United Kingdom excluding Scotland (per cent)

	Level	
	GCSE	A level
Female	53	66
Male	47	34

Table 5   Participation rates for female and male students at various grades in Scotland (per cent)

	Level		
	Standard	Intermediate 1 + 2	Higher and Adv. Higher
Female	52	76.5	76.4
Male	48	23.5	23.4

levels boys generally make up only between one-third and one-quarter of students. This is a significant difference given that these figures represent trends at national levels. It can therefore be expected that trends and differences at more local levels – of individual schools or classrooms – may be even more pronounced. This is certainly the impression gained from listening to the evidence which emerges through the voices of both students and teachers in the following chapters. The much lower participation rate of boys at the advanced, pre-university level has clear implications for the recruitment of men to post-secondary or university-level foreign language study, the training ground for foreign language teachers. The low representation of male teachers in foreign language classrooms contributes to the view that foreign language learning is a feminised area of study.

The gendering of language choice

We were also interested in following up the perception – supported by anecdotal evidence – that some languages are more 'feminine' than others, therefore attracting even less interest from boys. We were able to collect some data on enrolment and participation patterns in specific foreign languages for each of the countries, the breakdown by sex for the study of specific languages shedding further light on the gendering of foreign language study. Below we explore for each country to what extent the overall trend of girls' greater participation is replicated across different languages and whether a 'gendering' occurs in the selection of the languages studied. As the number and type of languages available for study vary across countries, we present our findings by country. Where possible we also report participation rates at different levels of study.

Australia

The greatest choice and variety in school-based language study was found in Australia, where more than 40 languages are available for study up to final examinations level (matriculation). Most states offer up to 10 languages, but Victoria and New South Wales offer many more, although not all of these are available for study in day school. In Table 6 we have included the gender breakdown for ten languages which are not only widely available but are widely studied across Australia. This is especially the case for Chinese, French, German, Indonesian, Italian and Japanese. The participation rates relate to foreign language study from Years 7 to 12 (i.e., secondary education).

Enrolments in French, German, Italian and Japanese reveal the greatest gender differentiation, with approximately 60 per cent of enrolments being female. Less pronounced differences relate to Indonesian,

Table 6   Female and male participation rates in 10 languages in Australia (per cent)

Language	Female	Male
Arabic	57.7	42.3
Chinese	45.4	54.6
French	62.0	38.0
German	59.0	41.0
Greek (Modern)	49.0	51.0
Indonesian	52.8	47.3
Italian	58.8	41.2
Japanese	58.2	41.5
Spanish	52.2	47.8
Vietnamese	51.9	48.1

Vietnamese, Spanish and Modern Greek. With the exception of Modern Greek, female participation is higher than male participation. In fact there are two languages (Chinese and Modern Greek) which record a higher participation rate for boys than for girls. For Modern Greek the difference is very slight but it is more substantial for Chinese. It is worth pointing out that quite a few of the 'foreign' languages in Australian schools are in fact 'community' languages used by local ethnic communities. This is especially the case for Arabic, Chinese, Italian, Modern Greek, Vietnamese and to some extent Spanish. Whilst the study of any of these community languages is not restricted to students from the ethnolinguistic community, the proportion of such students is quite high for languages like Arabic, Modern Greek and Vietnamese. Gender patterns around these languages may be influenced also by ethnolinguistic and cultural expectations about learning one's 'heritage' language.

Unfortunately we do not have national figures for these ten languages at the post-compulsory or final year level. We do, however, have 2003 figures for the state of New South Wales which is the most populated state of Australia and which has, together with the State of Victoria, the largest number of languages on offer and the largest number of students sitting final year exams for languages. We will discuss the data in Table 7, but won't compare them to the data in Table 6 given the discrepancy (i.e., national vs state figures).

The data in Table 7 show that only three languages, Arabic, Chinese and Vietnamese, attract more than 40 per cent male students at final year level, and that the most marked gender differentiation exists in relation to French and Italian, with more than three-quarters of students

Table 7 Female and male participation rates in ten languages sitting final year exams in New South Wales, Australia (per cent)

Language	Female	Male
Arabic	55	45
Chinese	52	48
French	77	23
German	68	32
Greek (Modern)	67	33
Indonesian	68	32
Italian	77	23
Japanese	61	39
Spanish	70	30
Vietnamese	58	42

Table 8 Female and male participation rates in six languages in New Zealand (per cent)

Language	Female	Male
Chinese	52	48
French	64	36
German	65	35
Indonesian	62	38
Japanese	53	47
Spanish	60	40

being female, followed by German, Modern Greek and Indonesian, with the gender imbalance in favour of girls being around two-thirds.

New Zealand

For New Zealand we have data for six languages: three European languages – French, German and Spanish – and three Asian languages – Chinese, Indonesian and Japanese. The gender breakdown provided in Table 8 is based on foreign language study between Years 9 and 13. This table reveals that girls outnumber boys in the study of each of these languages. Least gender-differentiated are enrolments in the study of Chinese and Japanese, whereas participation in the study of German and French is most gender-marked with approximately two-thirds of students being female.

For New Zealand we can also provide a gender breakdown in the final year of study – Year 13. Table 9 shows that gender differentiation increases markedly for all the languages other than Chinese. For French, German

Table 9   Female and male participation rates in Year 13 in six languages in New Zealand (per cent)

Language	Female	Male
Chinese	42.7	57.3
French	77.0	23.0
German	74.5	24.5
Indonesian	77.0	23.0
Japanese	59.0	41.0
Spanish	66.0	34.0

Table 10   Entries for A level foreign language learning in United Kingdom (per cent)

Language	Female	Male
Arabic	56.0	44.0
Chinese	52.0	48.0
French	67.0	33.0
German	65.0	35.0
Italian	65.0	35.0
Japanese	50.0	50.0
Russian	53.0	47.0
Spanish	68.0	32.0
Turkish	62.5	37.5
Urdu	66.0	34.0

and Indonesian less than a quarter of the students are male. Interestingly, the situation is reversed for Chinese with more boys engaging in the study of Chinese in Year 13 than girls.

United Kingdom excluding Scotland

For the United Kingdom we do not have overall figures for foreign language study which provide a breakdown for sex. We do have data for male and female students undertaking A level (Advanced level) study in the ten most widely studied foreign languages on offer in the United Kingdom (see Table 10) and we also have data on six languages at GCSE level (see Table 11). The trends emerging from Table 10 are in line with those found in Australia and New Zealand. Female participation is greater for almost every language with the exception of Japanese, where there is equal participation. The most marked gender differentiation occurs in relation to languages such as French, German, Italian, Spanish and Urdu, where approximately two-thirds of the students are female. For Arabic, Chinese and Russian, the differentiation in participation rate is less marked.

Table 11 Participation by sex at GCSE and A level in selected languages in United Kingdom (per cent)

Language	Level	Female	Male
Chinese	GCSE	50	50
	A level	52	48
French	GCSE	53	47
	A level	67	33
German	GCSE	52	48
	A level	65	35
Italian	GCSE	56	44
	A level	65	35
Japanese	GCSE	46	54
	A level	50	50
Spanish	GCSE	58	42
	A level	68	32

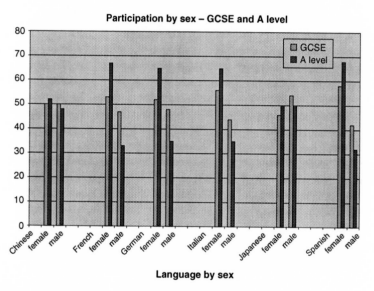

Figure 1 Participation by sex and education level for six languages in the United Kingdom (per cent)

In Table 11 we compare the participation of girls and boys at A level and GCSE level for six languages: Chinese, French, German, Italian, Japanese and Spanish. We have also included a graph comparing participation by sex for these languages (see Figure 1).

At GCSE level the greatest difference in participation by male and female students is found for Spanish. Also interesting to note is that boys outnumber girls in relation to Japanese.

Scotland

Information about female and male participation rates for Scotland is less detailed than that for the other countries. Table 12 shows participation rates by sex for four foreign languages consolidated for all grades (standard, intermediate and advanced). Given that the Scottish data contain consolidated figures for all grades, it is best to compare them to the Australian and New Zealand overall data. In Scotland boys participate more in the learning of French and German than their counterparts in New Zealand and Australia, whereas for Spanish and Italian their participation is less than in these countries (Italian data are not available for New Zealand).

Comparisons of the participation of boys and girls in selected foreign languages across the countries are restricted because of the limited overlap of languages: only the European languages – French, German and Spanish – are taught in all the participating countries. If we exclude Scotland, we have a slightly greater pool of commonly taught languages: Chinese, French, German, Japanese and Spanish. When comparing participation by sex for these languages across the countries, the evidence for a gendering of language choice is not too convincing, especially if we compare enrolments across all levels. However, there is some indication that French attracts consistently more female enrolments in all countries and at all levels: the 'feminisation of French' is particularly striking at final year level, with girls making up between two-thirds and three-quarters of the total enrolment in French. Although there is no evidence of a foreign language consistently attracting more boys than girls, Chinese could be seen as a language with the most balanced enrolment patterns across countries and levels.

Table 12   Participation rates by sex for all grades for selected languages in Scotland (per cent)

Language	Female	Male
French	55.2	44.8
German	54.6	45.4
Italian	69.4	30.6
Spanish	68.2	31.2

The statistical information presented in this chapter confirms that there is a degree of gendering in the study of foreign languages in all the Anglophone countries we examined. Boys participate less than girls and their participation diminishes significantly, at least for most languages, the more advanced the study of the language gets. It is significant that trends observed across four different countries/regions are so similar despite significant differences in education systems. Although there is some degree of difference for enrolment patterns in specific languages, the overall figures presented in Table 1 show that boys demonstrate similar levels of disengagement and disinterest in foreign language study irrespective of whether they study in Australia, Scotland, New Zealand or the United Kingdom. Unfortunately the absence of more detailed statistical data about language learning at lower levels means that we have not been able to refine this rather crude picture. If we had access to more detailed and more consistent data in relation to different types of schools and programmes (e.g., private vs public, or co-educational vs single-sex, immersion programmes or language as subject ones), different composition of classrooms (numbers of boys in individual classes), we could provide more detailed commentary.

This chapter, then, has provided the 'rough outline' to our study; the general shape and characteristic trends of the boys–languages relationship. In the following chapters, the more detailed profile emerges through the narratives of the main players in this scenario: the boys themselves, their teachers and some of the girls who study alongside the boys.

3
The Gendering of Languages Education

The statistics and trends examined in the previous chapter suggest the overall shape and direction of the boys–languages relationship in the contexts in question. As we have noted, these figures mask every-day classroom realities, reflecting macro-trends but failing to differentiate clearly between compulsory and post-compulsory figures or between male and female student numbers. They point none the less towards a clear 'gendering' of languages education, with boys seen as less likely to participate – or to continue to participate – than girls. The crucial point is the 'post-compulsory moment', when students make their own decisions about whether or not they continue with language study. We saw this point to be differently located in different countries, even within different regions or states of the same country; but regardless of when and where it happens, the data presented in the previous chapter indicate the trend common to the Anglophone countries we examined: post-compulsory language study is a fragile enterprise and one which is significantly skewed in gender terms. This is the shape of foreign language programmes. In terms of direction, there is little evidence of increased enthusiasm or engagement in response to either changing global conditions or changing curriculum initiatives. Post-compulsory language study continues to be an under-subscribed curriculum option, refused by the majority of boys. English, it seems, is still regarded as 'sufficient' by most young male speakers of the global language.

The two countries from which most of our data are drawn, Australia and the United Kingdom, are both multilingual communities. Australia, where we work, is one of the most culturally and linguistically diverse countries in the world. According to the 2001 Census, more than 206 different languages are used in the community, approximately 16 per cent of Australians using a language other than English at home

(Clyne, Fernandez and Grey, 2004:1). The United Kingdom and the United States are similarly rich in terms of linguistic and cultural diversity. The real-world reality in major English-dominant communities, therefore, is of significant numbers of young people living bilingually and bi-culturally, with first-hand knowledge of operating in more than one linguistic code. Yet interest in school language study remains weak. There seems to be little connection in young people's minds between real-life linguistic experience and in-school language learning. In the previous chapter we noted that Australian students have a wide choice of languages, reflecting both community interests and economic imperatives (for a detailed comparative analysis of community languages and 'national priority' languages studied in Australian schools, see ibid., 2004); yet there is a clear disjunction between in-school learning of languages and out-of-school experience of them.

As we noted in the opening chapter of this book, official educational policies in the major English-speaking countries of the world focus increasingly on educational objectives of intercultural competence and global literacy. Young people are exhorted to recognise (or to imagine) themselves as inhabitants of the global village; intercultural players negotiating global flows of information; learners for whom traditional boundaries are fast disappearing, new opportunities presenting. While additional language proficiency would appear to be an obvious component of global literacy and experience, support for language programmes in schools remains poor and interest among young people low; and boys' particular disinterest in languages appears to be accepted as 'how it is'; rarely commented on, poorly documented, accorded little critical attention (Sunderland, 2004). As noted, this is difficult to understand, sitting as it does within the context of the larger relationship currently preoccupying educators, parents, and the community at large: boys' perceived poor relationship with schooling in general and with literacy in particular. It may not often be included in discussions of this issue, but it is crucially informed by them.

Gender and schooling debates: focus on the boys

Gender has been a key concern in educational debates for more than three decades in the United Kingdom, Australia, North America and New Zealand. From the early 1970s until very recently, the main focus of gender-related concerns were girls and young women. Research activity and pedagogical intervention centred mainly around the identified poor relationship of girls with certain curriculum areas (principally maths and sciences) and around classroom dynamics seen to privilege the voices of boys and to disadvantage girls in terms of pedagogy, curriculum content, classroom interaction patterns and teacher attention (for an overview of the research and analysis of this period, see Swann, 1988; Sunderland, 2004). The last ten to 15 years have seen a shift in focus away from girls and an increase in attention to the relationship between boys and schooling (Davison, 2000; Davison et al., 2004; Frank, 1993; Frank and Davison, 2005; Kenway, 1995; Kenway, Willis et al., 1998; Martino, 1995, 2000; Mac an Ghaill, 1994, 1996).

While this concern with boys emerged at a time when there appears to have been a move to 'write out' gender differentiation in policy and curriculum initiatives, it continues to work from a recognisably 'girls versus boys' paradigm. In Australia, the 1987 *National Policy for the Education of Girls in Australian Schools* (Schools Commission, 1987) was superseded by the 1997 policy document, *Gender Equity: A Framework for Australian Schools* (Gender Equity Taskforce, 1997); and when Education Queensland reviewed its approach to gender equity in 1991, it formulated a *Gender Equity in Education Policy* intended to identify and respond to pressures arising for male and female students in relation to 'gendered expectations in both schooling and the wider society'; the unmarked term 'gender' clearly intended to acknowledge the universality of gender issues as they impact on both sexes. However, boys are unmistakably the current locus of concern (Lingard and Douglas, 1999). They may not be explicitly named in the new framing of gender and education at policy document level, but the sub-text to current discourses of gender and schooling is definitely '*what about the boys?*'

Boys in crisis, boys as victims

Scholarly work around boys and education, framed by theories of discourse and identity, has increasingly argued against over-simplification of the gender-schooling relationship and for recognition of the complexity of gender performance in school as in broader cultural contexts, critiquing the continuing binary frame to gender debates which assumes essential gender differences and reads off the needs of boys via previously assembled understandings of the needs of girls (Kenway and Willis, 1998; Yates, 1997). This critique appears to be having minimal impact on broader discussion, however, judging by the current proliferation of 'boys in crisis' discourses currently driving broader community debates; what Davison and colleagues describe as 'media frenzy' – familiar now in the United Kingdom and Australia – but recently emerging also in the Canadian press, where a systematic elaboration of the narrative of the 'victim boy' is constructing Canadian boys as 'short-changed' in the world of schooling (Davison et al., 2004). This narrative recounts the implicit – and often explicit – dominance of 'pro-girl women teachers', the losses for boys that came with the gains for girls, from the 'push' from feminism; the reported underachievement of boys accounted for via explanations of what schooling is 'doing' to boys, rather than by anything that might be happening with the boys themselves (ibid:51). The 'state of emergency' discourse in relation to boys and schooling is now well-established in the British and Australian press: editorials in newspapers, TV news segments, daytime chat shows, late-night studio discussions: all regularly construct boys as disenchanted, disengaged, and – according to some of the more strident accounts – disenfranchised. These accounts feed into and out of the rhetoric of writers such as Biddulph in Australia (1997, 1999) and Bly in the United States (1992), who speak through men's rights discourses, arguing for a restoration of masculinity, blaming the 'feminised' culture of schools for the identified under-performance of boys. This crisis account, driven by the binary categorisation of an essentialised model of gender, depends for its effect on the concept of victimisation: *'In a school system dominated by women, boys are suffering while girls pull ahead'* (*The Australian*, 27 July, 1995: cited in Alloway and Gilbert, 1997:49). Similar emotive declarations appear regularly in the British press, with boys being constructed as 'lost', disadvantaged victims of what is identified as the feminised experience of schooling generally and of literacy in particular.

These discourses have all the hallmarks of male backlash politics against the gains of feminism and are a significant component of the driving force behind the 'boyswork' programmes currently gaining momentum in Australian schools (Mills, 2000:221); and they are a significant influence in terms of shaping wider community attitudes and rhetoric. Boys are constructed as an oppressed group; oppressed by the over-advantaging of feminist-inspired gains for girls, in tandem with larger social changes seen to be undermining the cultural identity of men and boys. These are emotional narratives, often supported by statistical evidence relating to teenage suicide, youth violence, imprisonment and unemployment. Slippage between such statistics and the idea that schools are serving boys badly is easy. Boys are declared to be in urgent need of positive and affirmative intervention to help them deal with what is seen as an increasingly boy-hostile milieu (Lingard and Douglas, 1999). Calls for boy-affirming policies and programmes, funding and consciousness-raising programmes are supporting the 'boys–work' agenda referred to above (see, for example, Browne and Fletcher, 1995; Mills, 2000:221). These calls include a plea for a 're-masculisation' of schooling; the restoration of a culture which allows boys to 'be' boys. Mahony (1998) quotes a recruiting advertisement in Denmark for an early childhood pre-service education programme which specified that the college was looking for interest from 'Real Men' (by implication a scarce commodity) who could serve as role models for presumably 'real boys'. Such texts support the current argument – not only in Denmark – that school has become a 'terrible place', in which boys are dominated by women who 'cannot accept boys as they are' (Kruse, 1996:439). Release from such domination and emasculation, it is argued, will make school a more comfortable, equitable and confirming place for boys, who will then achieve better outcomes. The 'trouble' that boys are 'in', in such accounts, requires immediate intervention to make schools less hostile milieux – the trouble clearly being with schooling rather than with boys themselves or with wider social processes. This is one of the strong framing narratives of the current boys–school crisis discourse as it proceeds in broader community discussions.

There are some points of commonality between these popular and populist narratives of boys, crises and schooling, and some more academically framed analyses. Similar calls are being made by some educationists for classrooms to become more 'boy-friendly' – although what such an environment might be would differ in both substance and style in the two accounts. Some theorists and curriculum planners engaged in boys–schooling work argue for the implementation of strategies identified as 'boy-friendly': tasks that are more cognitively challenging; increased autonomy and active learning opportunities; the inclusion of more 'masculine' materials and resources; more interactive classroom dynamics; more explicit focus on the goals and aspirations of male students. These suggestions are very similar to the call for girl-friendly approaches to maths and sciences which characterised the 1980s affirmative action for girls agenda, and are currently proliferating in both Australia and the United Kingdom (e.g., Gilbert and Gilbert, 1998; Jones and Jones, 2001). Collaborative partnerships between school and tertiary-based researchers are being developed to further this agenda, involving action research projects and mentoring programmes designed to improve boys' performance (Gorard, Rees and Salisbury, 1999; Jones, personal communication, 2003).

'Boys' as problem . . . and 'school-unfriendly'

The focus on more boy-friendly pedagogy is one response to the perceived crisis. Another more critically and sociologically informed response shifts the focus away from what is being 'done' to boys on to boys themselves, and what is perceived as *their* 'unfriendliness': their reluctance – or inability – to 'be' the kinds of students who might connect productively with schooling. These more socially oriented accounts locate the problem as much with the boys and with the cultural construction of gender as with the processes of schooling. They are more interested in interrogating and destabilising established norms of masculinity; in critiquing the social and discursive construction of 'boy' (Frosh, Phoenix and Pattman, 2002; Mahony, 1998); in considering alternative repertoires, which might include persuading boys to engage in *less* stereotypically 'masculine' behaviour: to be more communicative, self-reflective, caring, sociable: in short, to cross the gender divide into the marked 'other' territorial space of gendered behaviour now regarded as more 'school-friendly'. This alternative response examines the characteristic behaviours of boys which appear to align least productively with schooling, such as the reluctance to communicate (in particular to express emotions or personal experience), the desire to be 'cool' and therefore disengaged from academic effort, the reluctance to assume leadership positions, the use of aggression and violence in conflict resolution, and the inability/disinclination to develop literacy and oracy skills – in either first or additional languages.

These are the points of axis in current boys and education debates. On the one hand, a push for boys to be allowed the opportunity to 'be boys' in school; a call in fact for a return to more 'boy-like' behaviour and for schools to become more attuned to this model of behaviour; on the other, the argument for the unstitching and reconstruction of dominant hegemonic versions of masculinity and for possibilities of wider repertoires of gender performance.

Theoretical framing

At this point it is appropriate to sketch out the theoretical frame which shapes this project. Our exploration of the boys–languages relationship, like all research projects, is framed by theoretical positions which inform what we found as well as what we looked for. Both of us work in teacher education, in fields informed by critical theory, feminist, poststructuralist and postcolonial theories; both have a background in gender and language studies. Given the context of our work and the focus of this study, the frame to our analysis is unsurprisingly discourse-oriented, informed by an understanding of gender as socially and culturally constituted performance and of language and culture as co-constitutive phenomena (Carr, 2003; Pennycook, 1998).

Discourse and safe houses

The 'discourse' which informs our discussion is not the version of discourse usually associated with language classrooms – that of discourse as top-level organisation of text. Our version is the one long-since strategically accorded a capital D by James Gee (1991), a defining move now widely embedded in critical literacy and critical language awareness undergraduate programmes. This capitalised Discourse involves not only lexical and grammatical items – 'language' in its linguistics sense – but equally the less visible components of communication and social practice that go with these items: behaviours, politics, ideologies, ways of enacting and valuing: in short, ways of 'being in the world':

> A socially accepted association among ways of using language, of thinking, and of acting that can be used to identify oneself as a member of a socially meaningful group or 'social network'.
>
> (Ibid:3)

This widely quoted definition of discourse is followed by advice from Gee to think of it as an 'identity kit', which comes complete with 'the appropriate costume and instructions on how to act and talk so as to take on a particular role that others will recognise' (p. 3). While this description can lend itself to over-simplification, suggesting ease and equity of access to different 'costumes' or discursive repertoires which does not characterise all individual experience (for a critique of this model of discourse 'performance', see Pennycook, 2004:16), it provides a first level point of entry to thinking about the interrelationship of identity and language and to the processes of 'recognition' via discourse which inform our study.

Many education-oriented research projects adopt a discourse-frame to analysis, even when language is not the explicit focus of the study (e.g., Grieshaber's study of parent–child relationships, 2004); and all acknowledge a foundational debt to Foucault, whose genealogical elaboration of the relationship between discourse, power and knowledge (1977, 1979, 1982) forms the basis of poststructuralist accounts of cultural knowledge construction, of the place where 'truth' and 'reality' are constituted. The individual 'subject' – in this case the boy in the language classroom – is seen to be constituted systematically and ineluctably via the regulation of discursive formation: he can 'be' whatever version of 'boy' is sanctioned by the discourses to which he has access. Some of the most recent critical work which looks closely at discursive framing of language learning (e.g., Pennycook, 2004) insists on the circularity of this process of subject constitution, arguing that the constituting subject is in fact 'performing' the discourse as well as itself, in such a mutually constitutive way that the discourse too is 'called into being' by the very identities which it 'permits' (ibid:8).

Foucault's genealogies trace in detail the multiple and interconnected ways that discourse operates in the social world: how it shapes, rationalises and regulates the power–knowledge relationship which drives both broad social and institutional practices and individual subject formation. Foucault argues that the power in question is not the visibly repressive, brutal kind of power graphically detailed in the opening paragraphs of *Discipline and Punish: The Birth of the Prison* (1977); nor is the knowledge commonly associated with official sites of knowledge construction – such as academies, schools and libraries. Both the power and the knowledge are constituted, exercised and enacted 'everywhere', circulating via the 'capillaries' of social networks, the small processes and practices that constitute and regulate the social world just as effectively as more obviously dominant or oppressive *régimes* of power (Foucault, 1980, 1982).

When thinking about the connection between Foucault's work and this project, the knowledge component of the equation appears at first sight to be more relevant, but is in fact inseparable from the power component, having – as Foucault argues – very material effects. The power lies in the *régimes* of truth which resonate throughout our data, framing repertoires of possibility, sanctioning particular ways of being in the world and in the classroom. This 'truth', progressively constituted and solidified through discursive reiteration, becomes internalised and owned by the very individuals it constitutes. It slides comfortably into 'common sense', that most powerful of sites, working via the 'technologies of the self' (Foucault, 1988), turning the subject into the ultimate self-regulator; never having to defend its empirical basis nor its epistemological credentials; calling into being both belief systems and material practices. 'How things are' is the ultimate normalised point of comfort and of 'knowing'. Our data provide significant evidence of these kinds of ways of knowing. Gendered curriculum practices and individual students' relationships with school options – in this case foreign languages – might appear to have few points of connection with the oppressively imposed *régimes* which regulated hospitals, prisons and schools in earlier, less gentle times. To all extents and purposes, there are currently few material impediments to either girls or boys in terms of options in school in Anglophone countries in the Western world. Yet the real, material effects of the gendered narratives collected in the course of this project suggest the enduring, regulating influence of truth *régimes*, constituted, reinforced, regularised via dominant discourses; reminding us of the post-structuralist proposition that 'discourses produce meaning and subjectivity, rather than reflecting them' (Weedon, 1997:102).

Foucault's account of the discursive shaping, enabling/disabling of bodies and minds – collectively and individually – provides a frame for reading off our data. Talk of disciplinary power, docile bodies and compliant minds may seem worlds removed from the learner-centred, constructivist discourses of current educational practice; yet it resonates through the seemingly self-defeating influence of both collective and individual senses of self and of masculinity which can be seen to drive so many of the comments from boys in our data. While much has changed in terms of offered options and pathways for learners in schools, one of the most powerful forces impacting upon young people's in-school behaviour continues to be the power of the normative, discursively protected, gendered and classed sense of self. What it 'means' to be a boy, or a girl, or a student in school continues to connect very directly to the same kinds of dominant truth *régimes* – internalised technologies of the self – tracked in different detail by Foucault. These technologies work gradually, at times imperceptibly; accumulatively constructing a position which becomes difficult to refuse; arriving ultimately at the impregnable status of the 'natural' and 'normal' way of things. Many of the 'truths' which inform curriculum planning, pedagogy and wider community understandings about education, about gender and about languages sit comfortably within these safe houses.

Gee (1991) foregrounds the significance of the act of identification by the individual subject in discursive formation, the act which involves recognition, both of self and of others, as acceptable, appropriate players in imaginable worlds; worlds which interpellate and position sanctioned versions of self into appropriate subject positions (Butler, 1999:20). Of course, as Butler also argues, the offered subject position can always be refused or renegotiated; but, as many educational research projects have indicated, and as our own data confirm, refusal or renegotiation of sanctioned norms requires courage and good strategies.

Gender

Our study sits squarely within current debates around gender and education, alongside talk of crises in masculinity, gender and educational performance. Gender, therefore, is the second key concept which assists in the framing of this project, a term used loosely and uncritically in many of these debates, often conflating with sex and with biology. Our interest is in boys who choose to study languages, or – more specifically – in boys who choose *not* to study languages; and it's important to make the distinction between gender and biology. Our interest is in gender as a social construct and key cultural organising principle, not in biology. The subjects in our study are not the essentially male, biologically determined, coherent, subjects of cognitive science: believed to be pre-determinedly hardwired for certain kinds of cognitive behaviour, with brains arranged in ways that predispose them to do well in certain curriculum areas (such as maths and sciences) but less well in others (language-related areas). The boys in this study are theoretically quite other boys: they are socially constituted, culturally performed gendered boys (Cameron, 1998; Frosh, Phoenix and Pattman, 2002). Butler talks about being 'transitively' gendered: how the 'calling' of the individual as 'girl' or 'boy' produces the effect (1999:20, in Pennycook, 2004:13). Leaving aside for now the issue of biologically based and scientifically narrated accounts of differentiated brain formation and function (see later in this chapter), we emphasise that our interest lies in the impact of *socially constructed* 'biological' accounts of difference and in the implications of these 'understandings' in relation to foreign language study. Grosz details the thorough ways in which essentialism does its work (1995): shoring up the belief that characteristics, traits and capacities defined as women's and men's 'essences' are shared in common by all women and men in all times and contexts, underlying all apparent differences and variations which differentiate women and men. Such essentialism is sustained and protected by governing frameworks of 'knowledge'.

Our understanding of gender has obvious points of connection with the account of discourse formation outlined above. Gender, unlike biology, is recognised as a social, cultural and discursive construct; one of the most salient and 'load-bearing' key principles of cultural organisation. The poststructuralist, discourse-informed view not only sees gender as socially and discursively constituted, but also, importantly, as always intersecting with other key social and cultural variables, such as social class, ethnicity, health status; as fluid, unstable, capable of reconstitution (Johnson, 1998; Cameron, 1998). It emphasises instability and incoherence, at the same time recognising the power and influence of the individual and collective cultural desire to *be* both stable and coherent. It refuses the notion of generic 'boy', immutably formed, set in stone and accounted for via prescribed versions of masculinities. Rather than being essentially formed – predispositions, characteristics and attributes mapped out from the beginning fact of biology – the socially constructed 'boy' is recognised as ineluctably shaped, prompted and ultimately 'hailed' into socially sanctioned versions of the self. This is the end result of Foucault's truth effects, which congeal, settle and stabilise into 'how things are'; the process described by Pennycook as 'sedimentation' (2004:13–14). The end result may often seem every bit as unchangeable as any biological given, but the process which leads to this product indicates otherwise. The individual socially formed boy can shift into unboy-like configurations if he chooses: the price may be high, he may choose not to take up the option, but the option is there. The poststructuralist, discursively accounted-for gendered self is always in process; and is on the far side of the divide from biology.

Gender as performativity

Judith Butler's work in the early 1990s made the conceptual move which has since informed much of the theoretical work around gender, identity, language and education: that of theorising gender as performativity (1990a, 1990b, 1993). Butler argues that 'gender' in fact constitutes itself rather than being something already in existence; it is 'brought into being' by the idea of itself, 'constituting the "identity" it is purported to be':

> Gender is the repeated stylization of the body, a set of repeated acts within a rigid regulatory frame which congeal over time to produce the appearance of a substance, of a 'natural' kind of being.
>
> (1990b:33)

And language plays a core role in this constituting process. 'Masculine' and 'feminine' ways of talking, of performing speech acts, identification with different communicative practices (e.g., foreign language study) are seen by Butler as 'acts by social actors' who are engaged in the crucial cultural process of constituting themselves as 'proper' men and women/girls and boys (ibid:49). More than a decade ago, Brian Street (1993) famously argued that 'culture is a verb'; a proposition which accounts not only for the complexity of collective and individual options as to how we 'do life', but also for agency in negotiating this complexity. Gender, too, is a *verb* (Pennycook, 2004). According it the status of a verb in the grammar of meaning-making acknowledges both its fluidity and the agency of the subject who enacts this verb; as Gordon and Lahelma argue 'We *are* and we *have* gender, but we can also do gender, avoid gender, ignore gender and challenge gender' (1995:3).

Our data provide solid evidence of the 'doing' of gender; but also remind us of the dangers of slipping into benign accounts of performativity: implying freedom of choice, free decisions as to which of Gee's 'costumes' will be worn at any point in time. More critically and socially informed accounts of gender performance emphasise the particularities of individual relationship to the variables involved in such choices. Performance is always dictated by available repertoires and material, social and psychological circumstances. What version of 'boy' – or 'girl' – can be performed varies significantly according to time, context and material circumstances. Being a 'girl' in Taliban-controlled Afghanistan, for example, offered different performative options than being a 'girl' in middle-class London or New York during the same period. Being a 'girl' in New York or London, in turn, varies according to the intersection of variables such as class, ethnicity, educational opportunity, health status. Gender is never performed on a free-floating stage. It is always affected by the complex intersection of cultural and social conditions which constitute individual life circumstances. The connection between gender as performativity and the power–knowledge dimension of discourses is close; and, as Danaher, Schirato and Webb (2000) remind us, discourses determine the ways in which 'truth' is inscribed on bodies as well as minds. Our data provide additional evidence of the embodied nature of the gendered sense of self.

Discourse, gender, identity performance and language learning

The final move in establishing our theoretical frame brings the discourse, gender, identity relationship back to the site of our study: the foreign language classroom, where the performance of both gender and 'language learner' is enacted. The intersection of these two performances turns out to be a difficult one.

Mainstream twentieth-century linguistics and applied linguistics have operated from a predominantly scientific, cognitively oriented model of language learning. The learner in this model is an individually bounded cognitive performer, and language learning is seen to happen primarily inside this individual learner's head. It is commonplace, therefore, to hear talk of 'good language learners', of 'ability' and 'linguistic intelligence', of 'effective language learning strategies'. In this study we collected many comments from both students and teachers about the fact that girls are 'good' at language learning and boys are not. This cognitively based, information-processing model of language learning assumes fixed facts, fixed learners, stable meanings residing inside the language, conveyed and received provided the necessary skills and capabilities are in place. While context and the 'ecology' of classrooms

(Holliday, 1994) are acknowledged as relevant, they are not generally recognised as having real impact on either the meaning that is being made, the process that is doing the making of this meaning, the material effects of the learning experience. This cognitively based account provides part of the story, but is now widely recognised as an inadequate account which fails to engage with the powerful influence of material, social, cultural and affective circumstances.

The discursive turn of critical theory as it has informed educational analysis and research over the last two decades has shifted attention to the other – for us more relevant – part of the story, which accounts for the individual learner as socially constituted, socially situated, negotiating cultural and material circumstances which are never 'given', never stable and which impact significantly upon the nature and the outcomes of the language learning experience (Norton, 2004). Interestingly, the discipline whose core business is language education (applied linguistics) has been slower to engage with these socially oriented moves to retheorise the relationship between language and the social subject than have areas whose core business is, on the surface at least, quite other (e.g., cultural studies, gender studies, sociology and literary studies). Drawing from poststructuralist, postmodern, postcolonial and feminist theories, researchers from these disciplines were exploring the interconnectedness of language and social and cultural practice long before more than a handful of people in the official business of language study were making similar moves.

However, the last few years have seen the development of a strongly theorised 'critical applied linguistics' position which refutes notions of fixed positions, knowable and stable languages, learners or learning experiences. This more critical, social evolution of theories of language and of language learning moves beyond the tracking of contexts and situations to tracking the less visible dimensions of language practice: the politics, ideological and material investments, the more complex and invested issues of identity, social spaces, ownership, equity and access; even to a critical tracking of the 'critical project' itself (Luke, 2004). While the official agenda of the language classroom is the 'learning' of a new linguistic code – accessing new ways of communicating and experiencing different cultural contexts – research evidence and critical scholarly work from very different contexts around the world now collectively argue the case that language classrooms are much more than 're-coding' sites: they are complicated places, of social, cultural and political action and interaction, where identities are negotiated, where learners encounter not only new linguistic coding systems but also new value systems, new social worlds, speaking positions and meaning-making systems; sites in which 'uptake' can never be 'given', where the nature of the individual learning experience can never be 'known' (Canagarajah, 1999; Hedgcock, 2002; Kramsch, 2004; Lin, 2004; Morgan, 2004; Norton and Toohey, 2004; Pennycook, 2001; Ramanathan, 2002).

Like the longer-established tradition of first language critical literacy and critical language awareness, the critical applied linguistics position takes an interrogative approach to analysis of language practice, including language learning, moving beyond the traditional sociolinguistics concern with texts/contexts relationships, with the 'how', 'where', 'when' types of questions to the 'why' and 'to what effect' ones. It concerns itself directly with the discourse–knowledge–power nexus discussed earlier in this chapter, with the enactment of Foucault's truth *régimes*, and with acknowledgement of the involvement of the 'speaking subject' (subjectivity, identity, the performance of the self) in the language learning project. Social relations, and intra-individual 'social relations' (identity negotiation) are as much in play as are cognitive processes. A 'grammar of the self' – both the individual and the collective self – is up for negotiation as well as the grammar of the target language. Learning an additional language presents possibilities of new ways of making meaning (Carr, 2003), and this meaning is always socially constituted, always 'dialogued' with, through and in opposition to other voices.

The work of Bakhtin is also helpful here (1981, 1986) with his key concept of 'dialogue' involving an understanding of consciousness as 'otherness', what Holquist describes as 'the differential relation between a center and all that is not center' (2002:18); individual consciousness constituting a drama always involving more than one actor, always enacted in social, discursively shaped conditions (Day, 2002:17). Bakhtin saw the individual voice as involving 'an intense interaction and struggle between one's own and another's word' (1981:354), constructing utterances from available resources constituted from all the voices – all the utterances – that have gone before (Bakhtin, 1986:96). This dialogic, social account of language underpinned his critique of the Saussurean view of language as a closed, individually located system (Day, 2002:10), as did his understanding of the self as inherently dialogic, in 'relation' only through relationship with other(s): what Holquist summarises as 'a permanently in-process social "event"'; an 'event with a structure' (2002:21). This 'structure' depends on the connection of the event to social history, drawn from and through the many and varied social processes, practices and voices which make up individual lives.

The points of connection between Bakhtin's theory of dialogism, Foucault's theory of discourse and Butler's theory of performativity provide the structure for the analysis of our data. In different but complementary ways each accounts for the 'forging of the self', described by Pavlenko and Blackledge as the all-important 'interactional accomplishment' of identity formation:

> In sum, we view *identities* as social, discursive, and narrative options offered by a particular society in a specific time and place to which individuals and groups of individuals appeal in an attempt to self-name, to self-characterize, and to claim social spaces and social prerogatives.
>
> (Pavlenko and Blackledge, 2003:19)

This 'self-naming' and 'claiming' invariably involves tensions and contradictions, as the 'voices' which constitute the available repertoires are themselves multiple and often competing; the 'identities' constituted always fluid, contingent, in process, never complete (Eckert and McConnell-Ginet, 1999; Grosz, 1995).

The issue of identities is very relevant to this study. The foreign language classroom turns out to be a particularly challenging site for boys in terms of identity constitution and performance. Norton and Toohey (2004), drawing on Bourdieu (1977, 1979, 1991), describe it as a social space in which learners not only engage with new linguistic systems but are required to reconfigure their relationship to the social world (2004:5), arguing that any analysis of individual language learners must involve analysis of this 'social space'. The boys who talk through our data are unmistakably individual boys, 'voicing' and performing themselves from individual speaking positions; but they are also indisputably socially situated individual boys, contextually located and impacted upon by intersecting social influences. The concept of 'communities of practice' may be relevant here: what Lave and Wenger define as 'a set of relations among persons, activity and world' temporarily situated and socially constituted (1991:98). The boys who speak through the following chapters narrate their thoughts about languages and language learning, about themselves as boys and as language learners, from within particular communities of practice which are constituted via particular discursive resources. Lave and Wagner argue that the relations established in these communities of practice often have more influence on learning outcomes than does whatever is happening in terms of methodology or instruction: 'The practice of the community creates the potential "curriculum" in the broadest sense . . . .' (ibid:92–3). This proposition will be revisited later in the book, when we reflect on the evidence gathered and presented in terms of the theoretical frame presented in this chapter.

The trouble boys are in

Returning to the context which frames the boys–languages relationship, it is probably helpful at this point to go back one step and look more closely at the nature of the 'trouble' that boys are supposedly in. We already noted that the main locus of concern is literacy. Research data indicate that there are established patterns of differentiated perform-ance between male and female students in terms of literacy proficiency in both Australia and the United Kingdom (Gilbert and Gilbert, 1998; Martino, 1995). Girls are reported to consistently out-perform boys in early basic literacy skills tests and in final year secondary English scores. The 1996 National School English Literacy Survey, for example, under-taken by the Australian Council of Educational Research, found that in reading, 34 per cent of boys in Years 3 and 5 did not meet national stand-ards compared with 23 per cent of girls, while in writing tasks, 35 per cent of the boys in Year 3 did not meet national standards compared with 19 per cent of girls; and in Year 5 testing, 41 per cent of the boys compared with 26 per cent of girls did not meet the standards (Gilbert and Gilbert, 1998:19). Similar statistics are available from UK-based research (e.g., Epstein, Elwood, Hey and Maw, 1998), and this evidence is widely circu-lated and used as the basis for much of the framing of current interven-tionist policy.

The evidence is increasingly challenged, however, both for its reliabil-ity and usefulness (Raphael Reed, 1999). More finely grained analyses show that factors other than gender clearly impact upon these statistics, and that the current panic around boys and literacy represents a simplis-tic, uncritical reading of a complex intersection of variables. Australian studies demonstrate how a single-variable analysis provides an unreliable account of a complex scenario. Research in New South Wales almost a decade ago already demonstrated how socioeconomic factors play a sig-nificant part in determining educational outcomes, as do other variables such as geographical location and ethnicity. Gender, it was argued, is never a free-standing variable. This research indicated that not all girls are performing well in school, or are out-performing boys; and that not all boys are underachieving (Davy, 1995). In Queensland, more recently, Lingard and Douglas (1999) suggest that closer analysis of the 'under-achieving boys' suggests that the outcomes being read to increasingly alarmist effect are less to do with poor performance by boys in specific areas and more to do with improved performance by girls in traditionally 'masculine' curriculum areas. Like the earlier Australian study, this study foregrounds the interrelatedness of social class and school achievement along gender lines:

> A small group of mainly middle-class girls are now performing as well as, and thus challenging the dominance of middle-class boys in the high status 'masculinist' subjects such as Maths, Chemistry and to a lesser extent Physics.

(Ibid:278)

Recent studies in Canada (Davison et al., 2004), have also queried the reliability of the crisis account. Studies in Nova Scotia show that girls' reading and writing scores are higher than boys' in some measurements, but data collected in 1998 indicate that boys across the board are not in fact falling further behind girls: 'In fact, in numerous cases, males are showing *improvement* at several levels, and some boys are doing very well' (ibid:55). Like researchers in the United Kingdom, the Canadian team point out that differences in literacy performance have in fact been an object of concern for over 300 years (Cohen, 1998). Griffin, analysing the 'boys' underachievement' debate in the United Kingdom, argues that the failing boys narrative represents 'a form of collective and selective forgetting', which totally ignores previous debates about the underachievement of working-class boys in poorly resourced schools, about girls' relative underachievement in maths and sciences, and about underperformance among particular ethnic community groups (2000:167). The hugely significant intersections between gender, social class and ethnicity are excluded from current discourses of crisis. The comparatively poor performance of large numbers of boys is not a new phenomenon; what is new, is the changing context in which this performance is now sitting; and what is sliding by many of the louder current debates is the fact that there are very different levels of achievement among boys. Some boys are doing very well (Harris, 1998). Gender remains a powerful predictor of literacy performance in relation to *some boys* in *some contexts* (as it does for *some* girls in *some* contexts); but it is crucially impacted by other variables. Any discussion of boys and literacy performance which leaves such variables out of the explanatory grid is unlikely to be helpful.

The debate has become increasingly oppositional recently in the United Kingdom, with conflicting evidence emerging from differently framed research projects. On the one hand, as in Australia, there are official reports which document clear and increasing patterns of gender differentiation, with boys showing comparatively poor and declining outcomes (e.g., Brookes (NFE), in Carvel, 1998; Speed, 1998; Stobart, Elwood and Quinlan, 1992). On the other hand, there is growing research evidence – as in the Canadian study referred to above – of quite different patterns, challenging the gender gap account, suggesting that any such gap is actually shrinking if it were indeed ever actually there (e.g., Arnot, David and Weiner, 1996; Gorard, Rees and Salisbury, 1999; Mahony, 1998). These more critical accounts argue that boys in general are not underperforming at senior levels of schooling, but that working-class boys are (Pyke, 1996:2); and that, for a variety of reasons, this poor performance is becoming more visible. Research data analysed by Murphy and Elwood demonstrate that in some contexts male students continue to outperform girls in maths and sciences, but are also now outperforming them in English (1997:19). There is a growing sense of dissatisfaction with both the research methodology which produces the 'gender gap' model of analysis (see Gorard, Rees and Salisbury, 1999, for a more detailed review of this literature) and with the translation of the results into wider community discourses which construct boys as a homogeneous category. The totalising logic which works beneath this model not only ignores the complexities of gender identity and performance, and the differences and possible shades of positioning which get played out by individual girls or boys, but ignores the significance of the intersection in individual lives of variables such as gender and social class.

It is interesting to consider the timing of the boys–education 'crisis'. The argument is made in Australia, the United Kingdom and North America that problems now being identified and reacted to have in fact been around for a long time (Davison et al., 2004; Lingard and Douglas, 1999; Mahony, 1998); and that current moral panic over boys' perceived underachievement has close – and largely unscrutinised – connections with current politics of 'standards' debates, which in turn have significant links to changing social and economic conditions (Slee, Weiner and Tomlinson, 1998). What is relatively new is the tendency to blame the 'failure' of the boys on the perceived 'success' of the girls (Lingard and Douglas, 1999:54). Attention might also be directed to the connection between anxiety around gender-based literacy performance indicators and current imperatives of educational policy and management. As Ali, Benjamin and Mauthner (2004) remind us, there *is* a 'politics' of gender and education, whereby micro-politics and macro-politics act on, shape and inform each other. Alloway and Gilbert (1997), for example, query the framing of the boys–literacy crisis in Australia as a recent, urgent issue, suggesting that boys' lower achievement in language and literacy has not been of concern before now because these areas were seen as less important than those of maths and science; therefore the literacy performance of boys was not seen as something to be concerned about. Changing circumstances in the wider cultural, social and employment fields, for example the increasing move to wide-scale employment in the service industry (with its requirement of good communication and literacy skills), are identified as significant contributing factors in the current flurry of attention to boys and literacy. Frosh, Phoenix and Pattman (2002) point out that 'as educational demands have shifted and increased, boys' ways of expressing masculinities have become less compatible with the gaining of educational qualifications, at a time when it is increasingly important for them to do so because fewer unskilled jobs are available' (p. 196).

Acknowledging these interconnections brings into focus the relevance of the 'which boys?' question. The boys who are underachieving are mainly boys from lower socioeconomic backgrounds and NESB boys, who have been doing badly in school for a long time. McDowall (2002), in her discussion of young masculine identities in the context of the transition from school to work, details the huge impact of economic change on working-class boys' options, through what she describes as 'deep transformations in the labour market of mature industrial economies in recent decades' (p. 40); changes in the labour market having further consolidated existing social inequalities. She comments on the easy slippage between recognising working-class boys as 'victims of economic and occupational restructuring' and seeing them as 'victims of changing school circumstances: victims of schooling' (ibid.). (See also, Arnot, David and Weiner, 1999.)

Mahony (1998) challenges the recent concern agenda with boys and literacy in the United Kingdom as a diversionary strategy which preempts attention to connections between schooling and broader cultural processes, to the part played by schools in the social and cultural construction of the very kinds of masculinities now identified as problematic. She too suggests that the underachievement of boys in school must be seen within broader contexts of social change in wider cultural sites, processes and practices. Changing understandings and imaginings in relation to nation states and global economies combine with changes in the shape and requirements of traditional workplaces to increase cultural anxiety about gender roles and the perceived loss of patriarchal dominance (ibid:46). She identifies ways in which concerns now being both discursively constituted and discursively responded to are effectively obscuring the 'internal orderings of masculinities' in which schools are centrally implicated (ibid:37). It is the issue of such orderings – of both masculinities and femininities – which is regarded by more critically oriented analysts as the appropriate locus of concern. As Mahony reminds us, referring back to girl-focused gender work two decades ago, it took a long time and much critical effort to move policy makers on from thinking in terms of innate capacities for explanations of underachievement. The same reluctance to step out of the biological binary account and to think in wider, more critical terms is now characterising the 'what about the boys?' discussions.

These debates provide the backdrop to the context and the climate within which discussions of boys and schooling are proceeding. Clearly there are different informing investments and understandings in play. The one conclusion which can be reached with any confidence is that the issue of boys' relationship with schooling is a complex and invested one, currently being co-opted for different purposes and serving different interests. The underlying 'fact' which sits at the heart of the debate, however, is solid: some boys, many boys – and which boys these are requires closer analysis – are visibly alienated from the processes and practices of schooling. A recent study in Canada showed that 'girls are overwhelmingly more positive about all aspects of their school life than boys' (Davison et al., 2004: 56); 70 per cent of girls responding positively to the statement: 'school is a place where I like to be', compared to only 54 per cent of boys. (See also Lightbody et al., 1996.) Data collected in the course of this project suggest similar levels of disaffection and that this alienation connects directly with a wider malaise around the major cultural project of 'negotiating masculinities' (cf. Frosh, Phoenix and Pattman, 2002). Boys invest a lot of energy and considerable strategic resources in crafting and maintaining their oppositional stance to schooling.

Language, languages and in-school masculinities

To return to the specific focus of our study, the poor relationship of boys with foreign language study needs to be considered within the wider frame and frostier climate of boys and schooling described above. As noted, this broader focus has called for closer critical attention to the construction and negotiation of masculinities and femininities through what actually happens in schools, alongside what happens through broader cultural processes; to school practices and pedagogies which contribute to the constructions of particular kinds of masculinities (or femininities), particular kinds of 'students' and particular kinds of 'curriculum areas'. In some respects discourses of masculinity offered and circulated in school align comfortably with broader cultural scripts of young masculinities; but, as Alloway (2002) argues, basing her analysis on extensive interview data collected across Australia, dominant discourses of masculinity also frequently collide with discourses offered to boys in school. Such misalignments – and resultant resistance by boys – were evidenced in earlier data collected in the United Kingdom by Mac an Ghaill (1994). These tensions and collisions are most visible in the traditionally 'feminine' curriculum areas of English and foreign languages.

To define the problem simply as one of boys and literacy and language – or, in our case, of boys and foreign language study – is to ignore the evidence that is both informally before our eyes and more formally documented: that boys are impressively literate in out-of-school literacy practices. They engage powerfully and creatively in a range of literacy practices which are rarely drawn upon in classrooms (see, for example, Lam's study of an ESL learner's engagement with out-of-classroom literacy practices, 2000). Unlike classroom literacy activities, out-of-school literacy practices tend *not* to collide with boys' broader cultural version of what it means to be masculine: technology, virtual reality, computer literacies of all kinds, key in to dominant cultural discourses of masculinity (Alloway and Gilbert, 1997). School-based literacies, on the other hand often involve practices generally perceived by boys as inherently 'un-masculine'. The English classroom, and the languages classroom in particular, involve ways of working and learning which run counter to the dominant versions of masculinity which frame boys' preferred out-of-school experience (Gilbert and Gilbert, 1998).

Language – before we even begin to think about 'languages' – sits at the heart of this malaise. It is centrally implicated in the discursive collision course outlined above. Hegemonic masculinity of the variety offered and largely taken up in wider cultural contexts accords little importance to communication, oracy skills, literate practices of the traditional written text-based types (Coates, 2003). Personal expression, exercises in personal identification with literary characters, introspection, self-narration and disclosure, exploration and performance of interpersonal relationships – these are part and parcel of the work around language that goes on in both English and foreign language classrooms. Hegemonic versions of masculinity head in quite different directions, choosing rather to concentrate on things outside the self (Alloway and Gilbert, 1997). Data collected from boys in high schools in Western Australia (Martino, 1995) indicate the depth of resentment felt by many boys of what they see to be the expectation that they behave in totally inappropriate ways in the English classroom: '*English is more suited to girls because it's not the way guys think* . . . . *I hope you aren't offended by this, but most guys who like English are faggots'* (ibid:354). The fear of being seen to engage in behaviour associated with girls emerges consistently through our data. Identities, as argued above, are forged in social spaces, and the pressure to conform to dominant cultural norms is particularly acute around adolescence – the stage when most boys opt out of language study. As Rankin and colleagues argue, 'adolescents are . . . characterised as being particularly concerned about how others perceive them . . . highly susceptible to peer influence and easily embarrassed when detected in peer-disdained activities' (2004:2). Our data suggest that language study for many boys is just such an activity.

Gender and foreign language study

In spite of considerable attention accorded to the relationship between first-language education and gender, as noted earlier, there has been surprisingly little critical discussion of gender in the foreign language classroom context. Sunderland (2004) suggests that this may be due to the fact that historically the gender–classroom–language lens has looked primarily at disadvantage and girls. As girls are seen to be 'good' at languages, performing better than boys, being more likely to continue with languages, there was not seen to be an equity or social justice issue (ibid:223). The fact that far fewer boys choose to continue with language study, and that language classrooms are perceived by boys as 'boy-unfriendly', has not been generally picked up as an issue of concern or as a relevant research question. It seems to have been generally accepted that 'boys don't do languages'.

Curriculum areas are gendered places. Students on the whole have a strong sense of what are gender-appropriate curriculum choices, these choices reflecting not only what actually happens in classrooms and schools, but also what circulate as *régimes* of truth (Foucault, 1977). Wertheim's analysis of the gendered dimension of the construction of maths and sciences (1995) details how this sense of gendered curriculum territory works. As we commented in Chapter 2, it has been interesting to track the changing market value of foreign languages in the curriculum stakes (Lo Bianco, 2001). In the early nineteenth century, Western universities required their students to study Latin and Ancient Greek as a prerequisite for entry into all courses – study of another language (even a 'dead' one) being seen as a reliable indicator of students' intellectual ability. In more contemporary times, until the 1960s students applying for university entrance in Australia needed a language; but Australia has shifted significantly from this position. In spite of the period of strong commitment to linguistic and cultural diversity which saw the formulation and enactment of the 1987 Australian National Policy on Languages (Lo Bianco, 1987), recent public and political discourses have regressed community attitudes backwards, away from acknowledgement and legislation of the importance of cultural literacy and linguistic plurality to what Lo Bianco describes as the current official 'One Literacy' position which characterises government policy, practice and rhetoric in Australia (2001). Real support for languages education is weak. Shifting attitudes at policy level in the United Kingdom and the United States convey similar messages about the value and importance of additional language study. None of this helps to improve young people's interest in language study. Equally unhelpful, however, and more relevant to our study, is the clear perception among students, teachers and members of the wider community, that foreign language study is an appropriate 'girl' curriculum option. Boys on the whole reject – and are expected to reject – the languages option (Carr, 2002).

The status of languages in the curriculum is low. Students asked to rank-order curriculum options consistently place languages either at the bottom or very close to the bottom of listed offerings (Carr, 2002; Clark, 1998b). Languages appear to be regarded in two quite different but equally problematic ways. Less academically focused students, especially boys, see languages as a 'hard option', a suitable choice only for 'brainy' (and female) students. Ironically, the more academically oriented students – again especially boys – see languages as a 'soft option', one which has little to offer in terms of the hard-edged competitive curriculum stakes (Carr, 2002); 'soft' in terms of potential value in career terms, but also in terms of cognitive challenge. It seems that foreign language study is poorly valued in all constituencies: soft option or hard option, on the whole it is an unpopular one (Lo Bianco, 1995).

This fact appears to be of little general concern, except of course to language teachers, who find themselves increasingly marginalised, often having to teach composite classes at senior level, with numbers too low for viable classes; at times required to reconfigure themselves as teachers of different languages (in which they may have minimal proficiency) or teachers in other curriculum areas. Interestingly – and discouragingly – recent discussions about the possibility of increasing compulsory language study further up the high school years in Australia produced a flurry of anxiety among language teachers, grown used to working with small, motivated post-compulsory groups of students (mainly girls), horrified by the prospect of replicating the compulsory year experience of large, mainly unmotivated classes of resistant learners (especially boys). This reaction shows how some teachers have, ironically, become comfortable with the marginalised status of their curriculum area.

The gendered profile of post-compulsory language classrooms is now so well established that it is rarely commented on: it is 'how things are'. Boys are not expected to be interested in – or good at – languages. As long ago as 1693, English philosopher John Locke was worrying about his observation that girls seemed more able to learn languages than boys: noting that while boys failed rather consistently to master Latin, in spite of years studying it, small girls seemed to have no problem in learning French rapidly and successfully just by 'pratling it' with their governesses (quoted in Cohen, 1998:21). (Locke was equally critical of men's first-language oracy skills – their inability to 'tell a Story as they should', or to 'speak clearly and persuasively in any Business', Cohen:22). The gender–language ability connection has been around for a long time. Conversations with teachers, parents and students confirm its durability (Carr, 2002). Based on crude versions of cognitive psychology and theories of innate difference, the male brain is believed to be differently structured from the female brain. Girls, it is believed, are biologically programmed to develop better proficiency at language, predisposed to be more effective communicators and therefore language learners. Boys, on the other hand, are believed to be cognitively organised in such a way that they will perform better than girls in terms of spatial ability, speculative thinking and action (Raphael Reed, 1999:61).

The biological difference argument continues to inform debates around curriculum choice among parents, teachers and students themselves. Neurologically based evidence about the comparative shape, density or alignment of various areas of the brain is increasingly countered by educational theorists and researchers who insist that such evidence must always be viewed in light of the powerful environmental and social effects of cultural formation (Yates, 1997). The argument that girls are better able to learn another language makes little sense of the ease with which millions of small people of both sexes all around the world function quite routinely in two, three or more languages. Yet the biological argument is proving resilient to such evidence or challenge, as our data demonstrate.

The monolingual mindset

The cultural 'knowledge' about gender differences, cognitive ability and language learning outlined above combines with another powerful cultural characteristic of young people living in the major Anglophone countries: the traditional disinterest in other-language learning which has always characterised – and continues to characterise – the major

Anglophone countries of the world. This is a powerful component of the boys–languages 'problem'. Male students in colleges and lycées around France or in high schools in Hong Kong may not enthuse about in-school English classes (and there is some evidence to suggest considerable lack of official enthusiasm), but there is no hard argument that has to be made about relevance or usefulness. English language proficiency represents access to highly valued cultural goods, popular, globally mediated youth culture in all its multi-modal, hybrid forms. Boys in these contexts certainly negotiate similar tensions around the performance of in- and out-of-school masculinities, but their attitude to the study of the 'foreign' language that is English has a different relationship with the all-important 'cool' factor. English-speaking boys, in the contexts we are concerned with, have no such motivating circumstance.

Their disinterest is informally sanctioned. The monolingual mindset is neither a recent phenomenon nor a characteristic only of the younger generation. Current leaders in the major Anglophone countries – politicians, business leaders, academics – are for the most part unashamedly monolingual, unselfconsciously progressing their agendas of globalisation and internationalisation in English-only mode, apparently comfortable in the assumption that all business can be done this way. The occasional display of other-language proficiency by a high-profile figure (e.g. Chinese language proficiency by the current Shadow Foreign Affairs Minister in Australia), or by a celebrity with popular youth-culture appeal (e.g., David Beckham's recent display of minimal conversational Spanish) is cause for comment and surprise.

The disinterest is also more formally sanctioned. The discussions around boys and literacy referred to earlier in this chapter make almost no reference to foreign language study. There is an irony in this omission, given the current strong commitment to the multiliteracies agenda (Cope and Kalantzis, 2000), to helping students develop the wide range of literacy practices seen as a prerequisite for the successful negotiation of contemporary times and conditions. The multiliteracies project makes only passing reference to other-language literacy, and generally makes no comment on the skewed gender profile of optional language programmes. In spite of the fact that other-language proficiency is recognised as a core component of intercultural competence, the wide-scale rejection by boys of the languages option is not seen to constitute a 'multiliteracies' problem. Girls continue to be targeted for additional support in areas such as maths, sciences and IT, and boys for support in communication, literacy and social skills; but this support is framed only in terms of first-language development. The fact that foreign language classrooms are staffed mainly

by female teachers and occupied mainly by female students is not officially recognised as a problem. Curriculum documents and policy statements on the whole make no reference to the variable of gender; nor is it
generally identified as an issue in pre-service or professional development
programmes for language teachers.

Research interest and evidence

The last two decades have seen some first studies into the boys-languages
relationship in the United Kingdom (e.g., Clark, 1998a and 1998b; Clark
and Trafford, 1994; Harris, 1998; Jones and Jones, 2001; Powell, 1986);
studies which have investigated trends and patterns and developed
pedagogical suggestions for increasing levels of engagement by boys; but
until the beginning of this project, there had been few such studies in
either Australia or the other major Anglophone countries around the
world. Apart from some first mapping of Australian statistics and trends
of gender distribution (e.g., Zammit, 1993) and some discussion of gender in terms of motivation and attitudes (e.g., Baldauf and Rainbow,
1995), there had been little investigation of what lies beneath these patterns and trends; and no exploration of what boys themselves might
have to say about their disinterest in languages.

Work in both the United Kingdom and Australia has recently begun to
redress this investigative 'empty space'; to look more closely at the variables in play and to canvass the opinions of boys themselves. This study
contributes to this project. The commentaries collected and presented in
this book identify key issues; we believe they also help to theorise what
we find, and to think about possible moves forwards in terms of improv-
ing the boys–languages relationship. Our data align closely with data
collected recently in the United Kingdom (Clark, 1998a; Jones and Jones,
2001). While there are some differences in the framing and the narra-
tion of our respective projects, the overall conclusions are very similar.
Boys in both Australia and the United Kingdom share some very foundational beliefs about language study: it is not something that boys do;
not something that boys are good at; it is very much a 'girl thing'.

'Boys don't do languages'

Different groups of boys provide different explanations. Some boys –
many boys – present a straightforward biologically based argument: boys
are not 'by nature' good at languages; not 'clever' enough to deal with
something which is perceived to be difficult; not capable of doing the
kind of sitting still and talking associated with language study. Biological
accounts of what it is to be a boy are alive and well (cf. Mahony and Frith,

1995), boys repeatedly commenting that the ability to do well at languages is really beyond their control: 'It's in yer brain', as one boy in a British study commented (Mahony, 1998:48) – or isn't ('in yer brain', i.e.). Interestingly, the biological account is less often articulated by girls, who frequently make comments along the lines of: 'If you work harder, maybe you get to like it and maybe you get better at it.'

In our data there is a strong sense of a culturally constructed and sanctioned model of masculinity; of what it means – socially, physically and academically – to be a boy in school; and this sense emerges from a very physically articulated discourse of embodied masculinity. Boys' talk of school identity consistently privileges the body, with sport frequently cited as the defining masculine activity. Boys' inability to 'sit still' is offered on several occasions as an explanation for disinterest in languages or in English lessons. There are repeated comments about 'real boys', and real boys, it seems, are active, to be found on the football field, in the metal or woodwork shops, in the science and computer labs; their presence in language classrooms usually in reluctant and resistant mode. A collective sense of embodied masculinity comes through the data, very similar to that identified by Martino (1995) in reporting his research into boys' relationship with English in Western Australian schools, and by Archer and Macrae (1991) and Mac an Ghaill (1996) in the United Kingdom into curriculum options and gender (see also Connell, 1995). Data collected from these quite different contexts all feed into and out of mainstream hegemonic discourses of 'real men': the 'deep masculine' version of boy, steering a determinedly wide berth around any activity seen to be unmasculine. Our data call to mind Connell's claim that 'true masculinity is almost always thought to proceed from men's bodies' (ibid:45); and that cultural scripts which 'write' the masculine body – producing and stage managing it with the support of disciplining institutional processes and practices such as schooling (Foucault, 1979) – result in very embodied identities.

As indicated this study represents the first principled move to explore the boys–foreign languages relationship to have originated in Australia, although – as also noted above – recent years have seen the beginnings of critical attention to the issue in the United Kingdom, where concern has manifested at official policy as well as at more scholarly levels.

In 1998, the then British Minister of Education, Stephen Byers, signalled the government's recognition of boys' underperformance in modern foreign languages as a problem, committing government support to investigate the issue. A project was designed and implemented, carried out by Homerton College, Cambridge (Jones and Jones, 2001), on behalf of the Qualifications and Curriculum Authority (QCA). The impetus for the study grew out of the findings of the Office for Standards in Education in the United Kingdom some years earlier (OFSTED, 1993) which had identified two main areas in which there was clear evidence that boys were performing less well than girls (Arnot et al., 1998). One was the earliest stages of literacy development, when girls were seen to get off to a better start in literacy; the other the 11–16 age stage, in which girls outperform boys quite markedly in language-related areas. The main evidence for these trends came from the English curriculum, but there was a similar, though less publicised, pattern in relation to modern foreign languages (Jones and Jones, 2001). The OFSTED Report had identified various possible explanations for gendered differences in performance outcomes, which included many of the issues which emerge from our data. These include: gender socialisation and educational practice; gendered patterns of classroom learning; gendered interaction patterns in classrooms; the nature of learning tasks and of teaching styles; the 'gendering' of the curriculum; the impact on educational experience of wider societal and cultural changes. The Homerton College team examined how these various issues impacted on the foreign language context (ibid.).

The one-year study involved the collection of data from both students and teachers. It took as its starting point the statistical evidence that showed a gap of 16 per cent over the previous four years between the achievement outcomes of female and male students; and evidence that fewer boys than girls choose to continue with language study to senior level, or to enrol in specialist language degrees at tertiary level. Two age groups were targeted for the study, Years 9 and 11, in seven comprehensive schools in the United Kingdom. Data were gathered via individual interviews and focus groups. The key findings were unsurprising in some respects, confirming more informally collected impressions; and aligning closely with our data (this connection will be discussed in more detail in later chapters when we analyse our own data).

The recommendations for policy and practice formulated in the Homerton Report relate closely to the findings. The initial stated intention of the project had been very specifically to 'listen to learners', and recommendations clearly reflect the tenor of boys' commentaries. Many connect directly with the relationship between boys, teachers and classrooms, with suggestions that content be made more engaging and relevant; that connections be established where possible with native speakers and the target culture; that the role of the teacher be made less central, and more ownership of the experience be accorded to students; that learning tasks be more interactive and challenging (ibid.). Such recommendations sit comfortably alongside pedagogical models currently informing educational reform in Australia, (see, for example, the *New Basics Framework* in Queensland, 2001), and there are clear reflections of the project's intention to accord priority to students' perspectives. As Hodgkin (1998) advises, students have a central contribution to make as active players in the education system and in educational reform, and educational researchers around the world currently insist on the inclusion of the pupil perspective – too often missing – in the process of school improvement (e.g., Ruddock, 1999).

The Homerton Report recommends that discussions take place with students of all ages about what makes or could make foreign language learning a more positive, productive and worthwhile experience (Jones and Jones, 2001:48). It argues that such discussions must involve not only canvassing students' views, but also providing clear explanations to students of teacher and programme intentions; clarifications of how certain activities or tasks fit into overall learning strategies; explicit discussion about the process of learning a second or foreign language and the relationship between learning a first and a subsequent language. This kind of explicit work is similar to the move to develop a language awareness dimension to first language and literacy which is now well established in Australia and the United Kingdom. The argument now being made is that a similar dimension to foreign language work is equally important.

An earlier United Kingdom project, jointly conducted by the Centre for Information on Language Teaching and Research (CILT) and the Barking and Dagenham Local Education Authority in 1998, provided comparable data to the Jones and Jones study. The focus of this project was 'the invisible child' in the language classroom: the student who is neither the 'star' nor the 'problem' in the average language classroom; the much more representative 'ordinary student', who occupies the middle ground, often passing unnoticed, 'untouched and unseen' by the experience (Lee, Buckland and Shaw, 1998:1). This study also worked from student commentaries, collecting data from both boys and girls. 62 Year 9 students identified as being of 'average ability' were interviewed about their perceptions of, and attitudes towards, learning a foreign language. The report is shaped around analysis of their commentaries.

In some ways, the report challenges the received wisdom that these students on the whole are not overly interested in learning languages. The majority of them believed it is important to learn another language and generally expressed a positive attitude. However, many of them seemed to lack a clear view of what learning a language means; what they are supposed to gain from the experience. There appeared to be limited understanding of either the nature or the process of learning a language (ibid:58). Some conveyed a strong sense of enjoyment and a sense, too, of progress in their work, but the value of much of what they do seemed to escape them. This lack of understanding was seen to be a key factor in terms of motivation. While some could articulate quite a strong sense of extrinsic motivation – learning a language for purposes of employment, travel, intercultural contact – the intrinsic interest and appeal seemed almost non-existent. What students reported as happening at classroom level appeared to have little appeal, impacting on their overall evaluation of the experience. When asked to rank-order curriculum options, languages were overall placed sixth out of seven possible placings.

While gender was not a key focus of the study, there was one gender-related question used in the interviews: *Do you think girls are better at language learning than boys?* to gauge whether students considered gender to be an issue: 71 per cent of students thought there were no differences; 27 per cent thought girls were better. When asked to explain, those who thought girls were better listed the following reasons: girls listen better; concentrate better; settle down to work; learn better; have a better memory; have a better attitude; pick things up quicker; have a better relationship with the teacher. In terms of explaining why boys are worse at languages: boys tend to 'muck around' (explanation offered by both girls and boys); are not interested; argue about who does what in group work; think they know it all and don't need to listen; think they are better although they are not (ibid:47). These comments can be read through the performativity lens discussed earlier in this chapter, as well as through the well-established educational discourse of 'learning styles'. Interestingly, only one of the students surveyed in this study seemed to believe that girls are in some unspecified way 'naturally' better at language learning. Key factors clearly relate more to attitude and behaviour than to innate ability. Girls emerge as being more on-task, compliant and ready to work. There was less of a sense that languages are a 'girls' subject' in the data from this study than there was in our study.

A third study to come out of the United Kingdom, also published in 1998, was by Ann Clark, of the University of Sheffield, who assembled a team of writers and researchers with an interest in gender and curriculum choice. In 1996 she conducted an investigation into the reasons for the comparatively low uptake by boys of the post-compulsory languages option. She was interested in two dimensions of the issue: why fewer boys choose to study a language; and why those boys who do select this option often perform less well than girls in the same group. Analysis of the data collected by Clark identified three key issues: the perceived relevance of language study; its perceived difficulty; and what she termed its intrinsic appeal.

Data from the study showed that students' views about the relevance of language study were very stereotypically framed, centring around possible jobs or careers, with languages being seen as useful only for travel agents, flight attendants or people involved in the tourist industry. These were clearly seen as girl-appropriate career choices. The other area of possible relevance related to holidays: languages might be useful if travelling abroad. As Clark concluded, these comments reflected narrow, insular attitudes, presenting sharp contrast to comments from cohorts of non-English speaking European students about what they saw to be the relevance of foreign language learning. As speakers of the global language, young British students – like young Australian ones – clearly have little sense of urgency about gaining other-language proficiency. Other influences in terms of student motivation included parents' advice – that they had 'managed fine' without languages, and that their children would be well advised to select more 'useful' subjects; and anti-European attitudes, which appeared to have been aggravated for some students by the impact of clashes between rival supporters of European soccer matches. These comments were similar to commentaries by some boys in our study which clearly showed the influence of racism on attitudes to language study.

In terms of difficulty, 36 per cent of the respondents in Clark's study identified languages as the most difficult of all their subjects and 62 per cent placed it in the top three of their ten most difficult subjects. A strong sense emerged that languages constitute a hard option which poses particular challenges. Students talked about the high level of concentration required, of having to memorise a lot of material; of having to do a kind of rote learning which was rare in any other curriculum area; of the need for great accuracy and finely tuned listening skills. They talked about being presented with an enormous amount of disparate parts which do not hang together to form the kinds of narratives they found in other curriculum areas, and were therefore much more difficult to remember. Their comments suggested an overall sense of decontextualised learning, which brought with it little sense of relevance or achievement. One student commented:

> I think with languages I don't actually feel I'm getting anywhere – at the end of the lessons I feel I've learned another 10/15 words, but it doesn't feel I'm any closer to a goal, whereas with science I've learned a new section or something and it feels like I'm getting somewhere, with languages it just seems that there is so much I don't know.

The developmental, accumulative nature of language learning was seen as a huge challenge. The overwhelming sense of difficulty seemed to obliterate any sense of enjoyment.

In terms of intrinsic satisfaction or appeal, the results from the study were overwhelmingly discouraging. Students talked repeatedly of a sense of frustration and lack of progress; about learning the same things 'over and over'. They complained about the emphasis on decontextualised transactional language, which they found inauthentic and boring. A similar kind of mismatch between the intellectual and social sophistication of pupils as that reported in a 1986 study by Powell came through the data. In terms of gender-related commentary, Clark reports that girls seemed more 'tolerant' of boring tasks than boys; that they seemed more malleable and eager to please (1998:38). The female Head of Department in the school where the data were collected made the following overall commentary in relation to gender patterns of interest:

> Essentially languages is a communicative subject and you are talking and expressing things and I think there are very few 14-, 15-year-old boys in England who are good at expressing themselves . . . Lads at that age are much more into doing things with their hands and doing things with machines, rather than interacting with people very much.

A final more recent UK-based research project which has relevance to our study is the "Young Masculinities" project, funded by the Economic and Social Research Council in the United Kingdom, and carried out by Frosh, Phoenix and Pattman (2002). The project began in 1997, spanning several years and involving more than 200 boys and a smaller number of girls. The book which grew out of the study, *Young Masculinities: Understanding Boys in Contemporary Society* (Frosh, Phoenix and Pattman, 2002) explores aspects of 'young masculinities' that have become central to contemporary social thought. While the study has no explicit focus on language study, it connects directly with many of the issues identified in the research projects discussed above and threaded through the data presented in the following chapters. The analysis is both psychologically and sociologically framed, covering areas as wide as the place of violence in young people's lives, the function of 'hardness', homophobia and football, the racialisation of masculine identity construction and – most relevant to our study – boys' underachievement in schools. Like us, the authors of this study work from the understanding of masculinities as performed, or achieved; performative acts which constitute specific cultural ways of 'doing gender' (cf. Butler, 1990b;

Wetherell and Edley, 1998). Their study tracks what they identify as 'major canonical narratives about masculinity current in London schools', which emerge progressively and powerfully from rich data. The aspect of their account which resonates most clearly with our data is their evidence of the driving imperative of so much of boys' 'gender work': the maintenance *at all costs* of their difference from girls which lies underneath the crafted sense of indifference and coolness about schoolwork, the competition and the teasing, the determinedly physical, embodied sense of selves.

Real boys

This initial survey of the context, the shaping and the current state of research in the area of the boys–languages–schooling relationship has touched several times upon the issue of 'appropriateness'. Our data suggest that boys have well-developed understandings of what is gender-appropriate behaviour – in school and out. These understandings come in large part from the shared storehouses of cultural knowledge – what we have called truth *régimes* – which we have argued not only describe but often determine what girls and boys can, should, must do. The data we present from conversations with teachers show how they too draw upon this notion of fixed gendered behaviour, talking easily about 'boy/girl-friendly' pedagogy, 'gendered learning styles', 'appropriate content'. What is deemed 'appropriate' seems to slip easily across into what is 'fact'.

Cohen's (1998) historical analysis of discourses of schooling in relation to gender differentiation indicates that this is nothing new. Perceived patterns had already become 'facts' by 1923 in England, when the Board of Education institutionalised gender differences, defining girls as over-industrious and conscientious, susceptible to 'overstrain', and therefore needing a different kind of curriculum. This 'understanding' was a key determining factor in the differentiation of the curriculum on the basis of sex (ibid:27). Boys were considered safe from the risks of overuse of intellectual energy because 'it is well known that most boys, especially at the period of adolescence, have a habit of "healthy idleness" ' (Board of Education 1923:120, cited in Cohen, 1998). Traces of these early versions of the construction of girls as over-conscientious, 'morbidly' diligent and of boys as healthily unconcerned, can be tracked more or less continuously throughout the educational literature over the last 80 years. Present-day remarks by teachers about girls' willingness to work even when they dislike the subject, compared to boys' refusal to do so, show that discursive constructions of boys and girls as differentiated students have developed along some very traditional lines.

The boys in our data construct themselves determinedly and coherently as boys. The performances vary, but all share the defining characteristic of being recognisably 'other' in relation to girls. They range from the 'laddish' version of physically driven trouble-makers, dedicated to disruption and 'mucking up', to the more middle-class performance of 'effortless achievement' – the term used by Power and colleagues (1998:143) to describe traditional English aristocratic attitudes towards education. This position involves official resistance to the work ethic of schooling and scorn for 'swots' and 'sloggers' (usually scholarship boys); the assumption being that intellectual talent is 'naturally' (socially) inscribed and academic 'labour' demeaning. Vestiges of this class-based attitude, also tracked by Mac an Ghail in his 1994 study of the performance of in-school masculinities in the United Kingdom (he labelled this group the 'Real Englishmen'), come through our data: boys talk of having to work 'invisibly' for fear of being 'uncool'; speak contemptuously of boys seen to be hard-working (often Asian students) who they dismiss as being 'like girls'. This 'interest in disinterestedness', as Kramsch (2005) points out, is the kind of mark of symbolic distinction which Bourdieu analysed in detail in the French educational context (1984); boys appear to deliberately contribute to their own underachievement in order to reject the school-approved middle-class culture of hard work (Jackson, 1998:29).

In her recent book *Men Talk* (2003), which analyses men's narrative performance of gender, Coates brings into clear relief what she calls the 'constraining hand of hegemonic masculinity' (ibid:197). The corpus of data she draws upon – collected from adult men in a variety of contexts – tracks the tensions and ambiguities which constitute the sub-text to gender-language-performance work. It is these ambiguities – what Mahony calls the 'cracks and fissures' in gender *régimes* (1998:49) – that provide the evidence we need if we are to succeed in loosening up 'gender absolutism' (Jackson and Salisbury, 1996:82) to promote a more dynamic and relational view of gender, capable of destabilising the solid cultural sense of what girls and boys 'can' and 'can't' do, of what they 'will' or 'won't' engage with. Our study hopefully contributes to such gathering of evidence.

4
Boys Talking

So far we have set the scene and presented the broad outline of the boys–languages relationship, examining overall trends, tracking some of the history as well as the enduring characteristics of what is a weak and difficult relationship, providing a theoretical frame to assist in thinking about the next part of the book. We now take a different tack, and listen to boys themselves: talking about their experience of learning languages, about language and communication more generally, and about themselves as students in school. The text becomes, therefore, a primary source account of the issues we have been examining up to this point as interested language professionals working with secondary source material. It has taken until the fourth chapter to hand over to the boys, but the following chapters constitute the core of the book. Clearly it is not a total hand-over. How we organise these commentaries reflects our understandings of how the different dimensions of the account fit together, our reading of our data being informed by the theoretical frame outlined in the previous chapter.

Because the voices speak from different positions, different circumstances and through different discourses, and in light of the argument constructed in Chapter 3 that gender is always both performative and relational, we have tried to present the boys' commentaries as directly as possible, interfering minimally with the performance, providing space for the discourses through which the accounts are offered to emerge. In this sense these chapters are relatively free-standing, with minimal commentary or analysis. The final chapters of the book provide opportunity for further discussion and for reconnection with our theoretical frame. In structuring the book this way we follow the lead of studies such as that by Frosh, Phoenix and Pattman (2002) of boys in London schools, and the earlier British study by Mac an Ghail (1996) which accorded central place to the voices of the boys themselves with powerful effect. We believe our data have the same potential.

The issue of context is relevant. The commentaries of the different boys show how specifically they are anchored in particular cultural scripts and repertoires. The performed gendered positions are neither generic nor universal. While they share broad cultural characteristics – the most significant being the need to distinguish themselves from girls – they are affected and shaped by the particularities of intersecting social variables other than gender, most particularly social worlds and socioeconomic status. These particularities appear to determine in large part the nature of both the constraints and the possibilities of boys' relationships with in-school learning of languages. For this reason we have chosen to present the data in two sections, relating to two broad differentiating features. This chapter presents commentaries gathered in state school contexts – what are known as public or state schools in Australia and government schools in the United Kingdom (the term 'public school' in Britain, confusingly for outsiders, representing the private or independent sector), while the following chapter presents data collected in the independent or private school sector. This is clearly a questionable organising principle, there being variables and distinctions to be found in terms of general demographics and individual players in both sites; but we are using it as a first-level strategic organising principle; a blunt analytical tool, but one which illustrates how intersecting social and cultural variables impact on each other. As in the studies referred to above, which focus on the relationship between masculinities and schooling, the voices of the boys in this study drive the analysis in powerful ways. Their narratives often sound self-consciously performative; but their performances – like all cultural performances – carry traces of the tensions and contradictions identified by Coates (2003) and Mahony (1998) and referred to in the previous chapter. Much of the time they conform to dominant mainstream discourses of young masculinities; but there are moments when these regulating, normative discourses are contested, subverted or strategically rearranged.

Our interest as educators, academics and parents is to try to understand what it is that boys are saying about themselves and about languages education; and also what they are *not* saying; to discover the story that lies behind the statistics presented in Chapter 2. As in all discursive accounts, the silences and gaps are at times as informative as the statements. What is 'sayable' by boys in the school context is not always the full account. Sometimes what is narrated in negative terms – for example, descriptions of boys who are perceived as deviant from the sanctioned norms of hegemonic young masculinity – suggest possibilities of unsanctioned versions of themselves which are *not* narrated.

The data come from a large bank of commentaries collected from boys over a two-year period in Australia. They represent a fraction of the complete data set, 'excerpts' of performances. Ultimately, we will interpret and comment upon these performances, but for now, we will listen to the boys.

Background to the project and methodology

Poor relationship between boys and foreign language study is a feature of school experience in all the major Anglophone countries. Most of the boys presented here happen to be Australian, but they could equally well have been British, or New Zealanders, as is clear from the data presented in Chapter 2. They could almost certainly have equally been North American. As will emerge from comparative data along the way, their comments align uncannily closely with the commentaries collected from British boys by Jones and Jones (2001) and from anecdotal evidence from both New Zealand and North America. The voices which follow, then, speak with Australian accents.

As indicated in the introductory chapter, they were collected over a two-year period in the course of a research project which had small beginnings a couple of years earlier in Far North Queensland – a geographically isolated and culturally conservative region. The region is culturally diverse, with significant numbers of Italians (Bettoni, 1981; Douglass, 1995), Aboriginal peoples and descendants from the so-called 'Kanakas' (Pacific Islanders), who were originally transported to the region to work in the cane fields (Mercer, 1995); but it is not a region known for progressive engagement with cultural diversity. This pilot stage of the study unsurprisingly produced discouraging data from a language teacher's perspective, but it fuelled the interest to explore further. The subsequent stage of research, carried out from 2001–3, involved much wider sampling of opinion and commentary, including this time some interviews with teachers and with girls working alongside boys in language classrooms.

Unlike countries where English is not the mother tongue, the majority of English-dominant countries present the foreign languages option as exactly that: an option. In these countries there is usually a short compulsory period, after which language study becomes an elective subject, offered along with, or in competition with, many others. As noted, Australia's support and commitment to school-based languages learning is currently not in a strong phase. While important progress was made in terms of policy formulation and enactment in curriculum development and regional language policies in the late 1980s and early 1990s (Lo Bianco, 2001), the past eight years of Liberal and National Party Coalition governments have seen a substantial reorientation of languages education in the school sector which amounts to a significant weakening of commitment to languages education. This move at leadership level, involving legislative and funding moves as well as discursive renegotiations around national identity, has reconfirmed the Australian community's historically monolingual mindset. The agenda of internationalisation and globalisation, and targeted educational objectives of multiliteracies and intercultural competence, inexplicably continue to sidestep the core issue of the relationship between culture and language.

The State of Queensland, where this project began, is in fact one of the stronger Australian states or territories in terms of government support for languages education. A language policy was legislated and enacted in 1991 and funds were allocated to resourcing a compulsory three-year foreign language experience for all young Queenslanders. There have been good curriculum developments during this period, culminating in the recent introduction of a new languages curriculum and resource base, (QSCC, 2000) and all students in state schools continue to study one of the six 'priority languages' (French, German, Indonesian, Japanese, Chinese and Italian) for two years at the upper end of primary school and one year at the entry point to secondary school. At the end of this third year, the study of a language becomes optional.

The study

Over the two-year period in which the major study was conducted, I talked with more than 200 boys, many language teachers, some pre-service language teachers and teacher educators, and also gathered additional data via surveys/questionnaires. I also talked with some girls, to get their perspective on working alongside boys. The commentaries from teachers and girls provide complementary perspectives and additional information and are discussed in Chapters 6 and 7.

I interviewed students in Queensland, the Australian Capital Territory and Victoria, three important but quite different Australian states in terms of demographics, cultural profile, educational policy and history. In Victoria, for example, there is additional support for languages in the shape of favourable weighting within the VE 'loading' system, which determines students' exiting scores for tertiary consideration. This is a tertiary bonus system: students who successfully complete the final year of language study receive bonus points which enhance their chance of entry into university courses. This has some impact on numbers of students electing to continue with a language after the initial compulsory period. Students who took part in this study came in roughly equal numbers from state systems and from independent (private) schools; some were in single-sex schools, others in co-educational ones. While some surveys and questionnaires were used, the main data came from interviews which I conducted over the two-year period, in schools but out of class, in small groups of three or four students at a time, occasionally in even smaller groups, and occasionally one-on-one. I talked with boys who had elected to continue with a language, but more often with boys who had not.

I worked to a fairly rough, semi-structured, open-ended interview schedule, which always began with easy-to-answer factual questions (*how long did you study a language? which language? what electives did you choose?*), allowing the boys to get used to the interview process and to me and the tape recorder, before moving on to the more challenging questions about their reasons for choosing/not choosing to go on, their opinions about the relevance or usefulness of other-language experience, what they thought about how languages are taught, and what differences they saw in how female and male students engage with them. This general frame was always flexible, and our conversations often went in unexpected directions; unsurprisingly, some of the most interesting commentaries came as a result of these kinds of digressions.

The interviews were as relaxed and informal as I could make them – given the fact that I was an unknown outsider, coming at them with a microphone, talking to them about something which had often been a less than satisfying experience. I spent time up-front explaining what I was doing: talking about the book that we were working on, explaining my own concerns about the languages–gender imbalance, talking about my work as a teacher educator, and inviting them to come up with suggestions as to how we might improve the current situation. I carried out interviews in corners of libraries, small offices, outside under trees – preferably anywhere that was *not* an official teaching/learning space, although sometimes it would in fact be an empty classroom. These spaces varied enormously. In one school I found myself squashed with four large boys into a tiny Head Teacher's 'room' – 3 metres by 2 metres, located at a busy intersection between classes, with a high level of background noise and windows which wouldn't shut. In another, I sat at a huge mahogany table, in a spacious, gracious, luxuriously carpeted board-room, looked down upon by framed portraits of successive Principals, totally quiet, with afternoon tea served in china cups. Unsurprisingly, these different contexts produced different texts. Gender was never an independent variable in this study. I always asked to talk with students without the teacher being present. The one occasion when this request had been misunderstood, the teacher staying in the room (working at her desk, but none the less present) yielded the most unproductive data of the whole project. While I was the kind of adult the boys would have associated with teachers and authority (coming from 'uni'), I was still an outsider, with no apparent loyalties or responsibilities to the school agenda. This seemed to make for easier conversations.

What surprised me was the readiness of boys to talk. Given what we 'know' about the boys–languages relationship, I expected some degree of disinterest or reluctance to talk; but this wasn't the case. Nearly all the boys interviewed had plenty to say. The voices differed enormously: some were confident and strong, assured in their opinions, clearly accustomed to speaking out and being listened to, comfortable in the interview context. Others were more tentative and diffident, approaching issues sideways on, contradicting themselves, drawing on the full-range of boy-group strategies for protecting themselves from vulnerability (jokes, *badinage*, ridicule, exaggeration): going in fact to great lengths to *not* present as being too serious or thoughtful. Still others talked in ways that seemed to surprise themselves; often starting with a tone of voice and level of engagement which suggested suspicion about this whole project, cynicism perhaps about people really being interested in their opinion (several boys commented: 'I've never been interviewed before'), but then switching to a more animated and engaged tone, often expressing surprise at the fact that they had a lot to say, and that they enjoyed saying it. Several boys made comments along the lines of, 'That was fun!' when leaving; the intonation making it very clear that they hadn't expected it to be. Teachers of some of these boys subsequently told me that boys referred back to their interviews on several occasions, again saying how it had been 'fun', how they were going to be in a book.

I was often surprised, challenged and moved by the turns some of the conversations took. Preconceptions I took into the project about the difficulty of communicating with boys were often unsettled, at other times confirmed. In comparison to the interviews I conducted with girls, some of the boys' groups were certainly slower to proceed, needing more solid scaffolding, characterised by the kind of individual trajectory – as opposed to collaborative conversational work – described in the literature on gender and communication. But there was no problem gathering opinions.

The research questions framing the project were the following:

- How do boys regard the languages curriculum option? What do they see to be its relevance?
- Does it sit within a gendered sense of curriculum choice/appropriacy, and what are the effects of such a positioning?
- How do boys *experience* the languages option? What are their opinions about how it is taught and about what happens in language classrooms?
- How do boys feel about 'talk' in more general terms – in their first language? Is there a sense here of gendered position?
- What do boys see as ways in which languages could be made more attractive?
- What insights can boys provide to the constraints and possibilities offered by the discourses available to boys in school?

In the data that follow, the ordering of these questions begins with the last of them – which in fact frames all the others. In looking for evidence of how boys 'perform gender' when talking about themselves and about school, it is possible to glimpse the constraints, possibilities and trajectories that result from the influence of dominant discourses. And these traces of key discursive resources provide clues about how boys will subsequently talk about the languages option. Their commentaries constitute texts which make sense in very particular discursive contexts. In most of our conversations there was very little of what could be termed 'objective' commentary, although occasionally there was a discernible attempt to stand back and provide a more impartial account. For the most part, the commentaries were personalised and subjective, often articulated via emotive and accentuated linguistic choices. These were topics which the boys had strong opinions on.

The state school boys

Many of the commentaries in this chapter are provided by the boys in our study who, a decade ago, would have been referred to as 'the lads', the descriptor coined by British sociologists Archer and Macrae (1991) to refer to the working-class boys tracked in their longitudinal study across several communities and secondary schools in the United Kingdom. The lads embodied 'laddishness', the combined comportment, attitudes and discursive positionings which collectively add up to clearly defined resistance to the official academic and social ethos of schooling. Many of the boys interviewed in this data set come into this category, performing themselves insistently as lads. The descriptor has recently taken on different connotations in British discourses of sociology, and as it was always a 'British-context specific' term, not immediately meaningful to Australian or American ears, we regretfully abandon it, even though it fits some of our data so well, referring to the boys in this chapter rather as 'state school boys'. Some of them in fact are attending Catholic schools rather than state schools; but many of the Catholic schools visited during this project have more in common with state schools than with other schools in the independent/private sector. Clearly, it is impossible to make sweeping generalisations about boys in any of these schools; but the banished concept of laddishness sits very much more comfortably in the state and Catholic schools in this study than it does in the independent schools. Equally clearly, not all boys who talked with me in these schools were uniformly performing this version of boy-in-school; but even the boys I talked to who were operating in alternative discourses, and who explicitly identified themselves as *not* sharing this position, invariably talked about it as a central point of reference in relation to which they were obliged to operate.

The kinds of behaviours and attitudes reported by Archer and Macrae in the United Kingdom were very much in evidence in this section of our data. Many of these boys operate with minimal capital of the kind identified by Bourdieu and colleagues (1994) and other sociologists as necessary for successful negotiation of in-school experience. These are not on the whole middle-class boys whose professional parents encourage and support the development of academic and social ambitions which require serious engagement with school. Many of these boys come from less privileged backgrounds and have little expectation of gaining anything they really need from school. Few of them talk at all about imagined academic success. What they do expect to achieve is an in-school experience which develops their competence in what could be described as a collaborative and collective project of 'in-school masculinities': of 'doing boy' (Frosh, Phoenix and Pattman, 2002), acquiring culturally prescribed male adolescent social and cultural competences. The boys themselves describe this central project in much simpler terms – as 'mucking up' and 'having fun'.

Mucking up

> Girls are squares, kind of thing . . . all they want to do is learn!
> Like . . . I mean . . . what would be the fun of school?!
>
> (Tim, 13)

According to many of the younger boys in this cohort, having fun in school consists above all of 'mucking up'; a term which summarises a whole ensemble of comportment and attitudes which boys devote considerable energy and enthusiasm to developing. Nearly all the boys in this category eventually got to talking about mucking up, and it was at this point in the interviews that the tone invariably became most energetic and the body language most enthusiastic. We were clearly talking about the main business.

- Boys are more high-spirited – they like to do fun stuff – they like to muck up! We **have** to muck up!

(Alistair, 12)

- We choose to muck around – we choose to be this way – it's more fun! We get the enjoyment out of mucking up – and giving the teacher the hardest time we can!

(Tim, 13)

- We tend to muck up a fair bit more. Just to have fun. I don't want to leave school and find out that the last 18 years have been a drag, with no fun, just going to school . . .

(Jason, 17)

- Mucking up's what we *do*! You have to muck up if you're a boy!

(Michael, 13)

The boy who made the second of these comments – about *choosing* to muck up – pointed to a poster on the wall above us, clearly delighted to have such appropriate support at hand. It was part of a behaviour management programme running in the school, and its banner headline was: 'I choose my behaviour!' The 13-year-old was clearly delighted with its timely support for the case he was making: 'See? We **choose** the way we behave, like the poster says! We **choose** to muck up!' The sense of agency and control that came through his declaration was interesting. This was one of the strongest position statements about the hegemonic culture of being a boy in school to come out of the data.

Mucking up has a lot to do with being part of the pack and of conforming to the expected norm. Very disparaging comments were made about boys who don't conform, who *don't* muck up, who – like girls – actually work. An older boy in one school talked about his years at the lower end of high school and of how he had managed to weather this period when it really was required of boys to *not* work, to mess around, and of how he had still managed to (quietly) do the necessary to be able to continue with his language study into senior. The important point had been to work without appearing to work, without being seen to work, and therefore being identified as a nerd. He explained the connection between mucking up, being part of the group and being cool: 'Boys muck up because they want to be cool. You can't get on in school unless you belong' (Adam, 16). This sense of needing to belong to the dominant group came through repeatedly.

Mucking up involves disrupting, distracting, winding up the teachers, performing for the girls, attempting to ensure that the 'uncool' or 'nerdy' members of the class achieve as little as possible. I was given details about the subtleties and the technologies of mucking up (spit-balls, bay-blades, paper wasps), some demonstrations, and many confident and gleeful accounts of successful strategies for winding up the teacher (e.g., not *ever* doing homework, writing *nothing* in their books, *never* bringing books to class). There was a marked sense of pride and satisfaction in the more detailed accounts of how all this is played out; and clear indications of the price paid by boys who choose *not* to join in this core project (classification as 'girls', 'nerds', etc.). Overall, mucking up was narrated by these boys in ways which resonated with Mac an Ghaill's (1996) description of British boys' collective resistance to the processes and practices of school.

A second dimension to this politics of non-engagement was differently framed but equally insistent. It emerges more from a biological than a social account. The commitment to mucking up is shored up by an apparent understanding by many of these boys that they are not 'biologically programmed' to be successful in school. They talk a lot about their ability and their intelligence, which they see as being 'unsuitable' for school-work. They talk about what boys 'can' and 'can't' do, the general consensus appearing to be that girls are cleverer than boys, better designed (innately) to do well at school; that boys aren't as able. The biologically based account is alive and well.

Biology and the body

I listened to repeated explanations of girls' superior intelligence and ability. On the whole these accounts were offered quite comfortably, with no apparent sense of resentment or regret, just a statement of how things are. Boys repeatedly told me that girls are 'smarter' and therefore more likely to do well in subjects that were 'hard' – and languages were invariably included in the category of hard subjects. These explanations had all the assurance that characterises biologically based arguments:

- Girls are smarter than boys – they can do it (school-work) better

  (Nathan, 13)

- Girls are smarter – they work harder – they don't lose interest as quickly as boys

  (Tim, 12)

- Girls are smarter and have a good memory

  (Dan, 14)

- Girls are smarter and can think better

  (Michael, 13)

- Girls are better at it – they can sit still longer

  (Stephen, 12)

The grammatical and lexical choices which frame these statements – and many others like them – show the non-negotiability of the propositions. These are declarations, not suggestions. Boys appear to believe that girls' brains are designed differently, with different capacities in particular for concentration and memory. Girls' bodies are also seen to do well in school, apparently being better designed for long periods of sitting still – this in clear contrast to the many comments collected about boys' 'need' to be on the move. These comments are articulated with the same kind of assurance and conviction that characterised some teachers' comments about male and female students, keying into – and out of – the familiar cultural narratives about biology and ability which have 'sedimented' into truth status among teachers, parents and students themselves (Carr, 2002). The innatist, biological-difference narrative is, indeed, alive and well; and sits unhelpfully inside the boys–languages relationship.

The languages option and gender

The general comments reported above about girls being 'smarter' than boys were repeated in more detail when boys were asked specifically about the study of languages; and these comments need to be considered in the context of what has been described as the 'gendering' of the curriculum (Wertheim, 1995). The last few decades have produced substantial evidence to suggest that students, teachers and the wider community all have a clear sense of gendered curriculum divisions. For some this appears to be a cultural understanding of what is appropriate; for others a biological sense of what is possible. Attitudes have certainly shifted from the days when it was commonly believed that girls' brains just couldn't do the kind of work required for maths and science; and when the price paid by boys who wanted to study dance, home economics or music was too high except for the bravest of boys. Significant incursions have been made by both sexes into the curriculum territories of the other, but undergraduate enrolments in Australian universities still reveal significant gender demarcations in some curricular territories (e.g., only 4 per cent of first-year enrolments in engineering programmes are women; fewer than 5 per cent of Early Childhood Education students are men). Similarly, the gendering of the curriculum in high school continues to be a significant factor, and boys in our data talk easily about subjects that are 'girls' ones' as opposed to 'boys' ones'.

Curriculum areas seen as appropriate for boys include all the more physical and hands-on options, such as physical education, sports of all kinds, manual arts (wood and metal shops) and also the subjects seen as the most academically challenging, such as physics, maths, chemistry and IT. The subjects repeatedly identified by boys as 'girls' subjects' include the more obvious electives such as home economics and typing, art and music, but also English and foreign languages, with languages being repeatedly identified as a girl-appropriate option. When I asked boys to rank-order subjects in an imagined curriculum league table, languages invariably came right down at the lower end, usually just above home economics. Like English, they are classified as an inappropriate activity for boys. Comments about boys who do choose to study languages when they don't have to reflect the same kind of 'worries' as those identified around boys who enjoy reading in Martino's study of adolescent boys in Western Australia (1995). These are 'questionable' boys. I was repeatedly informed that 'real' boys don't do languages. As one 12-year-old explained: 'Only geeks go on.' When I pointed out that the captain of this particular school's football team was one of the few boys to still be doing Japanese in Year 12, this boy considered my point, seemed to think quite carefully about it, then shrugged and repeated: 'No, real boys don't do LOTE', repeating that boys 'can't' be good at both sport and languages. The durability and conviction of these 'understandings' – even in the face of evidence to the contrary as in the case above – is impressive.

Some boys' suggested that parents are also implicated in maintaining the gendered curriculum order. A Year 12 boy studying French commented critically on the ways in which boys are socialised into 'shape' by their parents:

> ... those kinds of opinions and beliefs are installed (sic) in them by their parents – the older generation, ideologies emerge: beliefs that you have your girls' subjects and your boys' subjects, and they continue to believe that and carry it through. One of my friends wanted to do French and his mum and dad pressured him into doing physics: there's certainly a strong belief – it's a problem.
>
> (Anthony, 17)

More biology ...

Moving back to the biologically based belief in girls' innate ability to learn languages, it was clear that many of the boys in this section of the data see languages as a very difficult option. I was told repeatedly that languages are 'hard', requiring the kind of application and 'smartness' that boys don't see themselves as possessing:

- Girls are better at it – it's too hard for boys.

  (James, 14)

- Because they're smarter than boys, they can do it more.

  (Stewart, 13)

- It's really difficult. Boys are no good at it.

  (Stephen, 15)

- Scientists say that girls can learn stuff better than boys ... because of the size of something in their brains.

  (Andrew, 13)

- Girls can do languages – that's how their brains are.

  (Luke, 14)

I tried to collect more detail about this brain connection, about what it is that boys see as making languages so difficult and beyond their capabilities. The following comments provide some clues:

- Girls can sit still for longer – they can concentrate more.

  (Stephen, 12)

- Girls can do more than one thing at a time: e.g., talk AND write; listen AND write; write AND remember what they've written.

  (Jason, 14)

- Girls can concentrate, because they want to learn. They just sit there and pay attention! Close their mouths and do their work.

  (Paul, 13)

- Girls can stay with something till they've got it. The girls in our class, they'll spend every afternoon looking at the same thing in Chinese till they've got it! Till they've got it memorised! Us fellas are a lot more laid back. They do better than us.

  (Nick, 13)

- Girls get answers quicker than boys – boys have to think more. I think we're not as quick as they are.

  (Sean, 14)

- Girls enjoy talk: it's what they do, what they're good at. They like talk – they like having conversations and stuff. Girls talk more . . .. Girls can express themselves more than boys.

  (Andrew, 15)

- We're not as social. I think girls tend to get on a lot better than boys. Girls can be part of a group of 20 girls – boys it's about five. They like working together!

  (Alan, 14)

- Girls will ask for help. If one of the girls is having trouble with her Chinese homework, she'll ring one of the other girls and get help. If we're having trouble, we don't ask for help. It's just not done. Boys don't ask for help.

  (Stewart, 13)

- Girls get on better with teachers. Girls are teachers' pets . . .. Teachers like the girls more than the boys. We talk a lot, but get into real trouble; more trouble than the girls. They talk SO much, but don't get into trouble.

  (James, 12)

- Girls are quite passive. They don't do anything. They just like sitting there in a room doing nothing – or learning. . . . Girls are squares. All they want to do is learn. All they want to do is learn!

(Geoff, 13)

These comments cover a whole range of relevant issues. The first point which emerges is the connection between boys' version of girls as passive – squares, with little interest in the kinds of physical activities boys identify with their own way of being in the world – and their explanation of why they do better at school-work. There is a default narrative working here. Girls are described as working because they have nothing else to do (i.e., nothing more interesting). This passivity also reconnects with the biological argument that boys are more physical and girls less so. The conversations about how boys 'are' repeatedly foreground the physical dimension of boys' lives. There is a strong embodied sense of identity:

- Boys are active, need to do sports and stuff.

(Sean, 14)

- Boys need to be moving around.

(Alan, 14)

- Boys need to be on the footy field – not sitting in a classroom.

(Andrew, 13)

- Sport is what boys do.

(Peter, 15)

The wordings of these comments – and of numerous similar ones – indicate the non-negotiability of the account. Declarative forms of the verbs 'to be' and 'to need' are used repeatedly: 'boys *are* . . .'; 'boys *need to* . . .'. The absence of any modality to shade the offered meaning (e.g. 'boys might be . . .'; 'boys could be . . .') indicates the solidity of the biological, embodied account. Sport is central to many of these narratives; as boys construct themselves insistently as the do-ers, the movers, the physically embodied actors. One 12-year-old boy summed it up in these terms:

We're just boys! We're more energetic, like to be up and about – not sitting still and learning stuff! Girls just have to think, think, think . . . but we need to do things, like run around the oval five times!

(Andrew, 12)

His use of the qualifier 'just' in 'just boys' came with a very deliberate change in intonation – combining logic and charm to dispel any doubts about the desirability or acceptability of this account of 'doing boy' (Frosh, Phoenix and Pattman, 2002).

Girls, on the other hand, are described as being physically inactive, still and passive. While boys 'need' to be on the move, girls, it seems are happy to be sitting still. They're described as rarely doing anything of interest – just talking. The 'girls as talkers' motif threads its way throughout the data, preparing the way for the association of girls with those language-associated areas of the curriculum:

- If you look around the school, girls are just walking around, or sitting talking.

(Paul, 13)

- Girls can sit still longer – that's why they're better at LOTE.

(James, 12)

- Girls just like sitting in a room doing nothing!

(Daniel, 14)

- Most girls are quite passive.

(Peter, 16)

- Some girls play basketball, but most just sit in a huddle and talk.

(Nick, 15)

- It's this girl thing – girls just **like** French . . . they tend to like talk all the time, they like having conversations and stuff, whereas we like to go out and DO things. It's just to do with interests. With girl games, they just keep on talking – they probably like to talk privately in that language, so people can't understand them. I think it's just the way men are brought up.

(Nathan, 15)

The dismissive 'just' figures frequently in boys' accounts of what girls do, suggesting a default version of being in the world. This is a different use of 'just' to the one in the 'We're just boys!' comment, where the 'just' suggests a softening of the fact, an artful invitation to indulgence on the part of the addressee in relation to what might be seen by some (e.g., teachers) as problematic: an assumption that their 'natural' way of being in the world will be accepted. The construction of talk as unimportant and uninteresting, the opposite of the interesting, active kinds of things boys do, connects directly with boys' resistance to curriculum areas seen as being predominantly 'just talk': English and languages. It explains, too, their dismissiveness about boys who don't conform to the norm, boys who appear to like to talk.

One Year 9 boy had been singled out in commentaries by some of his peers in earlier interview groups as 'a girl'; of not behaving like a real boy, not doing boy things. He was used as an illustration of what 'real boys' are like (or in his case 'aren't'). When I came to talk with him, he brought this up himself – buffered by two of his friends, who helped to narrate his account of how he gets positioned by other boys, seemingly complicit in the construction of himself as un-boy-like:

> I'm more like a girl than a boy. I don't have a dad. My dad died, and my brother. So I live with girls – my mum and my two sisters. So I talk a lot, because that's what we do. And I'm not really like a boy either in other ways. If someone at school comes up to me and punches me, I don't hit them back. I **want** to be like them. I want to be able to fight and stuff. But I just hold back . . . a bit like a girl.
>
> (Damien, 14)

His two friends were nodding and agreeing as he talked, chipping in with comments like: 'He is, he's like a girl.' There was no sense of ridicule or derision in their tone, more a supportive, friendly kind of agreement. The boy himself didn't sound distressed or ashamed of the version of himself he was narrating; simply stating how it is, though with some regret. It obviously poses problems for him, but he later commented that he thought it was quite 'good' that he was good at talking, and maybe that was why he was good at learning another language. One of his friends at this point offered the comment about himself that he lived just with his dad, because his parents were separated, and he wished his dad – like Damien's mum and sisters – was better at talking:

> He doesn't like talking about stuff. He doesn't talk much.
> He talks to the cat! But he doesn't talk a lot to me about stuff.
>
> (Adrian, 14)

This particular group of boys got involved in this question of talk far more thoughtfully than earlier groups had done, moving on from the 'it's just what girls do' position to thinking about some of the social variables involved.

Reconnecting with boys' continuing reference to the body, and the physical dimension of being a boy, some seemed to subscribe to a combined 'biological package deal' which takes in both the 'body' and the 'brain' (and there does seem to be a conceptual separation operating here). As indicated earlier, boys talk readily about girls' superior (innate) ability: describing them as 'smarter', better suited to classroom work, better able to listen, capable of doing more than one thing at a time, able to concentrate, memorise, work faster and retrieve information. These comments collectively constitute a solid view of girls' biological inheritance, which is seen by the boys to serve them well in school. Their comments about their own non-engagement with schooling suggest a similarly settled biological account, which means there's nothing to feel bad about, nothing to be done about it; it's 'how things are'. One Year 9 boy did offer an alternative account of the relationship between ability and mucking up:

> We muck around because it's too easy. Boys are better than girls! They just don't like the subject. We're smarter, but it's too easy for us. We just muck around because it's too easy and the teacher is too boring. Boys are smarter, and girls are trying to study to be as smart as we are! It's too easy for us. We're smarter than girls.
>
> (David, 15)

But this explanation was offered with a kind of defiance that wasn't totally convincing, and possibly needs to be read alongside the evidence from Jones and Jones's study in the United Kingdom (2001), in which boys describe their off-task behaviour as a response to *not* being able to do it: it's too hard, so they won't even try. The above comment – and the intonation of its delivery – suggests bravado and defensiveness rather than a serious belief in the proposition.

The social account

Some conversations with boys in this data set had a social dimension, with the occasional questioning of the relationship between socialisation and biology; but talk of social roles seemed to slip easily back into biology. The brief throwaway comment quoted above – the boy talking about how girls enjoy talk games, but they, the boys, like *doing* things – 'It's just the way that men are brought up' – suggests a combination account of nature and nurture. The nurture element is less often referred to by younger boys, but does crop up in conversations with some of the older boys, who occasionally talk about the kinds of roles they are 'expected' to play in life; of how parents influence their children – both sexes – in terms of what they think they should do and of how they think they should behave. One Year 12 boy made the following comment:

> I've read studies that say that boys are more mathematically inclined than girls: I personally think they're biased. But I think parents and teachers reinforce it, suggesting that English and languages are more feminine.
>
> (Dean, 17)

He went on to talk about his own experience in school after choosing to continue with French:

> There's a real social pressure. I've had friends come up to me and say: 'why are you bothering to do French? What's the point? When will you use it? Why don't you just do maths?' I find that girls are really good at it, but I think that's because they're expected to be – they're allowed to be! It seems to be a natural instinct to make distinctions between maths and languages and boys and girls.

He sees this 'natural instinct' – which he himself is arguing to be in fact far from natural – as engendering a definite anti-languages culture among the boys in his school:

> There's a real attitude: an anti-LOTE, anti-English – anti-anything that might be seen as girlish attitude among boys in this school.

One interesting characteristic of many of the younger boys' comments was their assertion that girls are more 'serious' about school not only because they have few other activities or interests to occupy themselves with, but also for more positive reasons, such as the fact that they actually seem to like it; actually *enjoy* the process of learning:

> • Girls are more interested. They pay more attention.
>
> (Tony, 15)

> • Girls tend to concentrate because they **want** to learn.
>
> (Adrian, 16)

> • Girls really enjoy it! They're obsessed! Like they all have their hands up – and they even speak it outside the classroom!
>
> (Toby, 13)

This last comment was offered in a tone of amazement: as if this level of engagement and enjoyment by girls – in this case in their French lessons – defies comprehension; some kind of 'other-species' behaviour – little understood, but observed with interest. At other times, the tone of bemusement shifted to one of incredulity: '*Girls really enjoy it! I mean really enjoy it . . ..*' These comments are qualitatively different in tone to some of those reported earlier (*girls are squares* . . ., etc.), which were much more derisive and dismissive.

This same tone of bemusement characterised boys' comments about girls' attitudes to life generally, which they saw to be very different to their own. Some boys accounted for girls' more serious approach to school as being due to the fact that they seem to be more focused on careers, on life beyond school, on what they want to achieve long term. They themselves report rarely thinking about this dimension of their lives:

- Boys, they just prefer to take it as they come. I'm just going to school, picking subjects as they come . . . if I do well at them. Girls set their futures more earlier . . .. The girls might be more focused on getting somewhere. I just want to have fun!

  (Peter, 16)

- Girls always seem to be working harder no matter what they do. Because they're worrying about their future more than what we are I suppose. They probably know what they want to do – most of the girls plan it, we just take it as it comes. Most of the girls in my classes they have an aim, I'm just doing whatever . . . I feel like I'll know where I'm going, but I just come here to school to pass, get good marks, and then get a job. Whatever.

  (Daniel, 15)

- Maybe girls just think that **whatever** they can get behind them is good . . . instead of just getting behind them mainly what they **want**, which is what we do. I think girls think about the future more . . .

  (Nick, 15)

In terms of choosing the languages option, there was also a sense that languages had more relevance to the kinds of things that girls might like to do in life – especially if the language were French:

Girls probably have more travel ideas in their head – going to France, and seeing all the places. I'd rather play sport than learn French, I know a fair bit of French, but what's the use of doing something that you're not going to use in the future when you could be doing something else that you would be?

(Dan, 13)

French was singled out as a particularly unsuitable choice for boys, clearly associated with girl-related interests – travel, old buildings and history, romance, fashion. This resonates with the statistical information presented in Chapter 1, which showed that studying French was highly gendered, with few boys choosing to study it. Some boys who had either lived or travelled in Europe, or had parents who could speak some French, talked in more positive terms about the usefulness of knowing French; but most saw it as having no relevance to their current interests or ultimate career aspirations. Two Year 9 boys in North Queensland, who were adamant that French had no relevance to them, told me of their plans to become a chef and an airline pilot respectively. They were unconvinced by my suggestion that French might in fact be helpful in either of these careers; they located it unnegotiably in the field of girl-related interests.

Many of the younger boys had few ideas about what girls might want to do with their lives, or in what ways their career aspirations might differ from their own; but they talked vaguely about travel and tourism and teaching – all of which they thought might see French as useful. This particular group of boys saw their own futures as revolving around physically related activities, such as the armed forces or trades, often related to the building industry. French had no possible relevance to their imagined futures as workers. One boy who had been studying Chinese for one year after the compulsory stage had been doing so solely because he was planning to apply to join the air force, and he reasoned that as China has a large air force, then Chinese would be a good thing to have. He had recently changed his mind about the air force, and had consequently lost all interest in Chinese and was planning to drop it at the end of the year.

Boys on the whole spoke of the usefulness or relevance of languages in very pragmatic, strategic and instrumental terms. Very occasionally a boy would reflect on the intrinsic nature of the experience – how it gave access to another way of thinking, made you feel 'different' in yourself, or made you think more about your own language and about language generally. One younger boy commented:

I don't mind learning new things. I want to be able to leave school with as much knowledge as I can . . . and I think this (Chinese) is helping me.

(Andrew, 12)

Another, older boy in the same school, who had reluctantly dropped French because he had to choose between it and chemistry, described why he'd been sorry to do so, and what he'd seen as the benefits and satisfactions of learning another language:

> Learning another language is really good for your first language. It's good for vocabulary and it enhances your listening skills. It's a very structured subject, French, and I found that by doing it I was also improving my English. In Year 10 we did so much grammar, so much structuring of the verbs and that, and when I finished it, and just looked at French and looked at English, I found there were so many comparisons you can make . . . and that's a good skill to have. It helps with English. There are patterns that emerge.
>
> (John, 17)

This kind of articulated understanding of the language-awareness benefits of additional language learning is music to the language teacher's ear. It's the powerful argument for other-language experience which is too rarely made. But there were few similar comments overall in the data set. Intrinsic motivation for language learning didn't loom large. The main arguments for studying other languages were clearly instrumental, such as the boy who had been thinking of Chinese as relevant to being in the armed forces. Japanese was the language most often identified as having some relevance to boys – although, significantly, it was boys who weren't studying the language who talked about it in these terms. They talked about technology, computers, and out-of-school interests, commenting that Japanese would have been a 'better' choice for them than whichever language they were in fact studying. Disappointingly few of the students studying Japanese – or who had studied Japanese – made this connection.

Boys' accounts of language teaching methodology

How languages are taught – what actually happens in language classrooms – is obviously central to how boys react to the offered experience; so this was a key focus of my conversations with boys. I was primed in some respects as to what I would hear through my familiarity with the workings of language classrooms in Queensland via my students' practicum experiences and my professional development work with teachers. I was also primed through my familiarity with the work that had gone before me in the UK context. The studies referred to in the previous chapter by Jones and Jones (2001) and by Clark (1998a), along with a Scottish-based research project (McPake, 2003), provide detailed and explicit commentary from students about teachers, teaching, programme content and the overall language learning experience. The British data had prepared me for what I would hear from our boys; and the closeness of fit was remarkable.

The subject itself

Boys made it very clear that languages are 'different' to other curriculum areas; 'different' plainly equalling 'more difficult'. Their comments suggest a very traditional model of pedagogy, in which reading, writing, learning by heart and reproducing for testing purposes are key features; suggesting traditional, grammar-translation approaches more than current models of task-based, communicatively framed second language teaching and learning. Boys talked a lot about the high level of concentration required, of memorisation and writing, of having to learn large amounts of vocabulary; what they identify as 'girl skills' – ones which they find difficult and boring. Judging from a cross-section of comments, writing appears to be the most featured skill – described by boys as the least interesting aspect of learning, and the one they are weakest in.

- There's too much writing! Writing down from the board, writing from the book . . . always writing. We're not good at writing. Girls like to write more than boys. They're so much neater than us! I like manual arts, not writing – you don't see many girls in manual arts classes – girls do writing classes.

  (Steve, 13)

- Girls love writing! You should see their books! If you look at a girl's book, it'll be all neat, and full of writing! If you look at a boy's book, there'll be nothing in it! Except Dale's book . . . he's a girl!

  (Mark, 14)

- When we go to class, we're just full-on writing stuff out and that – and you don't want to learn.

  (David, 13)

But reading and listening are also reported as difficult. When boys talk about listening activities, they are usually referring to listening to audio tapes which accompany the textbook; only occasionally do they refer to listening to teachers themselves, or other speakers of the language, 'live' in the classroom. When they do, comments tend to be more positive.

One senior boy who had opted to continue with his language study, and who would be regarded as a successful learner, commented that he thought a lot of the teaching he had experienced was inherently difficult for many boys, though he himself had fared quite well:

> The method used by most my teachers has been reading texts and listening to audio cassettes. I can personally pick it up, but I know a lot of boys who can't. Who can't just listen, can't take in what they're saying. They get lost and then they get frustrated. And when they read, they find the passages really hard, and then they lose focus. They'd find it easier to read if we used computers more, boys just don't like reading from books.
>
> (Mark, 17)

In Queensland, all first-year students in high school have completed two years of primary school language learning, and many boys referred to this earlier experience. They identified the main difference between their primary and high school language classes as the emphasis on reading and writing at high school; a difference they clearly don't appreciate. They talked nostalgically about songs, games, learning about the culture, *doing things* with the language – one boy talked about the 'taste' of French in his mouth; others about 'feeling a bit Japanese', and 'pretending to be Italian'. Now they talked about vocabulary, lists of words, writing things in their books and learning by heart, finding the content boring. Not all, of course, had positive memories of primary school experience. Some remembered it as a waste of time, where they learned a few songs, could count to ten, knew some colours, but really couldn't say they'd achieved more than that after two years' experience. Unlike the primary experience enthusiasts, these boys considered their entry into high school as signalling the beginning of learning the 'real' language. Different accounts reflect different teaching and learning experiences at both primary and secondary levels; but overall, there was much less enthusiasm for their high school language learning experience.

As well as complaining about the amount of reading and writing required, boys talked a lot about having to learn by heart, in a way that is now unusual in other curriculum areas. They described this as hard, but also boring and as having no connection with 'real' communication:

> We have to learn all these words . . .. All these words. Hundreds of them! And then we get tested on them. Boys find that really hard – girls

have got better memories than boys. Words about animals, or about colours, or about houses . . .

(Andrew, 14)

A sense of decontextualised learning comes through many comments, as it did through the British data; a sense that words have to be learned for the sake of learning them rather than for any real communicative purpose. Comments about learning lists or sets of words connected, too, with boys' reported sense of the difficulty of keeping up with the language. Jones and Jones (2001) reported that boys see languages as difficult because of their progressive and developmental nature; boys in our study made very similar comments, talking about the difficulty of catching up if they ever let themselves slip behind; of having to know everything that had gone before in order to be able to do new work:

> You might be starting 'family', and numbers might come up; so if you haven't learned your numbers, you can't do family. Or in the family they might have a pet, and if you didn't learn it properly when you were doing animals, then you can't do that either. It's like that. You have to keep **everything** in your head all the time!

(Tim, 15)

There were several comments along these lines, showing that boys understand the cumulative and progressive nature of language learning, flagging it as a major difficulty – and a major reason why many of them do badly. One boy talked about how he could have what he termed a 'bad period' in relation to other curriculum areas, such as English or social science, in which he would pay no attention, and not 'get' whatever was being taught. If a topic didn't interest him, or he had other things going on in his life, then he would go slow or opt out for the duration – knowing that he could come back on track once a new topic or unit of work was being introduced. If he was in a better state of mind at that point, more 'available', then all would be well. *'But in Chinese, if I don't work for a while, then I'm lost for the next bit – and for ever!'* (Ryan, 14). The sustained nature of the kind of application required is identified by boys as one of the hardest aspects of learning a language. Students talk about having to 'manage' their time and attention between curriculum areas. Even the most engaged and academically focused boys talk about juggling time and energy according to immediate priorities with assignments and exams. The way languages are taught, and the nature of language learning itself, makes this kind of variability of focus a problem.

Perhaps the most worrying aspect of boys' comments on teaching and learning relates to the interest level of the content. Concerns about the amount of writing and memorising, the difficulty of mastering grammar and scripts, feed into what appears to be boys' most fundamental problem with the language curriculum: what they actually learn *about* – the content of their programmes. They seem on the whole to have no interest in the notion that the language itself is the focus of what they're doing. They talk repeatedly about boring lessons, uninteresting content, lamenting the lack of 'real things to do'. A few boys talked about grammar as 'interesting' – a challenging system, like maths, another 'code' to be cracked; but most of the boys in this data set talked far more about 'unreal' and 'boring' tasks and activities. I asked them to suggest ways language learning could be made more interesting, and they talked about using language for 'real things', making connections with the 'real world', communicating about the things they were interested in. They used the word 'real' repeatedly – in the same sense that it is used in the L2 literature, as 'authenticity': authentic tasks which encourage the use of language for real purpose. Their comments on their own classroom experience indicate very low levels of satisfaction in these terms:

If you're just reading and writing stuff, then you don't want to learn. It's boring. If it were made more interesting, we'd want to do things. Doing things – not just reading and writing and learning lists of word.

(Alex, 13)

It's not like in other lessons – where we do interesting things. Worksheets!! We do so many worksheets, and exercises from the book. It's really boring.

(Aidan, 13)

The comments reported earlier about the need to 'have fun' surfaced again when boys talked about ways in which language teaching could be made more effective. The boy who talked about not wanting to leave school at 18 and find that all his school years had been 'a drag, with no fun', continued to talk about fun in relation to language learning – in his case Chinese: '*I try to incorporate having fun into my learning. If Chinese were more fun, I'd be much more interested*' (Jason, 14). When I asked him how he thought this could be achieved, he immediately compared Chinese classes with his lessons in his favourite curriculum area, agricultural science. His school has a well-developed vocational training programme, which includes a school farm – a very popular support for the agricultural studies programme. He spoke enthusiastically about this course, and about how Chinese could be made more interesting by using some of the same approaches:

> If we could get out more. Since we have an Ag farm – instead of learning about animals by holding up cards and repeating it 20 times till we fall asleep . . . we could go down to the farm, go for a walk, when we see the animals, talk about them in Chinese . . . instead of sitting in the classroom listening. In Ag. science we do hands-on stuff – learning about tractors, and driving them, and handling the animals, hands-on planting things . . . .. I do much better hands-on stuff. Down at the Ag. science I'm getting A+s, but up here I'm not doing so well. I find with hands-on stuff I do so much better, getting into it, having fun. If we could do that in Chinese . . .

One of the other boys in the group was nodding furiously throughout this comment, and added:

> For a couple of weeks last year she had us on computers doing stuff with Chinese – we all really got into that – we weren't mucking up then. We were out of the classroom.
>
> (Andrew, 14)

Getting out of the classroom can be virtually organised as well as in real time. Several boys talked about using computers, escaping what they think of as the normal classroom space. Using the Internet, communicating via email with native speakers, doing collaborative research projects: these were some of the activities boys suggested to make language classes more interesting. (These comments reminded me of boys' reactions when the new language syllabuses were trialled in Queensland in 1999, when there was a noticeable increase in interest when materials were introduced which used content from other curriculum areas such as science, social science and IT (Carr, Commins and Crawford, 1998).) Being confined to what is criticised as the unreal and artificial context of the language classroom was offered as a major explanation of frustration and boredom. Boys talked dismissively about 'pretend' scenarios: pretend you're at the market and want to buy a baguette; pretend you're at Tokyo airport, and want to find out about shuttle buses. Boys clearly find this kind of simulated 'real experience' unworthy of serious interest. There was some acknowledgement of the constraints associated with the realities of schooling, but a definite opinion that more effort could be made to shift the linguistic/cultural experience away from simulated unreal scenarios to ones which at least have some authenticity. Some boys had been on outings to restaurants, for example, and spoke positively about this experience; others identified this kind of activity as something that would help. One Year 12 boy, nearly at the end of his language study, commented:

> We never do excursions . . . and you need the context of the language. You need to be put in the environment – like a restaurant – where you can USE the language you've been taught. It would add life and a realistic dimension.

> (Nick, 17)

Teachers and teaching

I talked at some length with most groups about teaching; about what they see as good and effective teaching – the kind of teaching that might have encouraged them to carry on with their language after the compulsory year. This was something they had definite opinions about: they rarely had to think before listing what they see as the attributes of a good teacher:

- One that understands you.

> (Michael, 13)

- One that is happy and nice.

> (Tim, 13)

- One that talks to us properly – got to show the work more clearly – not just tell us once then say 'Now do the work!' Shows you how . . .

> (Jason, 14)

- One that isn't boring! They've got to be all and about!

> (Adrian, 12)

- One that's fun – but strict . . . .. Not too strict, but strict.

> (Dan, 14)

- One that does interesting things with you . . .

> (Damien, 14)

- One that's smart – but not too much!

> (John, 12)

These are very much the same general attributes identified in the United Kingdom data. A teacher in one particular school was repeatedly given as an example of a 'really good' teacher – by boys who, by their own account, were probably close to the top of the 'mucking up' league. They explained why she is so good:

- She has a really good personality.

(Ryan, 13)

- She makes us laugh and plays games with us.

(Peter, 13)

- She let's us talk quietly when we're doing activities.

(John, 14)

- She talks French to us – and even when we don't understand, she keeps doing it – in different ways, and giving us clues, until we get it. She believes in saying things in French – and that's what makes us want to learn.

(Joel, 13)

- We have fun with her, and she makes us laugh, but she takes consequences to us (i.e., she sets boundaries, and if they are overstepped, there are consequences).

(Colin, 14)

- She doesn't just give us worksheets or make us work from the book all the time. She plays games with us and we do activities that make us work it out. Instead of just writing it out, she makes it more interesting – and we find it out.

(Ken, 13)

- We have a short attention span, and if we just have to write it from the board and stuff, we're never going to go back and learn it or read it again. And she knows we won't! So if we visualise it and do things with it, it's easier for us to learn.

(Alan, 14)

- She's fun because she's also a drama teacher, so we get to do lots of activities and we learn a lot easier.

(Tim, 13)

This teacher works in both Drama and French, and has recently completed a Masters level research project which involved developing a Process Drama approach in the foreign language classroom. At the time I talked with her students, she was trialling some Process Drama activities and had been encouraged by the level of response. In a school where the numbers of students who continue with French into Year 9 is typically around 15 out of a cohort of about 80, and where there would usually be at best about three boys in any such group, she had already been told by at least ten boys in Year 8 that they were definitely going on with French in Year 9. This is anecdotal evidence, and when the pressures that operate around subject selection come into play, her numbers may well be lower; but it was interesting to see the level of enthusiasm. While a Process Drama approach can't be classified as 'authentic' communicative experience in the same way as communicating with native-speaker students in a target culture school, going on an exchange programme or even an excursion to a restaurant, its use of in-character, extended situational scenarios, where the teacher as well as the students is in role, comes closer to the kind of realistic exchange that boys report as being rare in their language classrooms.

The social dimension: peer pressure

Many of the comments collected in this data set provide further evidence that languages are 'risky options' when it comes to fitting into the hegemonic model of young masculinities in school. The comments about what girls and boys respectively 'do', 'are' and 'aren't' good at provided earlier in this chapter show how this works; however, some of the most convincing evidence came from the boys who *had* chosen to continue with the languages option:

- My friends have a good laugh when I say I'm doing Chinese!

    (Michael, 15)

- If you're a boy and you're doing French, you're going to get teased. If you're different from other people, you're going to get teased. And doing French makes you different.

    (Mark, 16)

- It's a perception – it's for nerds. Jocks wouldn't be seen dead doing it!

    (David, 15)

- If you're not careful, you're pushed into things. It's very stereotypical, people think boys should do certain subjects . . . you **have** to do those subjects! Of course you have a choice, but it's powerful in this school. If you're not sure yourself, it's hard to get over the pressure from other people.

(Ian, 15)

The Year 10 boy who made the last comment had been sure in his own mind that he wanted to go on with his language, and said he found it relatively easy to ignore the pressure; but he commented that if he *had* been wavering, been less sure in his own mind, he would probably not have gone on. He talked about the power of what he called 'socialisation':

Girls and boys are fully different – that's what everyone thinks! So if you're doing something that girls are supposed to do – like a language – then that's seen as a stupid subject to be doing. And because you're not doing the same as the other boys, you're seen as stupid, and not as good as them. At the beginning when you choose to do it, that's what it's like. You get heaps of comments. But eventually it wears off . . .

(Ian, 15)

This boy appeared to be comparatively well placed in terms of 'social capital' to counter-balance his (inappropriate) choice of languages. The hard times he was getting initially from his peers eventually wore off, but probably because he had other things going for him. Some of his peers talked about him during their interviews, citing him as an example of a boy who did do a language – therefore was uncool in this respect – but was cool in other ways; mainly because he was from England and his London accent was considered cool. He was also described as confident, not caring what others thought, which increased his status with other boys. Their opinion of his feelings about their opinion in fact was slightly off-mark, as he explained the tensions he felt, not only about choosing to study the language, but also about the fact that he liked to work hard – again going against the grain of the dominant model of boys in school:

I like to apply myself and do better and do extra work. Lots of boys don't. I know they think I'm uncool! But it doesn't bother me . . . in the slightest . . .. Well, it DOES . . ., but it doesn't affect me. I don't let it get in the way.

(Ian, 15)

These comments indicate the tensions experienced by many boys in school, especially those wanting to work and do well academically. This boy came across as focused in terms of his objectives. He knew what he wanted to do, where he wanted to be at the end of his schooling, and seemed fairly confident about his ability to achieve his goals. But his distinction between what 'bothered' him and what 'affected' him suggests the tension and the complexities involved in the performance of 'boy' in school. He talked about feeling out-of-step with a lot of his peers, because of the fact that he wanted to work:

> I don't think many guys understand that these are the times we **have** to work now. We've had our time for playing around – out of school is for playing around. School is for focus, and should be made the most of . . . got to grab it by the neck, or you're just not on your game! Like right now, talking to you, I'm trying hard not to focus on the fact that I've got two guys being clowns in the side window . . .

And he was in fact managing to continue to talk seriously to me in spite of the fact that two of the three boys from his class who had been talking to me in the previous group had stayed behind, just outside the room we were in, trying to distract and make fun of him while he was being interviewed – positioning themselves out of my view, but in his direct eye-line.

Other boys are less successful in ignoring the distractions and the peer pressure. A Year 8 boy who reported that he really enjoyed French, and really wanted to do well and continue with it the following year, then commented that he probably wouldn't be able to, because it was so hard to concentrate when all the other boys were being distracting:

> It's fun, I really like it; and I want to do it. But when you're sitting there trying to pay attention, there's guys flicking paper wasps, and talking, talking . . . and you can't focus. So you sit away from them, but then they tease you and there's always people butting in and laughing. Then you end up getting into the conversation, because you really have to . . . and then you end up getting into trouble.
>
> (Terry, 13)

Another boy in the same group agreed, adding:

> Even if you're really into it and want to learn, all the people who aren't into learning muck up and stuff it up for you.
>
> (Jason, 12)

Both boys seemed to accept that there was not much to be done about any of this; the kind of determination to stand their ground described by the older boy above not appearing to be in their repertoire of response.

Another boy, in a different school, also still studying a language at senior level, talked about another dimension of being a boy at school which he sees as difficult. He was explaining that he thinks boys are more easily distracted than girls, have a shorter attention span and lose track more easily. This in itself, he commented, was a problem; but what compounded the problem was the fact that he believes boys hate to be seen to need help, and so will rarely ask for it even though they need it:

> If you can't ask, or don't feel comfortable about asking – and boys don't – then you're not going to get what you're missing. I've noticed – especially in Year 11, when people feel pressured by asking – that you have a question, and you think everyone knows it except you, and to ask would make you look foolish . . . .. I've felt that way a fair few times . . . but it's really in your best interest to ask. That's one of the downfalls for boys! It's harder on the boys. Both boys and girls get criticised for asking and working, but it's harder on the boys . . . it's more a hero thing: NOT to ask!
>
> (Dylan, 16)

The 'heroism' referred to here might explain the comment cited earlier in this chapter, from a younger boy, who was talking about girls' sociability and their readiness to talk to each other when they got stuck with homework:

> Girls will ask for help. If one of the girls is having trouble with her Chinese homework, she'll ring one of the other girls and get help. If we're having trouble, we don't ask for help. It's just not done. Boys don't ask for help.
>
> (Stewart, 13)

The fact that asking for help is seen to be an inappropriate option for boys could well be a contributing factor to what the older boy above described as the 'downfall' of boys in the language classroom. The 'heroism' – or stoicism – of appearing strong and autonomous is almost certainly a relevant dimension of the boys–languages problematic.

A final dimension to the general account of boys' experience of the languages option in this data set is that of the small number of boys who talked about the positive dimension of their own low representation in language classes. The few boys interviewed who were continuing to senior level with a language invariably found themselves in a small class, with a majority of girls. Sometimes they were the only boy in the group. None of the boys talked negatively about this fact. Most seemed to find it a distinct advantage. One Year 12 boy summed it up in these terms:

> It's really, really difficult, working with boys. If girls are bored, they doodle and they draw. But boys actively make noise. They always talk, so it's very distracting and hard to concentrate.
>
> (Reece, 17)

So far, this comment seems to be revisiting the 'passive girls' narrative; but his additional comment is more positive:

> I've been the only boy in a class of girls, and I can say that I work **much** better with girls. They're much more serious, and they don't make fun of me if I work. My grades go up when I work with girls.

'You've got to be able to fit into school to learn!' (Sean, 15)

The contradictions which sit inside this declaration by a Year 10 boy could be seen as summarising the data presented in this chapter. The very process of 'fitting in' appears so often to work against the process of 'learning' – at least in the usual academic sense of the word. Clearly there are other types of learning going on. Cultural and social scripts and repertoires of behaviour are being developed, discourses and identities performed, inscriptions into particular ways of being in the world negotiated. Parents of adolescents – and adolescents themselves – will confirm that the major daily 'business' of schooling has far more to do with social and identity issues than it has to do with academic matters. Many of the commentaries presented in this chapter show how the boys in this section of our data, the state school boys, are negotiating discourses which make academic engagement (and the languages option) a challenging enterprise. Dominant masculinity discourses are clearly not languages-friendly. The ways boys think and talk about languages and communication, about study and school performance, show how alienated many of them feel in relation to the opportunity to 'be' in a different language; and in relation to language work more generally.

There *were* positive comments about languages. Some boys talked positively about their experience and about what they see to be the benefits of studying additional languages. One 16-year-old offered the opinion that it's 'intriguing' to learn another language, comparing it to seeing a musical instrument and wanting to pick it up and be able to play it: '*What you could do with it is endless*' (Adrian, 16). Another much younger boy confessed to loving the sounds of the language – in his case French: '*The words are really catchy – I really like how they sound*', and to enjoying imagining himself as French: '*I can imagine I'm from France – that I'm French, with a French name and a French family . . . and that moves me along to speak French!*' (Brett, 12). Another young boy, also still in the compulsory year of studying his language, imagined the satisfaction of defeating all the odds and doing well in the subject:

> Not many boys will do it . . . BUT, if you get through it and learn, think how special you'll feel! Because hardly any of the boys do it, and you'd feel special!
>
> (Jason, 12)

A similar comment was made by a Year 12 boy, who had talked about the strategies he'd developed for not allowing other boys' disapproval to affect him, commenting:

> I think, finally, among **some** of my friends I've been kind of respected, because I'm being seen as tackling something that's difficult, intellectually challenging.
>
> (Angus, 17)

The Year 12 boy who had talked about the difficulties of working with boys, also talked about the benefits of seeing inside another culture via language study, and of seeing another way of being in the world. He saw this as a significant benefit, and one really needed in Australian society:

> Australians are really arrogant! They don't understand what the world is about these days. They think English is the only important language in the world – that's really stupid and really arrogant. There needs to be more awareness of other cultures, and for that you need to be able to speak other languages. If these perceptions and attitudes changed in Australian society then I think more boys would be inclined to study a language.
>
> (Reece, 17)

Many of the issues which have emerged in this chapter emerge again in the following chapter, when we present commentaries from boys in the independent school sector. There are some similarities in how they are framed, and some key differences. The significance of context becomes apparent at this point.

5
Other Boys Talking

In the previous chapter, state school boys talked about themselves and about languages. They talked, too, about girls, about teachers and about language programmes; and their commentaries showed the closeness of fit between texts and contexts and between discourses and life worlds.

In this chapter we hear commentaries from boys in different contexts, boys attending private schools in various states across Australia. As noted earlier, this classification of the data represents a blunt analytical tool, some boys in private schools having more in common with boys in state schools in terms of socioeconomic background than with other boys in their own schools. Some private or independent schools – especially Catholic ones – may have more in common demographically and organisationally with local state schools than with other independent and private ones. We use the classification strategically in order to pull focus on the variable of class and social worlds, believing it to account for distinctions which are relevant to our thinking about the implications of what we discovered in the course of this project.

Again, our intention here is to allow the voices of the boys to stand alone as far as possible, observing the versions of 'boy', of 'student' and of 'language learner' which emerge from the data. We have, however, taken a different approach in presenting the data. Several schools were visited, and commentaries from students collected in all of them; but we focus in closer detail in this chapter on three individual schools, believing that more finely grained snapshots may bring into sharper relief the points of differentiation between these boys' experiences – and narratives – and those of the boys in Chapter 4. The conversations were similarly organised, and produced some very similar as well as some very dissimilar responses.

On the whole, these boys draw from a broader range of school-compatible subject positions than the state school boys, having access to a wider range of discursive resources, more options in the range of performable 'masculinities' and 'students'. Many of them come from the kinds of privileged backgrounds which give access to wider world experiences and different forms of cultural capital. This is reflected in their attitudes to schooling, to study and to their projected life-pathways. This is not to say that from a language teacher's perspective their attitudes are always more encouraging. While the versions of 'boy' and 'student' constituted in these conversations are at first glance more school-friendly, they are not always more 'languages-friendly'.

The models of masculinity which come through in this chapter are often just as coherent and normative as those constructed by the boys in Chapter 4, but are different in significant ways. On the whole, they are more academically framed. Many of the boys would be considered by parents and teachers (and themselves) as successful students, committed players in the curriculum stakes, who take schooling seriously, seeing it as the process of credentialing which leads to good life outcomes; outcomes which are imagined in very material terms. These boys typically talk about money, respect, power, the need to be providers and to bring credit to their family. They talk about careers: medicine, law, engineering; career paths which they expect to give them comfortable and respected lifestyles. They talk too about wanting to be active, significant social players, responsible members of the community. There is little of the 'laddish' desire to resist or to reject either the school or the wider community ethos.

These boys convey no sense of being less smart or less engaged with schooling than girls; nor do they identify differences between themselves and girls in terms of aspirations – unless to suggest that goal-setting is in fact more important for them than it is for girls, for reasons indicated below. But, like the boys in the previous chapter, they too appear to believe that girls are inherently 'better suited' to studying languages:

> I think girls are much better at communicating than boys. They're good at talking – they're always talking; and they tell us that we're no good at it – and that's a problem! That causes a lot of the problems with girls! So talking for them in another language is much easier. They **like** communicating. It's what they're really good at. We're good at more practical things – or more scientific things; things that need really hard thinking skills.
>
> (Joshua, 16)

The biological argument is alive and well here too. Again, there are no modal shadings in these comments, no suggestion that 'possibly' girls are better at communicating; these are declared 'facts'. I collected many comments similar to the one above: stories about talkative sisters who monopolise the home phone line, talking endlessly about 'nothing' and enjoying learning languages; about girlfriends with unreasonable expectations about communication. When pushed for more detail about the 'problems' referred to above, the 16-year-old detailed his recent experience of 'communication failure':

> My girlfriend has just broken off with me – and she said it was because I don't talk to her. I talk to her! But she reckons I don't communicate. She wants me to talk about how I feel and stuff . . . I mean, that's not what we do! Girls . . . they love all that. They want to talk about everything, all the time. It's different with boys – we're not good at that.

Many of the boys talked in similar fashion about key differences in communicative styles, and about girls' predisposition to enjoy talk-related activities (such as language study), which led into further 'explanations' that languages are more 'useful' for girls, not only because they match how they 'are', as girls, but also because they fit more appropriately with the kinds of things that they believe girls are likely to do in life. I asked what these likely career options might be, and nearly all boys mentioned teaching first – in spite of the fact that many of them are in all-boys' schools with a majority of male teachers. Teaching clearly sits squarely in their 'common-sense' understandings about what women do. Apart from teaching, they see girls as being likely to go into careers that involve communication and 'people skills', or jobs that involve travel; all career possibilities which boys see as making languages a more sensible choice for girls than for themselves. When asked to talk more about these imagined kinds of jobs, boys identified the travel industry, working as flight attendants, or nannying in overseas countries. It was interesting that they didn't talk about diplomatic careers, international communication systems, trade or business. The informing schema operating here appears surprisingly traditional, and not at all in line with girls' own comments about their life choices and possible future plans (see Chapter 7). A surprising number of boys in this data set appear to subscribe to a traditional and conservative version of the adult working woman; one which often includes mothers not engaging in paid work. Boys commented that girls are under far less pressure than they are to do well at school, high-status careers being less important for them, given that they would in all probability never have to support a family or be in the workforce for too long:

> Girls don't have to worry so much about careers – I mean, they usually get married, and have children . . .. Or they might be teachers. But they don't have to worry like we do about earning a lot of money.
>
> (James, 13)

This was not an isolated comment. Quite a number of boys appeared to work from the model of home-based mother and professional father; a very different model of family to that which frames many of the commentaries in Chapter 4, where both parents typically are workers, and where many mothers are single parents.

After this brief introduction, suggesting the tone and texture of this data set, we now present three snapshots of conversations which took place in three different independent schools, offered as 'informing moments', bringing into relief how issues identified in the previous chapter are differently framed in other contexts. This detailed contextualisation identifies more clearly how gender intersects with other key social variables; how boys' relationships with languages are always situated relationships.

School A: Beaconsfield College

This first snapshot comes from the school referred to in the previous chapter where the interviews took place around a huge, imposing table, and the conversations felt leisurely and enjoyable. The aesthetics of the physical environment were impossible to ignore, as was the school's powerful sense of space, place and history. If conducive physical circumstances contribute to successful learning experience – and evidence indicates that they do – then students in this school are starting from a good place. This is an established, well-resourced, internationally regarded school; and the campus I visited is a quite extraordinarily privileged physical environment.

This is one of the oldest and most elite schools in Australia, situated in a major metropolitan area. It promotes itself as a school which works from and to an international perspective, creating 'independent and confident learners', who, according to the school's prospectus, will contribute purposefully to an increasingly interdependent world. It has a strong and energetically maintained tradition of academic excellence, with graduating students moving seamlessly into professional tertiary programmes and sectors. According to a posting on the school's website, of the 98 per cent final year students who applied for tertiary admission in 2003, 92 per cent were successful. These are dramatically different statistics to those relating to schools attended by most of the boys of Chapter 4.

The ethos of the school is one of confident, direct and interactive engagement with 'the world', with an explicitly stated understanding that what happens in school works closely (and in complementarity) with what happens both at home and in the relevant wider community. This assumed closeness of fit between school, home and community shared goals and values is a given. The determinedly global school perspective in part explains the school's support for its languages programmes. There is a strong, well-established languages department, well staffed and resourced, which enjoys the support of an ex-language-teacher Principal. It is not unusual for students in this school to continue with two languages at senior level. The language teachers I spoke to have no sense of working in the margins, or having to fight for their position in the curriculum stakes. Languages are a valued core component of the school's academic culture; no apparent sense of stigma is attached to them as an academic option.

Student voices

The students who took part in this particular conversation were senior students, both male and female, studying various languages. Talking with them reminded me of the school's mission statement. On the whole, these are very confident voices; confident not only about themselves and their futures, but also about the institutional processes and practices which are shaping their paths to these futures. Talking about teachers, programmes and classrooms, they convey little sense of school as a hostile or alien environment, to be navigated or sabotaged. They sound more like satisfied clients, describing what they 'get out of' school, how it's helping them to secure the kinds of future that they're pitching for. They talk about their educational experience in market-economy terms, through the 'education as investment/capital/commodity' discourse. Once again, the text–context relationship is hard to ignore. Academic achievement is clearly understood to be necessary, desirable and achievable. While there are variations in levels of engagement – and attainment – there is little apparent resistance to either the academic ethos or the broader social values shared by the school and home communities. The fact that students' families are paying considerable amounts of money for this educational opportunity is also part of the input–output relationship.

In terms of students' attitudes to studying languages, there appears to be a happier union in this school between academic ethos and practice and the social worlds inhabited by these students. Unlike many of the boys in Chapter 4, most of these boys have first-hand experience of overseas travel and intercultural contact. They know from experience the benefits which accrue from other-language proficiency. Some are planning careers in which additional linguistic and cultural competence might be seen as an advantage. Many have parents who speak other languages, do business overseas, host international visitors. Some are sons and daughters of interracial marriages, with first-hand experience of bi-culturality and bilingualism. The contrast is stark between these social worlds and those of boys in the previous chapter, most of whom have few points of intercultural connection or possibility. As the group was a mixed one, and as gender felt as if it were, on the surface at least, a less relevant variable than social class, some of the commentaries by girls have been included. The focus was still on the boys–languages relationship, but both girls and boys provided good data for thinking about the issue of social context. It was a girl, in effect, who first spoke at length about the experience of learning languages, setting the tone of much of the rest of the conversation.

She was in her final year of school, studying Chinese and had recently been to China. She talked excitedly about 'the most fantastic experience I've ever had in my life!' – detailing the thrill of 'being able to talk to people who had never met a foreigner before'; of the sense of venturing into totally unexplored territory; the excitement of going to this 'massive country – millions of people – and knowing you can talk to them and get into their culture!'. She described the experience as 'the most satisfying thing I have ever done', which 'took me further than I had ever imagined possible' (Adrienne, 16). This is the kind of enthusiasm and intellectual energy that dispirited language teachers would love to bottle, preserve and uncork at strategic moments to invigorate disinterested students. Her enthusiasm was infectious. Her plan at this stage was to finish her final year at school, go back to China for a few months, return to study Chinese at university and then go back and work in China. And all this was clearly an achievable planned trajectory in the world she inhabits. She spoke excitedly about the benefits of stepping outside her normative world, of rethinking her view of life, of making important personal gains. This articulate, confident, enthusiastic and interested 16-year-old was the archetypal 'good' language student, with the kind of motivation, curiosity, readiness to explore and to take herself out of her comfort zone that textbooks identify as characteristics of the 'ideal' language learner. She herself was also a 'text' in a very culturally-specific context, drawing on resources not on offer to all young people in school.

The literature tells us that this kind of expressive, enthusiastic account of personal cultural experience is typical of 'women's ways with words'; and the data presented in Chapter 4 suggests that these views are right: boys' performance of talk steering clear for the most part of any such displays of detailed enthusiasm of experience or ways of thinking, talking and feeling which would be considered 'personal', enthusiastic and therefore 'girlish'. But this is one of the distinguishing features of the two data sets in this project. In this school, even in this mixed group, where masculinity and femininity were always in play, some boys talked as easily and volubly as girls about these kinds of experiences.

One boy had recently spent three months in France. He talked about the 'huge sense of satisfaction' of being able to negotiate the French language and culture – from basic routines to more complicated situations: '*I loved the whole experience – really satisfying, being able to fit into the culture – so different, such a different world! I felt so good when I got it right!*' (Damien, 15). He talked about being 'adopted' by a French family for these few months, of feeling 'almost French', seeing life 'through a different lens' and about returning to Australia a different 'self'. He talked a lot about feelings, using words like 'excited' and 'happy', clearly very pleased with the idea that he could become a more 'expanded' self, with a different repertoire, ways of being in the world: '*I felt different – and it was great! Doing all the kissing on the cheek, eating their way – managing to make myself understood. I felt like I was really French . . . it was such a great feeling!*'

Another boy had been to China twice. He, too, talked enthusiastically about the way this experience had changed him: '*A really fantastic experience – it opens your eyes, makes you think differently – very satisfying*' (Adam, 16). He went on to say that he thought everybody should be 'made' to live in another culture for a while, to make them understand that there are other ways of 'being'. Several boys in this group talked in similarly enthusiastic terms about opportunities to travel, to try out the language they'd been studying in school; about seeing the world differently as a result of their experiences. Their comments showed appreciation of the benefits of other-language experience, not just in the 'cultural capital' sense of valued gains, but also in relation to more personal dimensions of growth and experience. The majority of boys in Chapter 4 were struggling to find any working model to connect with the offered languages option; these boys seem able to draw on both the 'languages as investment' and the 'languages as personal growth/experience' models. Their comments

weave between both discourses, the emphasis varying, languages sometimes appearing to be valued more as components of future professional
skills packages, other times as important and enjoyable opportunities for
personal enrichment. One boy combined both models, the following
comment showing how he juggles the two. He'd been talking very critically about his experience of learning Indonesian at primary school:

> It was really a waste of time. We learned nothing – just played games,
> and coloured in and sang songs. When I came here and started French,
> it was so exciting! I learned more that first day than I'd learned in all
> my primary classes! I felt so much energy, I was so excited, such a rush –
> it seemed to come naturally! I loved it, thrived on it, great fun! Now it
> was serious. Now I knew I was really learning something, getting
> something out of it.
>
> (Simon, 16)

This comment illustrates nicely how the two models can work together.
On the one hand he talks about the excitement of cracking a new code –
the exhilarating sense of moving 'naturally' into this new experience;
on the other he positions himself as a dissatisfied consumer in one context, not getting value for his money, then really feeling 'value-added' in
the next. This is a confident, critical response from a boy who appears to
have worked out his own understanding of the value of things. He's anx-
ious to gain what can be gained from the languages experience, and
dissatisfied when it's not delivered. He's also confident enough – like the
students above – to let himself enjoy the experience of the 'shifting self'
(Carr and Crawford, 2005).

Occasionally the balance between the two models dips, and when it
does, the outcome is usually less good for the 'personal enrichment'
model. One boy from a different independent school, in another state,
had talked persuasively about the importance of other-language and
cultural experience:

> I think it's really important to learn another language, because it
> pushes you out of your comfort zone! It makes you understand that
> there's more than one way of being . . .. My Mum's Japanese, and my
> Dad's Australian. And my Mum says she feels like two different people,
> and that means she can get inside two cultures, and choose who she
> wants to be. I think that's cool. I can't speak Japanese, but I can speak
> French – a bit – and when I went to France, as an exchange student,
> it felt really good because I could feel myself sounding different, and

using my hands and that, and I could see how you might even think a bit differently, be a different kind of person . . .

(John, 15)

But then he told me that he wasn't continuing with French at senior level. When I asked him why, given his positive comments, he shrugged and said:

When it came to choosing my subjects for senior, I had to think about which ones are worth most, which ones are what they're looking for if you want to get into the really hard courses at uni . . . and French isn't seen as a hard option, it's not like physics or chemistry or Maths C . . . it's not what I need.

Another boy from the same school, who was studying Mandarin at senior level, had talked about how angry he gets when boys criticise him for having chosen a 'soft option':

It's ridiculous! It's the hardest subject I do! It's harder even than physics or Maths C. I don't know why everyone thinks languages are easy – aren't important, like the hard sciences. They should try doing Mandarin . . .

(Michael, 16)

In my conversation with our snapshot group, I had broached the issue of 'value'. The status of languages appears to be more variable in the independent school sector than in state schools. Students commented that among the less academic boys – usually the 'cool' boys – languages are considered a 'girls' option'; a similar position to that tracked across the data in the previous chapter. However, there were significantly more boys in this context who don't share this view of languages as 'feminine' in any identity-impacting or investing kind of way, but who do consider them as a 'soft' option in terms of academic value. Like the boy who had reluctantly given up French, there is a sense of languages carrying less value than other, 'harder' options – hard in both the 'hard currency' and in the 'difficulty' sense. The language which is the exception to this model in this school is Latin, which will be discussed further later in this chapter, and which for various reasons rates highly in the value stakes. Given the strong sense of school as a preparation and investment for future careers that comes through students' commentaries in this context, the issue of perceived currency of language study is clearly relevant to our research and analysis.

To summarise so far, the distinguishing features of boys' relationship with languages in this school include recognition of the value of other-language experience in both extrinsic and intrinsic terms; easy connection between social worlds and other-language and cultural experience; and the sense that while language experience is recognised as valuable and useful, it is not at the upper end of the curriculum 'capital league'. The differences between these features and those which typify the boys–languages relationship constructed in Chapter 4 are easily identified. The relevance of social class and cultural scripts and repertoires is clear; the framing educational and social discourses of this conversation are more languages-friendly. It was interesting, none the less, to find that some of the key impediments to boys' connection with languages identified in the previous chapter were also an issue in this more language-friendly zone.

Being cool in a different context

This educational context is more privileged in obvious ways, but it too involves complexities, hazards and casualties in relation to the identity–gender–cool relationship. The strong academic ethos of the school makes it easier for boys to achieve academically; but it doesn't eliminate the pressure to conform to culturally prescribed ways of being 'cool'. While there are far more boys in this school who are willing and confident enough to go for the benefits they see attached to languages, there are still traces of social disapprobation in relation to this choice. Boys in this group talk about being mocked for choosing to do languages by the boys who do *not* make this choice, who are, invariably, the 'cool boys'.

As indicated above, one of the languages offered in this school is Latin. While Latin has obvious 'saving graces' for boys (discussed below and in more detail by the teacher in the following chapter), it is still regarded by some as uncool, as a Year 12 boy explains:

> I do science, two maths and Latin. And Latin is my hardest subject. But I still get mocked for doing it – cool boys don't do languages. But what's cool? It's just as hard as everything else I'm doing. The people who are doing languages are the ones who are bright and striving to succeed. It's something hard, but it gives you something that you can keep for life.
>
> (Nick, 17)

The question of 'what's cool?' is a vexed one for boys in this school too. Even though there is far more official recognition of academic effort and achievement, boys still navigate tensions between competing versions of (and investments in) 'young masculinity'. What's cool is closely connected to social cool; and collides head-on with the middle-class model of 'bright and striving' boy – the dominant explanatory grid to in-school experience. The boys in this group (the language learners) self-identify as belonging to the bright and striving group rather than the cool; and while lexical and grammatical choices in their commentaries about cool, un-academic boys suggest little respect for this option, there are tensions here. The case of Latin is an interesting locus of the tensions in play. Very few Australian schools still teach Latin, and this school has one of the largest cohorts of senior Latin students in the country. Most are boys, some of whom were in the group I spoke with. The teacher's comments about his Latin students are included in the following chapter, but boys' comments are interesting.

They told me that they enjoy studying Latin for various reasons. The first is the default case: Latin involves no oral communication, unlike other (modern) languages. For boys, this is a significant argument in its favour. More positively, Latin involves close encounters with texts which detail great masculine exploits – military campaigns, heroic deeds, great leaders. All this sits comfortably with what boys are 'interested in'. Most of all, according to these boys, Latin is regarded as cognitively challenging; 'more like a science than a language':

> You have to learn all these formulised rules and patterns – declensions, tenses, cases and things. That makes it interesting in the same way as maths or sciences – you're really challenged to get it right, work it out, build things up. That's the kind of work we're good at.
>
> (Christian, 17)

Being good at this kind of cognitive exercise keys into what boys identify as innate masculine skills. The final motivator in choosing Latin reconnects with the 'cultural capital' model of education discussed earlier: Latin is identified as an elite, exclusive option. Boys told me – with pride – that only 200 students were studying Latin at senior level in the state that year; and that the additional weighting accorded it in the VE ratings reflects its status as a difficult option for an academic elite. It represents, therefore, highly valued curriculum capital, with an exclusive appeal. In spite of all of this, however, Latin, as the comment by the boy above indicates, is not cool. I tried to get more detailed explanations of this, but boys stayed at the very general declarative level of comment: *'It's just not – it's not cool. Cool boys don't do languages – even Latin'* (Rick, 16). Girls in the group, however, had more to say:

> The cool boys, we all know this, they're not very bright. We all know that. They're the ones who do sport and stuff – they don't do languages. The ones who do languages aren't cool. They're the ones who want to work, they stay in the library; not the common room. They're the people who are bright and striving to succeed. The cool – the popular – boys are doing sport and hanging out – not studying. It's a more masculine thing. They go out a lot, hang out with girls a lot, play sport all the time.
>
> (Megan, 16)

The reiteration of the 'bright and striving to succeed' descriptor may just have been a case of this girl echoing what the boy had said a few moments earlier; or it may indicate the solidity of the tension between these competing discourses: the 'bright, academic student' versus the 'cool boys'. This tension surfaces repeatedly in the following two chapters, when teachers and girls in independent schools talk more explicitly than boys themselves about this dimension of the boys–languages 'problem'.

School B: Pensborough College

This school is an independent, co-educational Christian school, also located in a major metropolitan area, which offers a broad range of curricular and co-curricular options. Organisationally, it is structured around a Junior, a Middle and a Senior School, and languages are a core component of all three programmes. The group of students in this second snapshot are in the first year of Middle School, where languages are a high priority. In this first year, (Year 7), students study two of the six languages on offer (two Asian, three European languages and Latin), with compulsory study of at least one language for a further two years. Retention rates after this compulsory period are good. Figures for the year preceding my visit (2002) showed impressive retention rates for both Asian languages (Chinese and Indonesian) and French. The school offers the International Baccalauréat, which involves significant language study, and this increases the languages profile in the school. From Year 9, students are offered a range of study tours and international exchanges, which also makes languages an attractive option. The group of ten 12–13-year-olds interviewed in this snapshot were at the time each studying two languages. They were talkative and interested, arguing with each other and with me, seemingly interested in our research project and in the issue of gender and language. And they repeatedly assured me they could talk for as long as I liked – as it meant they were missing Form Class.

We began by talking about languages, but they were most animated and interested when they propelled the conversation towards talking about broader issues relating to gender socialisation and cultural norms. They were studying different combinations of languages, but all had French in common. They seemed to be enjoying both the language and the teacher, but were quick to point out the problems associated with studying French. Like the boys in Chapter 4, they insisted that French is a 'feminine' language; one that they enjoy, but not as much as girls, 'because it's a girls' language'. Again, they were concerned that I understood that this doesn't mean girls are 'better' at it, just that they can relate more easily to it:

> When you think about France, you think of a more feminine place . . . maybe more girls would want to go over there . . . fashion, beaches . . . maybe France isn't really a more feminine place, but it's made to look like that.

> (Andrew, 13)

Asian languages, on the other hand, are seen as more 'masculine'. Several of the boys in the group were studying Indonesian, which they described as 'less appealing' to girls:

> Boys grow up thinking they want to party, go surfing . . . go to Bali . . . girls grow up thinking about going to places like France, seeing the old castles, going to the fashion stores . . .

> (Stewart, 12)

These are familiar comments, drawing on the familiar model of boys-in-action (in this case partying and surfing) and girls in more passive mode (shopping and dreaming). The additional comment was made that in Asia 'males are more dominant than females', and that Indonesian is therefore possibly seen as 'a more male language – which girls maybe can't relate to' (Ian, 13).

But thanks to the intervention of one boy, the conversation moved interestingly away from these normalising, stereotypical kinds of comments into talking about gender as a social construct, and into questioning the durability of the kind of role allocation they themselves had just been drawing from. It began from a very essentialising account of what girls and boys 'want' and 'can do':

> Girls have bigger ambitions . . . they want to grow up and travel to France, see the beautiful buildings and such . . . but boys at this age don't look that far ahead – if they did, they'd want to go to Hollywood or Los Vegas . . . and have more fun!
>
> (Stephen, 13)

> I think girls throughout the world don't enjoy sport as much as boys, so they have to look for more things to do. Boys have more opportunities to do things. That's why boys don't see languages as important. Girls do, because they don't have other things.
>
> (Brett, 12)

Continuing the theme of limited opportunities, the boys talked about how 'you don't see many girl engineers, or mechanics', and how 'the only female farmers you see are the wives of the farmers – men!'. So far the commentary resonated with the kind of traditional thinking about gendered life choices and chances that had surfaced in the conversations with the older boys. But one boy was thinking more critically about gender roles, challenging what the others were saying, arguing that, 'I reckon that it's beginning to change as we modernise'. He went on to talk about what he called 'stereotypical girls': who 'learn their flute, go to the library, do ballet, learn French'. He then pointed out that some of these same girls are 'beginning to get into sport; playing soccer, trying out for state teams . . . they didn't use to have those opportunities' (Matt, 13).

This contribution pulled the conversation up short, the boys appearing to stop and really think about what up until that stage had been a fairly easy re-run of what were obviously settled 'common-sense' accounts. The commentary became qualitatively different, at first via some rather tentative propositions (shored up by a lot of joking and laughter), but then leading into some quite serious discussion about social options in relation to gender. The same boy who had talked about the soccer-playing ballet girls, talked about language study, classroom talk and gender:

> Everyone says French is for girls, and girls are better at talking than we are . . . but I reckon that's not true any more. When you

see the girls' language choices for Year 7, most of the girls are doing French and German, or French and Chinese – and there are heaps more boys in Indonesian than in French . . . that's true; but at the moment in our class the boys are contributing just as much, if not more, to discussion. In fact I think the boys are contributing 70 per cent to girls' 30 per cent – the girls are the ones doodling, writing 'I love so and so . . .' – the boys are asking questions, putting their hands up. I did the Alliance Française competition, with all the other schools, and nearly all the finalists were boys. I reckon boys are doing really well . . .

(Matt, 13)

He then went on to talk about different 'kinds' of boys in different parts of Australia, commenting that the state in which he lives is 'doing quite well' in terms of allowing boys to 'do more things', contrasting this with Queensland, which he described as 'more a man's state' where 'everyone plays rugby and goes surfing', and where 'not many boys do languages'. The other boys seemed to agree with this analysis, chipping in with jokes about 'Queenslanders', drawing on the popular stereotype of northern, non-metropolitan Australia as the uncultured 'deep north'. This region-ally framed analysis had a discernible class dimension to it, the same kind of 'superior–inferior' inflection that came through when the boys talked about their school in comparison to other (state) schools; a sense of privilege, that their school – like their state – is 'doing it right', pro-viding them with more options (possible 'performances') than other schools. Like the older boys in the first snapshot, there's a sense of com-fortable appreciation of what's on offer. They see it as being easier for them than for boys in other contexts to cross gender lines: to sing in the choir, or play in the orchestra ('*Well, sax and clarinet . . . maybe one day flute!*'), just as it's easier for girls to play soccer ('*But that's really got more to do with 'Bend It Like Beckham' than with what the school says!*'). They also talk about the social difficulty of making untraditional choices: '*In Year 7/8 we have a choice of doing art or fabric fundamentals or wood/metal . . . they try to get us to do the girls' ones, and a few brave ones do the other if they have a huge talent . . .*'; but there was a sense of acknowledgement that in 'schools like this' (a phrase used several times during this inter-view) gender is an easier issue. As one boy summed it up: '*This school is doing well with boys.*' Part of the 'doing well' is evident in the more equal gender balance in language classrooms, and the same goodness of fit between school experience and wider social worlds that emerged from the conversations with the older boys.

School C: St Barnaby's College

The third snapshot selected from the independent school sector is of a small group of Years 11 and 12 boys attending an independent Catholic Boys' College, which draws its cohort of more than 1200 boys from several outer suburban areas of a major Australian city. These boys are studying French, one of three languages offered at the school and their commentaries represent an interesting discursive middle ground: connecting clearly with some of the commentaries from other boys in independent schools, but also having quite a lot in common with the conversations presented in Chapter 4. While this is a fee-paying independent school, the students represent a much broader socioeconomic cross-section of the wider community, the fees being low enough to allow wider community access; but the relevant variable in this snapshot turns out to have little to do with class and a lot to do with single-sex education, which appears to be a significant variable in the boys–languages relationship.

This is a very masculine environment. The Head of Languages describes the College as having thrived upon the traditional dominant masculine model of the 'active and competitive boy', prioritising sporting prowess and achievement, encouraging the competitive, physically embodied model of masculinity. He reports having had to work strategically and determinedly with other colleagues to raise the profile of language study in the school and to establish a culture in which academic achievement is valued as publicly as sporting success. Languages are reasonably well supported, and popular in the junior years, but retention rates are not high at senior level. Unlike physical education, sport and outdoor education, languages are listed on the school's website as elective options rather than core curriculum components. The school curriculum coordinator, who is also a language teacher, reports having to work hard to 'sell' the languages option to boys and to parents. The small group of boys who talked with me were part of a composite Years 11 and 12 French class which combined three Year 12 and ten Year 11 students.

The background context to these boys' language experience, therefore, is less obviously language-supportive, and less well resourced than either of the other two snapshot contexts. The closeness of fit between language experience and social worlds is also less ideal. There was only one boy in the group I spoke with whose out-of-school world had involved significant overseas travel or authentic intercultural exchange. He had spent six months in France, where he has relatives, and talked in similar vein to the boys in Snapshot 1 of the benefits of other-language and cultural immersion. He also speaks Polish, and commented that *'languages don't come hard for me. They just come – I get my tongue around them . . .'*. One other boy in the group had been on a school trip to New Caledonia, but the others had few opportunities for authentic connections with France or French people. In this sense, then, these boys are less privileged in relation to support for their in-school language experience; yet their accounts are positive and show how the successful combination of two key variables – effective teaching and a learner-friendly environment – contribute to good outcomes.

The boys talked a lot about their teacher. He is a native-speaker of French, and this is certainly part of what the boys enjoy:

> He tells us stuff about when he was a boy in France – the things he did, how it was at school, all that sort of thing – and we really enjoy that. It makes it real.
>
> (Jason, 15)

> He uses French a lot! It's fun to try to work out what he's saying – and he's really good at giving clues, and different ways – and it's fun to talk it, I really like sounding French! And we know we're learning it right, because he IS French.
>
> (Sandy, 16)

But they also detailed other reasons why he's an *'excellent teacher'* – and the reason for many boys continuing with French: He's *'got a whacky sense of humour'*, he's *'not too pushy'*, he's *'strict – but not too much'*, he *'respects us'*, *'he doesn't make you feel as if you're 2 years old'*, *'he's interesting and he gives us interesting things to do'*, *'it's not like a bludge – you learn heaps'*. These comments align closely with boys' descriptions of what constitutes a good teacher in the previous chapter, and also with teachers' own comments in the next chapter; and this teacher is clearly a major reason why boys in this school choose to continue with French; but there is another feature of this particular learning environment which appears to play a significant role: the absence of girls.

As indicated earlier in the book, when discussing the 'gendering' of the curriculum and the gendered economy of classroom interaction and performance, the impact of the 'gaze of the other' is clearly significant. We have noted variations in the performance of both masculinities and language learners in different contexts; but we have also noted the almost universal imperative for boys in school – across contexts – to differentiate themselves from girls. This group of boys, therefore, provided the opportunity to think about whether the absence of girls in the classroom actually makes a difference. And it seems that it does.

I didn't talk about the all-boys issue initially. I talked, as I had done with all groups, about their attitudes to languages and to language learning, about their reasons for choosing (or not) to continue with language study, about their teachers and their peers, about how languages connect with their real worlds. But what emerged quite distinctively in their responses to these questions was a qualitatively different sense of how they see themselves as language learners. There was no sense of apology or justification. One boy mentioned fairly dismissively the fact that 'people' think languages are for girls and boys 'shouldn't' do them; but he didn't give the proposition any serious response, moving on to talk about other things. There was no sign of the 'saving grace' discourse. This was a noticeable difference, and made a qualitative difference to how the conversation proceeded.

Having by-passed the familiar provisos, cautions, justifications and defence mechanisms, these boys talked directly about the nature and the quality of their French programme. They identified the challenges: having to '*make a commitment*', to '*study seriously*', to '*maintain the language, go over it constantly*', to '*think about the structure of the language*', to '*find ways of practising at home, out of school*' – ('*you have to go out and do more than school – watch French news – find friends in French*', Paul, 15) – something they described as difficult, as most of the group have no contact with anyone outside school who speaks French; but they also spoke comfortably about the pay-offs: managing to understand what the teacher is saying – '*love it!*'; learning about France and the French culture; feeling they can finally make the individual words fit into sentences that work – '*that's a really cool feeling!*'; achieving well in something that they're 'good at' and also enjoy. While I had been aware of the centrality and the impact of the 'inappropriate for boys' gloss on languages, meeting it constantly in conversations with boys and teachers, it possibly made its greatest impact by default, when talking with these boys. It wasn't operating, and there was a distinctly 'something's missing here' feeling. In all our conversations about the pros and cons of language learning, any sense of loss of face or ridicule was strangely absent. The skill of their teacher in establishing a learner-friendly environment is obviously part of this; but so, it would seem, is the all-boys' context.

This is not to suggest that single-sex classrooms magically eliminate the various complexities of the socialisation–gender–education relationship.

The teacher of these boys talked at length about strategies and aware-
nesses which underpin his teaching, and his frequent reference to
'working with boys' reconnects with the realities of gendered 'understandings' and behaviours; but the absence of girls in the classroom
would appear to improve some important aspects of the boys–languages
relationship.

I asked the boys whether they thought it a relevant issue. Their first
response was *'not at all'*. But one boy disagreed:

> I don't know, you know . . . in a mixed school . . . there'd be all those
> girls, looking at you! That would be hard! I'd probably shut up . . .
>
> (Jason, 15)

The others then backtracked, talked about 'cute girls', and 'wanting to
show off' – distancing this imagined behaviour from themselves – *'some
boys would probably want to show off'*; but just talking about this imagined
situation produced embarrassed laughter and a distinct change in body
language. The imagined addition of girls to their French classes was
clearly unsettling. They ended up agreeing that they would probably
speak out a lot less, tease each other a lot more, and that it wouldn't be
a good idea:

> We're all boys – and so it's easy. With girls, we'd probably get more
> embarrassed. With guys, it's easy – most of them are your mates – we
> all started off together, we've been learning together for four years
> now – we might laugh at each other, but it's not serious, we're really
> interactive and it's fun.
>
> (Kieran, 15)

Which brought us to the question of talk. I asked them if they enjoy
talk; whether they see themselves as talking more or less than girls; and
whether gender has anything to do with language study. Their first reaction was to stake their claim as 'talkers':

> People say boys don't talk . . . we talk!!! We don't shut up! Some boys
> are quiet, just like some girls are quiet. And girls spend more time
> talking than we do, because we spend more time doing things like
> sport. But that doesn't mean we don't talk! And it doesn't mean we
> can't talk! You should come and visit our English classroom – then
> you'll see how we can talk!
>
> (Noel, 16)

I reckon we spent most of last year talking! Boys **do** talk . . . just as much as girls. Out of school – with girls – no. Girls talk more then, for sure. But in class, here, on our own – yes, we talk!

(Peter, 17)

The distinction between single-sex and mixed-sex talk contexts is interesting. These comments are similar to several collected from teachers in this school and other single-sex schools visited during this project, who repeatedly challenged the model of 'uncommunicative and inarticulate boy' which features in discussions about classrooms, gender and language (in the literature but also in other sections of our data). Research evidence has shown that the absence of either girls or boys impacts significantly on interaction patterns and communicative styles in classrooms, and although there has been minimal exploration of this most communicatively challenging of all classroom sites, the foreign language classroom, it would seem that all-boys language classes have some distinct advantages. The same considerations relating to gender, communication and 'public/private voice' that led to the introduction of girls-only maths and science classes in some schools in the 1970s and 1980s are noted by teachers who have taught languages in both co-educational and single-sex classrooms. Performance freed from the presence of the culturally sanctioned 'gaze' of the 'other' has been tracked as allowing for broader possibilities. The teacher who works with these boys has worked in both kinds of classrooms, and has no doubt in his mind that there are definite advantages in his current context:

When I first came to this school, after teaching in a co-ed school, my first reaction was: This is great! I only have to teach to one agenda! Sure, I have to shape what I do because these are boys, I have to plan and teach in ways that are boy-friendly; but I don't have to worry about **all that stuff** that goes on simply because there are both boys and girls in the room! I don't have to juggle two agendas . . . just the one.

(T.M.)

The data presented in the previous chapter and in the first snapshots in this chapter seem to suggest that 'all that stuff' can be a major impediment for boys in language classrooms. The same boy who had talked about possible distractions from girls, and about it being 'easy' and 'fun' working just with boys, went on to explain that in an all-boy classroom it's possible to just 'get on' with learning:

> Like, because it's easy, with no girls there, and we all know each other, and it's interactive, we can just get on with it. Sometimes we muck around a bit, but some classes, everyone's concentrating, no distractions, and we get a lot done! That's really good. When we work, we work!
>
> (Kieran, 15)

This group was seemingly very comfortable in talking positively about working, achieving and enjoying what they do in their language lessons. There was a noticeable absence of the fear of appearing uncool or girl-like. This is a key point of difference in this context. While the boys acknowledged that there are stereotypical associations between language study and girls – 'out there' – they don't see it as an issue for them in school:

> Oh yeah – there's a stereotype out there that boys can't do languages . . . 'arty-farty gay guys' . . . but that's really not an issue at this school. It's not something we think about. We can do whatever we want. In a mixed school, you're going to be in with lots of girls if you go on with a language – they're nearly all girls. So that could make it difficult. But it's not a problem here.
>
> (David, 16)

Summary

These three snapshots of language learners in the independent/private schools sector provide no definitive account of boys' experience. The intersections of variables glimpsed so far make any kind of generalising impossible; but they suggest some useful points of focus for reflecting on the different data collected during this project, and of the variability and multiplicity of the masculinities which underscore the boys–languages issue. They highlight in particular the significance of the relationship between classroom experience and students' wider social worlds, of the 'cultural capital' brought by different boys to the offered languages option, in large part determined by their particular socioeconomic circumstances. They show, too, how gender performance – like all cultural performance – is always up for contestation, and how single-sex language learning environments may constitute different possibilities.

We have been selective in our focus in this chapter, concentrating on those aspects of the data which identify points of difference between the kinds of masculinities being performed in these contexts and those presented in the previous chapter. There has been only minimal reporting of boys' comments about teachers and teaching, for example, as many of these were similar to those collected across the data set as a whole, and therefore reflected in the previous chapter. These issues will be taken up again towards the end of the book. The next two chapters involve a shift in perspective, as we consider the commentaries first of teachers and then of girls who work alongside boys in language classrooms.

6
Teachers Talking

Having listened to what boys in different contexts have to say about the learning of languages, we now present comments from some of the teachers of these boys. These commentaries clearly come from different perspectives to those of the boys themselves, reflecting different investments and understandings, speaking through different discourses; but they have many points of connection with what the boys had to say. They were collected from various sources: some the result of impromptu conversations at conferences or professional development workshops with teachers who identified as having a particular interest in the boys–languages issue; others with teachers who had worked with me during their pre-service programmes, or who had responded to an invitation which I sent out through a language teachers' electronic discussion forum. They varied considerably, but probably represent a fairly typical cross-section of the language-teaching community. Some were recent graduates, others nearing retirement. Some had taught all their careers in single-sex schools, some in independent schools only, while others had taught across sectors and in a variety of institutions. All had an identified interest in the boys–languages issue – several of them talking about it as the 'sleeping dog' issue of languages education.

Their views varied quite significantly, some clearly subscribing to an essentialist, biological view about sex differences and learning, others more concerned about what they saw to be effects of socialisation processes which position both boys and girls in ways that are sometimes enabling but often constraining. There were some points of commonality across the teacher commentaries and some points of real divergence.

Nature or nurture?

One of the first questions to teachers, after initial context-establishing questions about their teaching background and experience, was whether they are conscious of teaching male and female students differently; whether they think of them as being in any sense different as learners. Only one teacher in the entire data set gave a straight, categorically negative response to this question, insisting that she teaches in exactly the same way, regardless of the sex of her students, and in fact makes it a point of principle and politics *not* to differentiate between them, nor to make any kind of prior assumptions about them:

> I try not to see them as male and female. I don't differentiate between them: they're students, I'm the teacher, and I'm what they get! I don't go easier on the girls, and I don't expect the boys to do less well. I expect them all to work and to achieve.
>
> (K.B.)

This teacher works in one of the most challenging sites visited, and has had to work long and hard to establish a culture of language learning in the school. She is popular with students and, in the context of this particular school, is attracting strong numbers into post-compulsory classes, boys as well as girls. Her way of 'doing teacher' could be described as deliberately unfeminine, as she resists what she describes as the traditional model of the nurturing female teacher (what she refers to as 'girly-girl' communicative style). She talked about her consciously adopted position in terms of constituting herself as 'teacher' early on in her career:

> I don't see myself as a girly-girl – and I wonder if that makes a difference. I'm really pleased with the numbers of boys coming through. Other LOTE teachers are very girly-girl: I'm not, and I have lots of boys coming through . . . I discovered early on that if I was nice to the boys, they didn't appreciate it – so I'm not very nice to them sometimes. Early on in my career one boy told me I was 'as weak as piss' because I was nice – my second year teaching . . . and I took that on board. I'm caring, but I try not to be too gentle – am pretty rough – they accept me as a person. When I'm stressed, I tell them: when I was doing my study, I talked to them about that . . . they would ask me questions, we'd have discussions . . . they can see who I am. I was told by someone at the beginning of my teaching career that I had to have two different personas: my own real self and the teacher. I tried it, couldn't do it. As a teacher I have to be me.

This is an interesting commentary, which suggests the complexity of what we do as teachers, and the dynamics of how gender in fact affects teaching styles. As she talked more about her teaching, her students, and the kinds of involvements they shared, it was clear that this teacher works to an inclusive, collaborative model of teacher–student relationship, which in part comes from the demands of keeping a Chinese language programme afloat in a school where she is the only language teacher, with minimal material resources, and where wider community support is hard earned, and in part from her own philosophy of education and personal communicative style. Her students seem to have a particularly strong sense of group identity, volunteering for all kinds of extra-curricular involvements – helping to receive Chinese visitors, taking part in cultural events and ceremonies, fund-raising for trips to China. Such is the level of engagement by some students that they continue to be part of the Chinese group even when they have stopped doing Chinese:

> We do lots of fund raising, we go to China together, we do so many things together . . .. The students and I are so involved with so many things outside the classroom – I'm who I am, and they see me. That's the model I had growing up: that I worked with grown-ups who expected me to take on responsibilities . . . and that's how I am with the kids – they work with me, take on responsibilities. They think they're stopping me from having a nervous breakdown – that makes them feel important! We work together.

These comments clearly go beyond gender considerations, confirming that what happens between teachers, students and curriculum is always as much to do with relationship as it is to do with pedagogy, and that 'doing teacher' can be every bit as variable as 'doing student' (or doing gender). This teacher talks about her relationship with her students as a partnership. The success of her programme depends crucially on the help she gets from students to keep the profile of Chinese strong in the school and the community – which in turn is crucial in terms of the acceptance of the programme by parents and colleagues and the students themselves. Her strong position on gender relations in the classroom can be seen as complementing her broader position in relation to working alongside her students.

What emerged subsequently in our conversation, however, was that while she was the only teacher interviewed who took a strong explicit position on *not* differentiating in terms of the sex of her students, and on *not* framing up her expectations about students along gendered lines, like all the teachers interviewed she did report significant differences in terms of how the students behave in her classes and programme.

The input in her practice may not be gendered, but the uptake certainly is. She may teach deliberately in a non-differentiated way, but she has no illusions about the gendered responses she sees to her teaching; and as she talks about some of the frustrations experienced when working with boys, she contradicts her own earlier statement that she doesn't teach them differently:

> I try not to see them as male and female – I don't consciously differentiate, but I **do** get annoyed with the boys when I'm putting in so much more work with them and they just throw it back at me – really annoying. I'm putting in so much more work with them.

The fact that she acknowledges having to put in more work with the boys indicates a differentiated teaching approach after all, although it is differentiated in terms of the effort involved rather than in terms of adopting different strategies with boys and girls – something many teachers talked about. She stands by her decision not to behave qualitatively differently with boys (although the comment above suggests a 'quantitative' difference), but she reports definite differences in what she describes as 'patterns of behaviour' among girls and boys. The main difference she sees is in attitude, describing boys as not realising that they actually have to participate in the learning process:

> I think they think it's like with SOS or English – they can just sit back and it will wash over them. Girls tend to be more involved in the learning process. Boys sit back and let it wash over . . .

She talks about differences in motivation, level of engagement with tasks, and of boys' 'need' for more scaffolding than girls. Like all teachers interviewed, therefore, she sees there to be significant differences in how boys respond to the languages experience, if not in the way she teaches. All the other teachers interviewed agreed that they did think in terms of differences and that this influences how they plan and teach.

The question of whether these differences are innate or socially and culturally acquired was a difficult one for most teachers. Most positioned themselves more on the 'nurture' and less on the 'nature' side of the debate, especially younger teachers more recently graduated from pre-service education programmes in which gender socialisation had been explored. There was a certain sense of political correctness involved in rejecting the biological argument, yet I was surprised how often teachers stated a socialisation position with conviction and confidence, then moved on to talk comfortably about how boys 'are' more physically active, 'need' to be more cognitively challenged, or 'have' a shorter attention span. While there was a discernible desire to believe that conditioning is a large part of the story, this theoretical understanding appears to float above – and stay interestingly separate from – an entrenched cultural common sense about how boys and girls respectively 'are'.

This disjunction fits with the misalignment identified in the literature on teacher knowledge between 'theoretical' and 'experiential' components of what teachers 'know' (Fullan, 1997; Wallace, 1991), providing further evidence of the challenges involved in aligning the two. Understanding of theories of gender socialisation in relation to language and communication seems to waver when confronted by the 'evidence' of real-life classroom experience; evidence which seems to reconnect so quickly and comfortably with the 'experiential', internalised knowledge which Wallace (1991) describes as the precursor to the 'received knowledge' of the kind delivered in academic courses. This tension between competing accounts is evident in our teacher data, which often travel fairly and squarely within traditional discourses of essentialism.

There were some key points of agreement about the detail of the differences teachers see as characterising male and female students; and they were points made by teachers working in some very different contexts. These points of difference were very similar to those identified by students themselves. There is a solidness about the collective account.

Boys are less motivated, less serious, less prepared to work . . .

There was almost universal consensus among teachers that girls apply themselves more seriously to learning than do boys, and that this is in large part due to their different level of motivation. Some of the many commentaries on this point included:

- Girls tend to be more involved in the learning process. Boys sit back and let it wash over them.

  (K.B.)

- Boys do the minimum. When I set tasks, I scaffold everything, give them models etcetera. Girls are prepared to go beyond what I give them, whereas boys stay pretty well with the model, don't tend to extend themselves, or be more creative. They want explicit guidelines, and when they've got them – they just do the task – as quickly as possible. Boys stick to the task. Girls will push themselves that bit beyond it.

  (D.C.)

- Girls seem more prepared to apply themselves – boys compete, but otherwise don't bother as much. Girls DO work harder, do their homework better and so on.

  (J.M.)

- Girls will get into it more, they'll take risks – once they get over their initial fear! They'll immerse themselves, have a go.

  (S.S.)

- Many boys don't know where they're going – it's a male thing, they seem to have the confidence that it will all work out, without them having to worry about it. Somehow it'll happen out. Girls aren't like that. That makes a big difference. Those who don't know where they're going don't get into it as much – it makes a big difference to how they work. If they're not worried, they don't work as much. Girls are so much more on task.

  (N.C.)

- Girls just want to please and work hard. Boys don't care so much about pleasing you.

  (P.L.)

- Boys are just lazy – and it matters more to boys what other boys think. It's not cool to be seen to work.

  (D.M.)

- I have mainly taught in boys-only schools but the few times that I have worked in our 'sister' school (a girls-only private school) I have been astounded by the energy and work ethic that prevails in the language classroom. My boys do work hard, but these girls seem much more engaged in what they were doing.

  (D.W.)

These comments connect with several of the issues which surfaced in boys' discussions: the tension for boys between working and being seen to be appropriately laid-back and cool about school; the version of girls as compliant and wanting to please the teacher while boys don't care if they please or not; the view that boys seem to have less clearly mapped out game plans in terms of future objectives, therefore less urgency in achieving specific objectives and that they operate more on a system of extrinsic motivation, 'needing' to see some real pay-off for any effort they might invest:

- Boys need extrinsic motivation, whereas girls seem to work more on intrinsic motivation. Because I'm inside – intrinsically – motivated, I expect that of my students. Boys don't seem to see the point if there's not some immediate, visible, tangible benefit.

  (S.P.)

- For boys, it's important to know 'what is this going to give me?' and unfortunately in Australia it's not easy to provide that motivation; we're so isolated, we're so monolingual, and with the global language – it's harder to get through to boys that it's worth doing it for the discipline – for its own worth – an intrinsic reward – like learning an instrument. For girls, they do appreciate the reward of learning something that's hard, and achieving, they can see that's valuable. There's a big difference in attitude there.

  (D.M.)

- From what I can see, girls will learn language, do language, and write language and make it pretty and do whatever, without it having to have a real use; just for the process of doing it. Boys aren't like that! If it has a real use, if they're actually going to write something to someone in France, and a kid there is going to read it and send one back – they'll be more inclined to do it. But even then, it won't be with the application and the dedication that girls will do it . . .

  (R.T.)

- The reason boys like me – I hate work sheets! They're boring, not contextual, take hours to devise. I did a work sheet – a 'fiche d'identité' – did Bart Simpson, all the characters they know, but it was still a worksheet – didn't lead anywhere, wasn't in any authentic context .. and the girls did it, and seemed to love it, but the boys just went '???' What's this? It's almost as if they couldn't grasp what it was, because it had no real purpose. What's the point? The girls happily did it. Now if I'd made it into a game, the boys would have done it. Then they can see a purpose to it!

  (R.M.)

- The structure of my classes with boys, especially the younger ones, is one of many short tasks so that they don't lose interest and especially concentration.

  (J.S.)

- You have to put that pragmatic thing on it – will help you get a job, when you travel. You can't sell it if you don't attach something to it. 'It will get me bonus points at uni, so I'll do it!' – weighting. Imagine if we didn't have that!!

(M.C.)

This final remark was made by an Italian teacher in an all-boys school in Victoria. She is the curriculum coordinator in the college, and uses this position and the access it gives her to both parents and students to 'sell' languages – seeing this as essential when recruiting boys for post-compulsory classes. She admits to emphasising the extrinsic rewards of other-language proficiency – career options, travel opportunities – but knows that the strongest argument in her armoury is the fact that in Victoria there is a weighting attached to languages in the exiting final scoring of school achievement in the state. Students studying languages at senior level therefore have an advantage in terms of their exit matriculation score which determines their competitive position in relation to university entrance. Teachers repeatedly assured us that the weighting system works as the extrinsic motivator *par excellence*. This teacher's additional, pragmatic strategy for recruiting boys to languages is to use her position as curriculum coordinator to promise boys that they'll definitely get their other two elective choices if they choose a language.

Many teachers worry about boys and motivation, and a lot of the thinking that goes into planning and teaching appears to be informed by this concern. One teacher in an independent school which enjoys strong language support described how he sees the first two years of secondary schooling as the prime site for affirmative action in terms of motivating the boys:

> Motivation is key at this stage! They're so locked into their 'being boys' thing. Years 8 and 9 are the critical years: whatever strategies work at this stage – use them! Physical activities, games, IT, whatever: you do that first. Later, when you've got them settled and in, you can work on the much bigger issue of socialisation into talking. That's more difficult in different ways, as it relates to wider issues in the school, but also in society.

(G.T.)

Sitting alongside motivation problems is another key component of the boys–languages relationship which teachers find frustrating: the reluctance by boys to be perceived as serious students; the 'being boys thing' referred to above, a combination of the 'healthy idleness' and 'effortless achievement' syndromes identified in Chapter 3. Another teacher summed it up as: '*Girls are more inclined to talk to each other in general, and boys are more inclined to make fun of each other!*' (G.H.). This comment will be re-visited when considering teachers' accounts of how students work in class, but the 'making fun of each other' syndrome is seen as a powerful de-motivator. This teacher talked about it at length, clearly concerned about this dimension of boys' performance in school.

His school context would be envied by many other teachers I spoke to working in more challenging situations where support for languages has to be continuously fought for. Until recently, this school offered a choice of five languages through the primary years and on into high school, but is currently narrowing the choice down to three. It has a strong culture of language learning, with an ex-language teacher Principal and strong parent support for language programmes. The students come from backgrounds which often provide access to travel and first-hand experience of other languages and cultures. There is, therefore, far less 'shame' attached to the choice of languages in this environment than in many other schools. None the less, in this comparatively ideal language-friendly situation, this teacher identified boys' 'need' to mock and criticise each other as one of the major impediments to their progress in the language classroom:

> Boys, even those who are excelling in the language, in the test results, and are enjoying it – they tell me frankly that they're enjoying it . . . they have problems in expressing that in class. They can't show it, and use the language like they'd like to, because other boys are willing to jump on any small mistake to embarrass them.
>
> (G.H.)

He sees this trait as a major impediment, commenting that it's almost *de rigueur* for boys to put each other down, to puncture anything that might seem like too serious an effort or contribution, to keep each other on the straight and narrow of *not* taking things seriously. In this teacher's comparatively privileged context, where the ethos of academic work is reasonably settled, he still identifies this trait – '*an almost universal component of boys' relationship with each other*' – as hugely unhelpful in the language classroom. For the less academically interested and engaged boys, he sees it being used as a deterrent pure and simple for being on-task; for consolidating social relationships and status and for keeping each other in the collective culture of mucking up. But for those boys who *are* on task, wanting to achieve, it is used just as effectively as a tool for competitive gains: by laughing at errors or failure to produce the right answer, subtler moves are being made in the achievement and competition stakes:

> Their main goal in some of these classes is to push themselves forward as individual boys – socially and academically. This is more important to them than supporting each other in their learning. Boys who are competing academically are quite comfortable with the fact they they're all studying – they don't get teased or mocked for that; it's alright to be academic, because it's an academic competition . . . and that's OK. The boys make fun of each other in that context to advance themselves.
>
> (G.H.)

He draws a clear distinction between girls and boys in this respect. The girls he describes as 'academic' also compete in their own ways (e.g., the investment they have in results and outcomes), but behave in a far more supportive way, helping each other through embarrassing moments, working collaboratively rather than competitively. He sees this kind of mutual support as being almost totally absent in boys' behaviour. He talks about the power and investment in 'ribbing'; a key strategy for preventing each other from achieving, which combines with the need to 'be a hero' – to *not* ask for help – to impede learning very effectively:

> It's very hard for boys to resist peer pressure, because it's harder for them to make mistakes in public. With the girls' support group, they'll say – that's OK we'll help you get over that problem . . . whereas the boys laugh and call each other idiots – 'you made a mistake!' Some boys are real rat bags – even in this school.
>
> (G.H.)

This comment was echoed by another teacher who works in a private boys-only school when he spoke of his frustration with this kind of behaviour:

> You know this – the most frustrating aspect: on the one hand the boys love performing, showing off – they don't want to spend time reading texts or writing scripts – but when it's time for them to perform something in class they just clam up and I think it's because they think that their mates will ridicule them if they make a mistake.
>
> (R.K.)

Using group work with boys – a core component of a task-based approach to learning – is fraught with danger because of this culture of mocking and criticising:

> Group work and boys can be really risky! The make-up of the group is extremely important, because if they're not carefully managed, if you let them self-select . . . don't forget that with boys the main objective is to embarrass somebody . . . and the language classroom is a pretty easy place to embarrass someone! So you really have to try to organise it that the least confident boys aren't with the ones most likely to give them a hard time.
>
> (G.H.)

Awareness of the high price paid by boys because of this culture of mocking motivated this teacher to develop a bank of computer assisted learning resources, so that boys can get additional help without the public shame of being seen to ask for it. They can make the mistakes they need to make along the way in private, without the humiliation of peer scrutiny. This is important for boys who are struggling with the language:

> The high academic students who are doing well in language anyway, they're still going to achieve that, but it's the middle-range students and the lower range that we have to look at, and that's where I'm trying to get more computer-assisted learning involved. By getting the language lab working, using CDs, putting a website up for the students . . . they can come and they can repeat pronunciation and they can do activities and email them to me directly. It takes the public display away, so that even the lower achievers who are embarrassed to ask for help in class, and who need to repeat the question several times till they get the pronunciation right, they can do it on the computer without anyone knowing.
>
> (G.H.)

This teacher had some good success stories which confirmed the patterns of motivation and performance discussed above. He described one context in which boys *did* support each other wholeheartedly, an activity related to that all-important masculine signifier in school: sport. He organises occasional language activities around sport, such as playing soccer in Japanese. To kick the ball, the player has to come up with a Japanese word; failure to do so means the ball goes to the other side.

When a goal is scored, the scorer has to produce a complete and correct sentence in the language for the goal to be allowed:

> The boys get right into this! Very active and motivated – and totally collaborative! They're calling out suggestions to each other, helping to get the grammar right and the words in the right order – contributing whatever they can. Doing all the things they'll never do for each other in the classroom!
>
> (G.T.)

The total change in behaviour engineered via the boys' favourite activity makes this the single most successful learning strategy with this group. The fact that only two of the girls in the class ever choose to participate means it's not one this teacher feels he can repeat too often; but he finds it interesting how this connection with boys' core culture makes the effort to produce language totally acceptable – and enjoyable. An individual boy who makes a mistake in this context is neither mocked nor laughed at. He is instantly supported and carried through by the others: everything is good, it seems, when it contributes to collective, competitive success in a culturally sanctioned activity. Team spirit is alive and well on the football field.

Another strategy used by this teacher to increase boys' levels of involvement and collaboration also capitalises on the much-reported competitive nature of boys' relationships. He uses an exercise with Year 9 students, boys and girls, for reviewing Japanese vocabulary. Students randomly select blocks with different characters on each face, are put into teams competing against each other, and have to run in turn up to the front, using a timer, to form a word using the characters on their block; they then run back, hit the timer, so the next team member can go. The exercise is popular with both boys and girls, but the teacher observed

> two boys who hadn't paid attention at all so far in the first five weeks, by the end of that 45-minute class, after three or four of these games, knew every item of vocab they were supposed to have done – whereas at the beginning of the class, they couldn't say more than 10 per cent of them!
>
> (G.H.)

Every time this teacher appears in class carrying the timer, there is a noticeable increase in energy and participation level by the boys, who work to get through the 'boring stuff' as quickly as possible in order to get to the 'fun stuff', the 'game'. Many teachers reported success with similar strategies that key into boys' enjoyment of competition and games.

> With boys, I deliberately make things more competitive. I say things like: 'you've only got 60 secs . . . see how many of these words you can learn!' Or: 'You've got 30 words to learn, let's see who can do it fastest, I'm starting timing now!' You've got to make it a challenge, or a contest, otherwise they find it boring and won't do it. If it's a contest, they'll give it a go.
>
> (J.W.)

I was repeatedly told that boys aren't prepared to do anything which they think is boring and that competition will usually solve this problem.

Resistance to languages

Teachers talked about two kinds of resistance by boys: the first they see as boys' version of broader community and cultural attitudes, while the second relates more directly to the resistant model of in-school masculinity discussed in Chapter 3. The conflict between dominant versions of 'doing boy' and the languages option is identified by teachers as a major issue. Walking out of step with dominant norms is described as difficult; and at this point teachers' comments reflect the issue of social worlds, and of resistance played out differently in different contexts. The socioeconomic profile of the schools in which teachers were working impacted on their accounts of how they view the issue of resistance.

Motivation to learn a foreign language is clearly impacted by class differences. Our analysis of the history of foreign language learning in Chapter 2 indicated that the learning of a European language in English-speaking cultures has traditionally been a privileged accomplishment. Jane Austin's young women needed some French as well as needlework, piano and sketching, to be marketable propositions in the marriage stakes; and proficiency in European languages was for a long time part of the capital required to be 'cultured' in the 'capital C' class-based kind of culture (Carr, 1999). Young working-class people have not historically seen language study as having relevance to their lives. Our data indicate that this is still the case today. Commentaries by boys in Chapters 4 and 5 were reinforced in conversations with teachers. A teacher in an exclusive independent school, for example, took it as a 'given' that her students would see the relevance of other-language proficiency:

> We start off ahead. These kids expect to travel. They know they'll have the opportunity to go overseas and use the language. They

have parents who speak languages, they know about watching films on SBS.

(C.T.)

The school has an International Baccalauréat programme, regular international student exchanges and school trips overseas. The small number of less economically privileged students in the school who don't have easy access to these experiences have a strong sense of being discriminated against:

> Those kids who can't afford to go overseas feel totally ripped off! They're surrounded by kids who **are** going . . . some of whom are doing the international bac . . . and they feel really ripped off.

The comparison is stark between this learning environment and that of a state school in one of the lowest socioeconomic areas of Queensland, where a survey of two Year 8 classes (60 students) revealed that there was not one parent with tertiary educational experience or who came into the work classification of 'professional', and that none of the 60 students had travelled overseas or had any expectation of doing so. The relevance of socioeconomic factors to motivation is brought into sharp relief.

Racism

> My Dad told me that the only good reason for me to learn Indonesian is so I can say: 'Stop there you bastard or I'll shoot you!' when they invade us.

This boy's father is a member of the Australian armed forces who had served time in East Timor; the comment can therefore be read as having contextual significance. Anecdotal evidence from many teachers, together with conversations with boys during this project, suggest, however, that this kind of attitude is not an unusual one. Racism is a key component of resistance to foreign language education among some groups of boys in the study. This is certainly not a new phenomenon in Australia which has at different times prohibited or strongly discouraged the learning of certain languages (e.g., German) because of national or international conflict situations.

As indicated earlier, the pilot study was carried out in North Queensland, and the timing as well as the location of this stage probably impacted on at least some of the data. Interviews were conducted only a short time after the phenomenon of the electoral success of the

One Nation Party in Australia, a small party which splintered off from the conservative Australian National Party, drawing its support mainly from rural and regional Queensland, and constructing its platform almost totally around a racist, xenophobic appeal for a return to a White Australia. Many comments received from some of the boys at that time resonate clearly with the discourses of racism and xenophobia circulating in the wider community at that time; discourses already embedded in the traditional cultural profile of this region of Australia. Boys talked confidently and comfortably in racist terms, with no apparent expectation that they might be found offensive. The *'Stop there, you bastard!'* comment quoted above was the most explicit expression of a racist discourse, but I collected many comments along the lines of:

- Why would I bother? If anyone wants to talk to me – they can learn English! If people want to come here – work here – they can bloody well learn our language!

  (Damien, 13)

- Why would I learn Japanese? We've got too many of them here – they're taking over! They're all over everywhere, taking all our jobs . . . I don't want to talk to them! You can't go anywhere on the Gold Coast without falling over them!

  (Leon, 14)

- I've just been to Europe with my Mum and Dad, and they don't speak French or anything, and we didn't need other languages – everyone speaks English, except people like taxi drivers, and who wants to talk to them?

  (Danny, 12)

As suggested in Chapter 3, the traditional monolingual, ethnocentric and often xenophobic character of Australia's relationship with itself and with the world is a key component of the boys–languages relationship in some school communities. Several teachers referred to this dimension of the anti-languages negativity, but more often in the lower socio-economic school communities than in the independent, middle-class sector. This is not to suggest that racism is class-based; but that it is differently performed in different contexts. And it appears to have a gendered dimension. There were fewer racist comments in the data collected from girls, and several teachers described boys as having more overtly racist attitudes. Similar evidence emerged from UK studies, where more actively racist discourses were more commonly articulated by boys (Clark, 1998a).

A key informant in the teacher interview data set – the Chinese teacher who talked earlier about her determination to teach all students in the same way – commented that much of the resistance to languages she has had to work with over the years, especially with younger male students, is to do with racism. She describes many of her students as 'totally racist' when they arrive in her class and refers to the 'ten-years' hard slog' it has taken to bring about a gradual change in attitude. As a teacher of an Asian language in a country where Asians and Indigenous people are the principal target of intolerance and racism, in an immediate community group which has minimal access to alternative discourses of difference, she has worked hard to destabilise racist attitudes towards her programme. After the ten-year 'hard slog', she feels things have eased considerably and that she has managed to overcome some of the negativity and intolerance:

> I'm finally beginning to feel that I have a really good level of acceptance. It's the kids. It's getting easier, I'm not having to battle that worst kind of racism and resistance because a lot of the kids coming through are little brothers and sisters of kids who have worked with me. I've had to work hard, but I don't feel that racist thing so much any more.
> (K.B.)

The 'cool masculinity' resistance

Like the students themselves, teachers identified the association of languages with being 'uncool', or – even worse – 'being a girl', as one of the major problems with keeping boys in post-compulsory programmes. While descriptions of this apparently basic boys-cultural organiser varied across different sites, there wasn't one teacher in the entire data set who did not at some point identify it as an issue. As suggested in the previous chapter, it appears to be less of an issue in all-boys schools, where the absence of girls weakens the power of the gendered curriculum paradigm; but teachers in these schools, too, assured me it is alive and well as a symbolic signifier of gendered identity.

Even in schools where language programmes are strong and well respected, teachers report a sense of it being a 'girls' project'. Apart from exceptions like Latin, and sometimes Chinese, the numbers of male students at senior level are weak. Teachers talk about languages being a difficult option for boys, the level of difficulty varying according to context. In the state schools where the boys in Chapter 4 are studying it appears to take considerable courage to continue with a post-compulsory language. The stigma attached to such an inappropriate option is a powerful disincentive. Teachers' commentaries support those collected earlier from the boys:

- In order to do LOTE in this school, boys have to be prepared to step up – and say: 'I'm doing Chinese!' and not feel bad about it! By making that choice they're signalling themselves out as somebody different, somebody who's prepared to take the challenge. And that's hard for these boys. Often they come through in batches – as a cohesive group, and I know it's because it's too hard on their own. For a boy to do LOTE – he has got to be prepared to cop it! And to get respect, he has to have extra things going for him – to make up for doing LOTE.

    (K.B.)

- The boys who tend to go on with French are really kids out of the ordinary. They get a hard time from the other boys! They really tend to be either very strong individuals, who don't care what the others think, or the rather sad ones . . . who don't have much of a social life anyway.

    (C.S.)

- You've no idea what they have to contend with! The other day I was talking in class about how I hoped some of the boys would carry on into Year 9 with me, and some of the boys called out 'I want to, Miss!' and you should have heard the response from the others! Loud laughter, 'REALLY?!!' as if they had just done the most embarrassing thing! It was awful. And I know that when it comes to it, some of the ones who want to go on won't – just because of all that.

    (R.M.)

- If I can stereotype the male students that I have in post-compulsory classes, they're nearly all the supposedly 'uncool' boys. The one boy I have who IS cool, is new to the school, and still working out how it all works – and probably hasn't sussed out that he's doing something uncool! One other boy – he's not in the 'in-crowd' – but he's not totally uncool, because he's good at drama, and is very confident in his own mind.

    (S.S.)

- I only have one student in my Year 12 German class who is considered cool by his school mates and that's because he's good at cricket, football and very popular with girls from X (neighbouring girls' school). It seems that in his case he can be excused for continuing with German because he is so good in the 'cool' department.

(D.W.)

These comments construct a very similar picture of boys who study languages to that assembled by the boys themselves. The first comment included above, about language students having to have 'extra things going for them', was reminiscent of the conversation with a group of boys who had worked with this teacher for Year 8 then decided to drop Chinese at the end of the year. They'd been talking about 'the kind of boy' who studies a language when he doesn't have to, exempting some individual boys from their blanket classification of uncool precisely because they had 'something else' going for them. Their attitude to boys who continued with languages on the whole was dismissive and contemptuous; but some individual boys – friends of theirs – apparently had 'saving graces': yes, they were going on with the language, *'but he's really good at footie'*, or *'but he's really funny, he's got this really Pommie (English) accent!'* or *'but he's really confident and doesn't care what people think'*. The need for compensatory factors in this inappropriate boy-situation is clear. Comments collected from teachers in quite different school contexts show that the 'cool factor' operates across socioeconomic groupings.

Teachers too commented on the fact that while all languages are seen by boys as girl-appropriate, some languages are particularly so; and the highest casualty of the languages-gender relationship appears to be French. As indicated earlier, Latin, Chinese and to a lesser extent Japanese (possibly because of associations with technology) appear to be almost acceptable as male student options due to the cognitive challenges seen to be involved. Scripts and Latin conjugations, it seems, can almost pass for science; the statistics provided in Chapter 2 bear this out. French, however, is relegated unforgivingly by most boys – and some teachers too – to the status of a 'girls' language'; again, this correlates with the patterns traced in enrolment numbers in Chapter 2. One teacher who had a predominantly female group of senior French students explained:

Girls are more inclined to do French because it's a more romantic language, more socially accepted as something that girls do. I think they see it as being 'attractive' – of making them more feminine!

(B.T.)

No similar associations were described in terms of either Asian languages or German, one of the other European languages studied in Australia. French appears to have the monopoly on femininity. The only other comment from a teacher that related directly to a linguistically or culturally-specific gendered dimension was a 'reverse-rationale' argument from a Japanese teacher, who offered the following possible explanation of why many of his female students rejected Japanese in favour of French:

> Japanese is a very sexist language! Japanese society is very male-dominated, and although this is changing very fast, it still comes through in the language. The language that men can use is very different to the language that women can use: right there from the beginning, students are learning about 'I: watashi or boku': boys can use either, girls can only use one, the polite one. That's one of the first things kids learn – and I have some girls who really pick up on this and don't think it's right!
>
> (R.W.)

Like the boys themselves, teachers also talked about the reluctance of boys to be seen to be working hard, identifying this as a major issue with learning outcomes. The popular model of masculinity identified in Chapter 3, referred to briefly earlier in this chapter, works against any overt demonstration of academic intent by many boys. Even in the most academic of schools, where working hard is part of the shared ethos, teachers believe boys still feel obliged to hide the extent of their efforts:

> I suspect that most of our boys do work hard, but it's not cool to admit it. Most of the work is done at home, out of sight; and in class they underplay what they're doing. That's so different from the girls. There seems to be a real fear among boys of being cut down if they're seen to be achieving too much, working too hard, or doing too much homework.
>
> (N.J.)

Other teachers talked about the struggle to establish the 'respectability' of an academic ethos in a culture which is traditionally very sports oriented:

> We still have that attitude here, of languages being academic and therefore less important. Traditionally this has been a school with a huge emphasis on sporting achievement. The boys have a bit of that attitude: not wanting to shine too much academically – because boys

basically want to be seen as lads – interested in sport, not doing too much book work.

(T.M.)

He described how this culture of masculinity has been challenged by the concerted efforts of a group of teachers in the school in recent times, who have tabled it as an issue of concern, and developed strategies for 'interrupting' this culture:

> We've been fighting it – we ARE fighting it. And in the last few years I've seen a change in the culture of the school. More students are prepared now to be seen as bright, as doing well academically. There's a stronger focus now in the school generally on academic pursuits, for example, in assembly there's now a recognition of achievement academically as well as in sport.

(T.M.)

'Boys need to be challenged'

We have already commented on the issue of boys and 'boredom' from the boys' perspective. Teachers also identified this factor as a major challenge. It is in fact a recurring motif throughout the data. The solution to the problem of boredom is seen by teachers to centre around 'challenge'; and it was around this point of challenge that the two narratives of nature and nurture appeared to become most entangled. Like the teachers reported in the Jones and Jones study in the United Kingdom (2001), many of the Australian teachers constructed boys as having higher expectations and as making greater demands of the language classroom. A Head of Languages in the UK data had talked at length of what you 'can't expect' boys to do: and principal among these she identified activities which are insufficiently engaging or challenging. She insisted that *'Boys are not prepared to be bored!'* There was a clear conviction in her comment that boys need a different kind of stimulus and higher levels of challenge, in a way that girls apparently do not. It was never too clear in these commentaries whether these needs were understood to be biologically or socially constituted; but there was an apparently comfortable acceptance of their significance. Very few teachers questioned the substance of these understandings. This was a very normative discourse of how boys (and girls) 'are'.

In Chapter 3 we talked about the fact that there is a historically established narrative which constructs girls as more passive and compliant, prepared to work for the sake of working and pleasing the teacher (and themselves), prepared to engage in activities which are inherently unexciting and 'boring'. This, it is understood, is part of being a 'good' student girl-mode. Many comments from teachers in this study echo this construction of the compliant, willing female student and the more assertive, demanding boy who 'needs' to be challenged:

- We have trouble on the rote learning front – boys don't like to rote learn, they find it too boring; so we have a computer programme – an Excel programme – we've made this up to help with this aspect, for revision, and boys are prepared to work at this.

  (J.W.)

- Boys don't seem prepared to do anything if they think it's boring. And this reflects pedagogically, because it encourages two different teaching styles – one for boys and one for girls. You have to always be thinking about how to get the boys interested.

  (S.S.)

- Girls are generally better at sitting still! They handle it better. They don't punch and throw paper . . . if they're bored, they talk; but they don't seem to get bored as easily. They're more prepared, for example, to work with worksheets. Boys hate worksheets!

  (M.N.)

Even when activities are more interesting and appealing, however, and the challenge presumably greater, teachers suggest that boys are still less prepared to put in the effort. One teacher talked about the annual visit to his school of a group of Japanese students, always a motivator for increased communicative effort; but he describes how boys still employ what he calls 'boy strategies' for getting through the experience with minimal effort:

Each year, in all my classes, the most successful classes are those in which I say, 'OK, next week, there's a group from a Japanese school coming over, this is what you're going to do with these students.' Even the least academically inclined set to – communicatively motivated, and try to work out how to speak to these kids, then come and check with me. But there's a real difference in gender terms: the girls will do so much more, working away at what they want to say, trying to make sure they'll get it right. It's like they really **want** to be able to communicate with the Japanese kids. The boys will try to wing it and charm it and poke fun at each other in English, and not bother about the language at all. It's as if they're confident that the Japanese kids will want to talk to them anyway! Even in a 'real' communicative situation, the boys aren't focusing so much on communicating, but on their social status, and on being cool.

(G.H.)

While complaining about – and being frustrated by – what they see as regrettable and undesirable attitudes in boys, many teachers appear to accept them as cultural – or biological – givens; and continue to talk about the need to find ways of making languages more challenging and interesting for boys. In our teacher data there is almost no problematising of either the attitudes or the connected pedagogical solution. There is surprisingly little critique of this position.

Ways of working

Teachers talked at length about what they see as gender-differentiated ways of working in class. The identified characteristics of girls include the capacity to stay with something and see it through, to employ different strategies and to put time and care into getting it right. Boys are seen to put in much less effort and to not care as much about getting it right:

- Boys are more likely to blurt out something and hope it's right; to be first out and win the competition. Whereas girls are more likely to think about it and get the correct sentence out.

(C.W.)

- Boys want clear guidelines, and they only want to learn a bit at a time.

(D.M.)

- Boys are different . . . I kind of think it's perhaps an attention span thing: girls perhaps have more maturity all the way through, you know? Like the girls in Year 5, if you give them something like a colour by numbers, they will spend hours on it – colouring it beautifully – making it look pretty; whereas the boys, you know, they'll do the minimum they have to do and then move on. It's not necessarily that they're not interested, but they're wanting to grab it, take a hold of it, and run to the next thing kind of thing. I'm not sure if it's to do with biology . . . I must admit when I think of boys, I do think of them like that. They will give their full attention to something for a certain period of time, then that's enough, and they want to move on to something else.

(C.B.)

The comment about boys only wanting to learn a 'bit at a time' ties in with the previous comments about boys having a limited attention span – a comment repeatedly offered by boys themselves, and which was to be echoed in turn by girls, talking about boys. It seems to have achieved the status of fact in the narratives of learning and gender.

Learning styles: biology and the brain versus socialisation

The enduring nature of cognitively based theories of gender-differentiated brain function has been discussed in earlier chapters; and conversations with teachers suggest that many of them think about boys and learning through a biologically based frame of reference. There was repeated reference to 'how boys/girls learn'; what boys/girls 'can do'. For some, the biological argument was interwoven with Howard Gardner's model of multiple intelligences, also biologically understood, and currently a popular and core component of most pre-service teacher education programmes (Feldman and Gardner, 2003). This model works from the understanding that learners learn in different ways – are innately designed to learn in different ways – which must be accommodated in the classroom regardless of teachers' 'own' learning style. It sits comfortably within current educational commitments to inclusivity and diversity, and when it combines with a gender-frame – as it appears to do in much of our data – it feels very solid. Professional development work around the boys–languages agenda in both Australia and the United Kingdom often works from this 'learning style' premise. Recent professional development work in Scotland, for example, designed to improve the outcomes of boys' experience in language classrooms, has drawn heavily on theories of brain differentiation. It accords central place to the idea that there are students who can be identified as 'boy-type' learners and others as 'girl-type learners'. Most boys and girls are understood to fit into the appropriate gendered category, but about 10 per cent of girls are believed to be 'boy-type learners', and 20 per cent of boys to be 'girl-type learners' (Dobie and McDaid, 2001). It is argued, therefore, that 90 per cent and 80 per cent of learners respectively are believed to behave – and to learn – in accordance with biological predispositions associated with different configurations of components of the brain; which leads to the argument that if we want to increase male representation in language classrooms we need to structure language learning experience in more 'boy-friendly' pedagogical ways.

The arguments referred to in Chapter 3, offered by more socially oriented educational theorists – that these cognitive predispositions/ learning styles are more culturally constructed than biologically given – continue to be sidelined by cultural common sense. As Mahony argues (1998), biological arguments are attractive because they align so easily with the social processes and practices which keep institutional wheels turning, reproducing established values and practices. In our data, the cultural argument is much less audible than the biological one. Some teachers certainly talk about socialisation, peer pressure and cultural orientations, but many more talk through normative discourses of how boys/girls 'are' in essentialist rather than constructivist terms. Like the boys themselves, teachers appear to be thinking – and acting – biology.

The influence of essentialism is not only 'commonsensically' delivered. Essentialist models of 'boy' and 'girl' drive much of the child development literature in teacher education courses, which works through a physiological lens, operating with classifications which are often described as physical dimensions of learning development. These include phenomena such as listening skills, concentration, sequential memory, fine motor skills such as writing, visual tracking, body and spatial awareness, sequencing and rhythm; and they are often explicitly accounted for as sex-differentiated. Parallel to these physical features of a child's early development are those skills loosely termed 'social', which include sharing space or time, taking turns, collaborating and co-operating, communicating – including listening as well as speaking skills; and all these dimensions of learning have clearly drawn sex-differentiated lines. Many of the teachers in our research made specific reference to the literature which provides this kind of classificatory assistance. There was a confidence in this kind of explanatory grid which suggests well-established 'facts' about male and female students. Individual views or observations were often prefaced with authority investing phrases such as: *'The literature shows that . . .'*, *'I've read that . . .'* or *'Research shows that . . .'*. Far fewer comments were made which in any way interrogated such established, biologically based evidence, or drew from more recent critical, socially oriented accounts of gendered learning development.

Physical and cognitive characteristics

Teachers on the whole, then, seemed comfortable in identifying what they see to be differentiated physiological characteristics. They seem to agree that boys have less well developed powers of concentration than girls. The following was a typical remark:

> Boys have a real problem with attention span. It's not necessarily that they're not interested, but they want to grab at something and do it quickly then move on. They can't stay with something like girls can. They'll concentrate on something for a short period of time, but then they have to move on to something else.
>
> (K.G.)

This attention-span issue is often interwoven with the account of boys as less confident risk-takers than girls, and as less prepared/able to extend or explore. This sits interestingly beside the account of boys' overall greater confidence socially, and also of their identified need to be challenged. Yet in terms of planning their activities and teaching strategies, many teachers talk about the need to teach boys in a more structured way, with additional scaffolding to support them and maintain their engagement in tasks, particularly in the area of oracy:

> Orally boys need a lot of support. Talking is not something they are comfortable with – not something they do! So you have to structure oral activities very carefully – things have to be very well prepared, well defined, so that they're not put on the spot.
>
> (T.M.)

This belief in the need to provide additional support for boys in relation to communicative activities appears to be part of many teachers' planning process. The teacher who made the above comment went on to explain how this affects the way he plans assessment activities:

> Apart from choosing topics which I know will interest boys, I'm very conscious of adapting assessment tasks to make them more boy-friendly: making sure I create an environment and tasks which aren't experienced as threatening for boys, in terms of communication.
>
> (T.M.)

He talked about boys 'needing to feel secure' . . . again an interesting opposition to the commonly shared view that boys are much more confident generally than girls; this confidence clearly not extending to language learning or communicatively based activities. This teacher talked about this contradiction, making a distinction between boys' social confidence and their apparent lack of concern for teachers' approval and what he recognises as their real difficulty in venturing out of their usual comfort zone into a new language, something which carries risks of losing face.

The notion that communication constitutes an experience which is for boys an alienating, challenging and 'foreign' one, one which needs to be supported and managed in order not to frighten them off, came through several of the teacher commentaries, and relates more to the social than it does to the biological dimension of the boys–languages discussion. There was a general sense that boys need to be apprenticed into the process of communication before progress can be made with oral proficiency of an authentically communicative kind. One teacher talked about communication as a mode or genre which boys have to 'learn':

> If you say to two girls: 'Sit down and have a chat', and give them a topic and say 'chat!' it's not giving them a new situation, it's one they have normally in their everyday lives. They know how to do chat. You're simply asking them to switch codes, to switch languages. Whereas boys, you're asking them to switch languages AND switch behaviour. They're not used to sitting down and chatting – this is a new genre! Boys don't sit and chat. It's not something they know how to do . . .
>
> (G.D.)

Overall, teachers' views on boys' relationship with talk align fairly closely with the literature on gender and communication (e.g., Coates, 2003; Romaine, 1999) and with the more informal cultural common-sense understandings evident in boys' own comments. The data reflect the general opinion that girls are socialised into talk, whereas boys are socialised into physical activity. For some this is understood as a response to the biological 'predisposition' of girls to language, and of boys to different kinds of skills and activities; for others it is more a result of cultural and social organisation. Whatever the informing belief system, just about all the teachers interviewed talked at length about girls' facility in relation to communication and boys' comparative difficulty. The fact that girls are seen as more competent and comfortable communicators is believed – and expected – by teachers to put them at a distinct advantage in the language classroom. As suggested by the earlier comment about girls being 'generally more inclined to talk to each other', as opposed to boys who are more 'generally inclined to make fun of each other', girls are seen as being 'half-way there' in terms of developing oral proficiency skills in the target language, while boys are starting from behind the eight ball. Like the boys themselves, some teachers talked about the perception that what goes on in language classrooms is 'girls' stuff'. Apart from the centrality of talk itself, seen as something girls are good at, there's the perception that what gets talked about is also far more girl-appropriate. Like English classes, language classes are often regarded with some resentment by boys for requiring them to 'self-reveal': to talk about themselves, what they do, what they like, their families, their experiences. These are not, typically, the sorts of things boys like to talk about. Some of the teachers I spoke to talked about choosing content and activities with boys in mind: Japanese teachers designing units around samurai and martial arts; French teachers teaching about sport and Resistance fighters; Latin teachers choosing texts which detail great military campaigns. Most teachers reported trying to keep a fair balance in terms of content between girl-interest and boy-interest topics. They all mentioned 'gender-safe' favourite topics, such as food . . . although one teacher commented that while this was always a safe bet with all students, what she termed a 'great equaliser' between boys and girls: '*they always want to do different things with it: the girls want to prepare it, cook it and talk about it – the boys just want to eat it!*' (M.T.).

A different perspective on boys' perceived difficult relationship with talk, communication and verbal performance of self was offered by a teacher who is himself working and living in a second-language environment. He suggested that boys' discomfort with communication in their first language can potentially turn into a positive component of their second-language experience. He spoke about his own experience of first learning English as a young adolescent in France, describing himself as a fairly typically awkward, self-conscious and uncommunicative teenager. He remembers feeling that this new code gave him an opportunity to escape from his uncomfortable 'primary self', to become someone else:

> It's an opportunity to step outside yourself; an opportunity to take on another persona . . . to forget about the problems you're having with a first language, and start again in a second one. In this sense it's a bit like drama . . . where actors are escaping to other selves.
>
> (T.M.)

A similar comment was made by the French teacher referred to earlier who was experimenting with a Process Drama approach, working with a group of boys who were expected to be resistant learners, but in effect were engaging in an unexpectedly positive way. She, too, felt that the strategy of putting students in role was an effective one in terms of overcoming the embarrassment and discomfort of performing self. She was seeing this as a particularly promising approach to working with boys.

In a much more traditional context, but following the same principle of 'escape from self', another teacher commented on the fact that she noticed a drop in engagement recently in a French class where she had changed the textbook from one which proceeded via a group of fictional characters to one which didn't:

> I've just changed the textbook. The previous one was character-based; and now it's as if I've lost the edge. The students were less self-conscious when they were taking on a character out of the book.
>
> (M.D.)

She also mentioned that one of her colleagues, teaching Italian, was reporting a huge increase in participation by her younger male students since she had started working with puppets.

Not all teachers interviewed agreed with the proposition that boys are poor communicators. Most of those who didn't worked in all-boys' schools, where the classroom dynamic was differently framed. One teacher in a large Catholic boys' school rejected very energetically the notion that it's difficult to make boys talk, seeing it as an unhelpful cultural stereotype, which can be used too easily as a 'cop-out':

> It makes me laugh when I hear people saying that it's hard to get boys to talk! They talk! They LOVE discussion . . . they do talk . . .. It makes me mad when I hear teachers and parents saying: 'boys are like this, BOYS DO THIS, boys can't do this' . . . we're selling them short! They ARE different, but it's because we let them be. We just don't encourage them to be any other way. A lot of that stuff is used to keep things how they've always been. But a lot of it's crap – I don't believe it. We're selling boys short, selling them short; and that's my worry. To keep pigeon holing boys as these 'aliens' – they're human beings, adolescents! They'll rise to the challenge if we expect them to be able to do something!
>
> (M.T.)

This was one of the most explicit rejections of essentialist versions of 'boys' to come through the teacher data. This particular teacher spends a lot of her time and energy trying to talk boys into continuing with their languages, continuously fighting what she sees to be the consequences of boys' own gendered assumptions about what they can/can't do, and of the impact of what she termed their 'pigeon-holing' by the adults around them. She talked about the self-fulfilling prophecy dimension of all this:

> They can't do languages because they think they can't do languages!' They don't ALLOW it to appeal to them! All they have to do is drop their barriers!

A teacher in a co-educational context made a similar comment in relation to girls' supposed advantage as more able communicators than boys, suggesting that here, too, cultural stereotypes and assumptions play a large part in the 'realities' experienced in classrooms:

> I think it's a self-perpetuating thing: girls talk about how they communicate better than boys; teachers do too. And the more everyone says it, the truer it becomes!
>
> (S.C.)

Several teachers reflected on the difficulty of untangling cultural notions from hard facts. One of the most reflective comments came from a teacher of Japanese and Chinese in a co-educational independent school. He had been talking about the vexed issue of what is perceived as gender-appropriate behaviour by boys themselves; and about how boys seem to sit more comfortably in a Chinese language programme in his school than in a European one. He, too, commented on the feminine connotations of French (fashion, romance), whereas Chinese can be regarded as a more masculine kind of code-cracking activity. He digressed from talking about his students in school to talking about his 3-year-old son, and the ongoing debate about whether relationship with language, communication and behaviour is biologically or socially determined. He talked initially about the fact that when his 3-year-old watches the ABC for children programmes on TV, '*he will be very loving and gentle and kind and give big hugs*'. When he watches a 'punch 'em up cartoon' on a commercial station, however, '*he'll be a lot less loving and a whole lot more aggressive!*'. He then talked about his son's relationship with the three languages he negotiates in his home language environment: English as first language, Thai as second language (his mother's language), and Chinese as a third language used at times by his father:

> When my wife speaks to him in Thai, he laughs and tells her: 'You're being silly!' But when I'm working on the computer with Chinese language CD Roms, he's at me: 'Can I come on the computer, please Daddy?' He watches and listens, hearing Chinese on the computer while I'm working with it, he tries to say it after me, then he'll run around the house saying 'Nihou! Nihou!' in Chinese – after we've played around on the computer together. It could be that he sees my wife as just talking – communicating with him, trying to get a response – whereas he sees me as 'playing' on the computer, and he's playing with me? Maybe this is the 'doing' rather than the 'communicating' thing with boys?
>
> (G.H.)

While this may appear something of a digression from the boys–languages in school issue, it provides some interesting connected thoughts. The situation described here involves variables which are individually complex and culturally and contextually specific, to do as much with relationships and culturally constructed values as with activities *per se*; and this snapshot of one linguistically and socially complex scenario reminds us of the complexities and variables which surround individual students' attitudes to, and relationships with, language in any single classroom.

Many of the teachers talked about boys' disinclination to work collaboratively. Where girls are seen to favour interactive group work, boys are seen to be more comfortable working individually. The familiar classification of boys as independent, competitive learners and communicators and girls as collaborative and co-operative came through repeatedly in teachers' commentaries:

- Girls like to work together. They work well collaboratively. Boys don't. So this certainly affects how I plan activities.

  (S.C.)

- Girls will always help each other out. They often ask if they can do assignments together – share the work. You never get boys wanting to do that.

  (M.T.)

- Girls really like being interactive and sociable with each other. Boys are much more competitive.

(K.B.)

One teacher talked about this difference in preferred learning styles in relation to using IT in his programme, explaining that he has to factor this difference into his planning:

It requires different strategies. With boys, you set the right task, give them the right soft-ware, and say 'Go for it, boys!' Whereas girls, you have to have two or three on one computer, so they can talk about what's going on. This isn't so much because girls need more help in using computers, but because they like to interact while they're learning. They're more into it being socially interactive than the boys are. The boys just want to get in and do it – they don't want to talk about it!

(M.M.)

Another key issue identified by teachers, related to the issue of concentration, is that of memory: boys talked about their problems with rote learning and memorising; teachers also identified this as an issue. While some teachers went on to explain that boys resist this kind of work because they find it 'boring', there was still a strong sense in their commentaries that this was only part of the story, and that boys in fact find this kind of work difficult. Again, this implied problem with memory doesn't accord with one of the most often repeated arguments about boys' ability to be more cognitively organised. Organisation emerged as a key issue for teachers when thinking about boys and girls, but there are clearly two quite different dimensions to this aspect of behaviour.

'Boys are less methodical and organised'

Teachers talked a lot about the fact that boys are 'disorganised' and need to be 'organised' more than girls by the teacher. The teacher who talked about scaffolding her students, when talking about levels of engagement, commented that she always felt she had to scaffold the boys more than the girls in preparation for any task. She saw them as needing much tighter preliminary help, so that their contribution ended up being much less than that of the girls. Similar comments were made by other teachers:

- the girls are more methodical: they read the task, and they think – OK, this is what I've got to do; and they do it. They really look at the criteria, they think about it, and process it a lot more, and think OK, to do well, I've got to do this, this and this. And they do it. My Year 12 girls in particular are very methodical. I give them guidelines, what I'm looking for – and they think about it, 'OK, how can I show her what I know?' And then they talk about that with me . . . They put the effort into the process, into organising themselves to complete the task well.

(M.W.)

• Girls are more prepared to work, and stay with things, and the organisation aspect . . . . I tell students from the word go, to be really successful at a language, you've got to be organised. And I try to get them into organisational habits, like: this is our vocabulary section in our books, we're going to do a set of words . . . try to get them into groups of words . . ., so at least if they need to look it up it's organised. If you look at the girls' books – they're organised. If you look at the boys' – different story!

(K.B.)

In terms of the surface level of organisation, therefore – writing in books, approaching tasks, time management, doing homework – boys are seen to be in need of greater support than girls. This doesn't seem to be a dimension of their role as student which is of interest to boys. There is, however, a different kind of organisation which teachers identify as being stronger in boys.

'Boys are more cognitively organised'

The teacher who made the comments above, relating to the more functional, surface kind of organisation, went on to talk about a different level of organisation: a cognitive level, which she saw as being more developed in boys. She was talking about the teaching of script in Japanese, and of how she approaches what is often the most challenging aspect of Japanese for English-speaking learners:

I tend to pattern-teach in the junior school – because I want them to get the script, I tend to try to get them to identify blocks of words: 'this is "des", it always comes at the end, this is what words look like' . . . a cognitive approach, and I find that boys respond to this better than the girls. Boys seem to think in patterns! They seem to find them more interesting than girls do. The girls seem to find it hard to see them . . . 'Look, we've got a gap here', the boys see that fairly quickly, whereas sometimes the girls just don't get it. Boys are better at patterns and building things.

(M.W.)

Other teachers made similar comments. Script-based languages are seen to be particularly 'suitable' for boys, as the mastery of the script is seen to be cognitively challenging in a similar way to maths or science, requiring an understanding of symbolic systems. In Chapter 5, the boy studying Mandarin at senior level commented that he found this language every bit as cognitively challenging as either advanced maths or physics; several teachers made similar comments about script-based languages – but also about European languages when taught from a grammatical systems perspective. The argument appears to be that languages which are script-based are cognitively challenging in a way that makes them boy-friendly. A teacher in a school in which three languages are offered – Chinese, French and Indonesian – commented that Chinese attracts the most 'able' students, as it is considered a hard and challenging option; and it attracts more boys than the other two languages. Indonesian is seen as the easiest option, attracting 'more of the boys who are considered as having behavioural problems'; and French sits in the middle, attracting higher numbers of girls, as it is considered a 'girls' language'. Similar comments from other teachers included:

- One thing that attracts boys to Japanese is the script. It's a challenge – it involves decoding, and it's hard. Girls who pull out often tell me it's because they feel overwhelmed by the script. It's possibly the same kind of reasons why girls tend to back off from sciences: too cognitively challenging, that's not how girls' minds work.

(M.S.)

- One of the reasons I think I get more boys than girls in Chinese is because it's a language that lends itself to visual and logical learners. We work around patterns, and this appeals to boys – allows for inductive learning.

(D.F.)

Another teacher talked about how she tries to help students learn characters in Japanese by looking for patterns, designing pattern games, showing them how individual components can be moved around while preserving the overall pattern system. She commented quite casually: '*Girls don't latch on to patterns as quickly as boys.*'

As teachers talked about the differences in how boys and girls work, it was possible to see the connection between pedagogy and perceived 'gendered' up-take. A traditional grammar-translation approach, with a focus on the structure of the language, appears to work both for and against boys, depending on who they are. For those boys with minimal academic engagement, and a less than serious interest in the subject, it definitely works against their involvement: they see language learning as decontextualised study of discrete language items, abstract systems with little relevance to anything interesting or real; sitting squarely in the category of 'boring' – and hard. It works well, on the other hand, for the more academically interested boys, described by teachers as enjoying the cognitive exercise of discovering and studying patterns and systems; the kinds of boys they identify as also enjoying maths. Teachers who talked less about the structural dimension and the grammar of the language, and more about communication and task-based learning, reported different kinds of engagement by boys. There were boy-related problems here too, but they were differently described and understood, and can be categorised as being more social than cognitive. One teacher spoke interestingly about both dimensions in relation to the teaching of Latin, which is clearly different in some key respects from other language programmes. While his comments are in some senses very Latin-specific, and also rather particular in terms of the context in which he works, they none the less pull into focus some key aspects of the gender–languages debate.

This teacher works in the first of our three snapshot schools, Beaconsfield College. In terms of resources, facilities, environment and school culture it can only be described as the most privileged of educational contexts. The school has a well-established, strong languages department and students have the choice of several languages, many of them electing to study two languages up to senior level. Latin attracts good numbers, and the balance between male and female students at all levels is fairly equal. It is seen as the most challenging language; the Head of Department commented: '*Only the very smart kids do it.*' The teacher is a maths teacher by primary orientation, but did a second degree in classics, and has always enjoyed Latin as much as maths, commenting that he sees the two disciplines as sharing key characteristics, and therefore finding his dual interest in them quite 'natural'. The fact that Latin is a 'dead' language, and that there is no communicative dimension to the programme, is seen by this teacher as partly explaining the high number of male students in comparison to the other language programmes in the school:

The oral component intimidates boys. They find French or German or Japanese harder because of this. Boys find it hard to communicate; it's challenging to verbalise anything beyond a certain level; it's a vicious circle – they're not as articulate, they don't read as much, don't have the vocabulary that girls have . . . I'd like to think it's nurture rather than nature! I hope so. There are exceptional boys around who do read, who like debating, are very articulate . . . but I'm not sure why it's so few.

The lack of an oral component in Latin, therefore, is seen by this teacher as one reason for the high number of boys who opt for this subject. However, he also subscribes to the belief that the kinds of skills needed to do well in Latin are the kinds of skills more likely to develop in boys than in girls:

To do well in Latin you need to be able to recognise patterns, understand the roles of different parts of speech, manipulate word endings. You need to understand the systems of the language, how it's constructed to work together as a whole. It requires a kind of cognitive and analytical approach which boys seem to be better at – it's more like maths than language. It's about working with abstract concepts and rules, which girls don't seem to be so good at, but which boys appear to enjoy. Some of the boys get excited by patterns – verb endings – they like to work with cut and dried things, rules – they like formal procedures.

The model of language learning which underpins these comments makes many more obvious connections with the kinds of developmental play which characterise early childhood experience for boys (building blocks, experimenting with spatial relationships, solving practical problems) than it does with girls' more communicatively oriented developmental play. It also clearly reflects the teacher's own orientation to language study.

Another dimension of Latin which this teacher sees as being of more interest to the boys is the subject matter of many of the texts they work with: gladiators, soldiers, heroes, battles, military campaigns. He worries at times about the relevance of much of the content for girls ('*in Roman society women didn't do things, there's not much there for girls to relate to*'); but sees girls as gaining more enjoyment than boys from the literary dimension of the texts:

Girls' reading skills are strong and reading is important to them; so what they lack in terms of their ability to deal with abstract concepts, rules and patterns, they make up for with their interest in reading and literacy – and in the characterisation of the different people. Some of the girls take to it because they like stories, characters, reading; perhaps the girls relate more to the history and literary content.

The normative discourse about what girls and boys are respectively 'good at' and 'interested in' which comes through this commentary is familiar. The 'ideal candidate' for his Latin programme was described by this teacher as being *'one who is good at maths AND has a love of language! That's what I am – I did an honours degree in classics and English, AND did maths'*. He summed up this happy relationship by explaining that *'Latin satisfies both sides of the brain'*. The durability of the biological account of what girls and boys can/can't do continues to be a major element of teachers' expectations, assumptions and pedagogic practice.

Teachers on 'good teaching'

Just as we canvassed boys' views on what constitutes a 'good' language teacher, so we were interested in what teachers themselves had to say on this issue. Again, their definitions had several points of connection with the kinds of things boys had said. It became clear very quickly that 'good' language teachers are seen to share the basic attributes of 'good' teachers *per se*; but as language learners are negotiating additional challenges, these generic good attributes are seen to be even more crucial. The following commentary came from a teacher whose students had repeatedly told me what an excellent teacher he is:

> What makes a good language teacher? I'd say a reasonable command of the language; a good knowledge of grammar, but as a tool and not as an ideology; an affinity with the students in terms of their interests – you've got to like them; and of course that means being equitable, catering for individual needs as well as working for the common good. I start with that with every group every year: I work hard on group cohesion – try to convince them that I'm on the same side, I want the same thing as them . . . sometimes you'll veer off what you're supposed to be doing, but you're building relationship, which makes it then easier to come back onto task.
>
> (T.M.)

This teacher is a native speaker of the language he teaches, and the students he works with talked about how important this is. They enjoy his stories about the target culture, about his own experiences when he was, like them, a boy in school. They appreciate the fact that he can always answer their questions about life in the culture. More importantly, however, according to the boys, he is interesting, fun, fair, knows when to establish boundaries and rules. And they have a strong sense that he likes them, finds them interesting and enjoys working with them.

When I asked him about his approach to planning and teaching, he spoke about the importance of using activities which would appeal to boys – of using technology and authentic situations and experiences whenever possible, of connecting with their real-life knowledge and experience and of challenging them continuously. He also emphasised the importance of using the target language as much and as authentically as possible.

> I try to use technology, but the arrangements aren't always easy. We have computer labs, and facilities – but it's hard. But most students have access to the Internet at home, so I push them all the time to use this. It's an amazing resource. We're working on getting a twin school – I'm in touch with a few schools, trying to establish regular exchanges and trips overseas. We had a trip to Bali – but now that's the end of that (the interview was carried out shortly after the Bali bombings in 2002). I've taken boys to New Caledonia – but that wasn't a very satisfactory visit, so I'm trying to establish solid exchanges with France.

He talked about his determination to make languages more accessible to more students, recognising that the way that programmes are currently constructed, and the nature of curriculum and assessment requirements which frame language programmes, make it hard for many students to succeed. He wants to establish a vocational strand for languages in the school, seeing real possibilities of relevant programmes:

> I would love to have a vocational strand of languages, where you would do it differently: e.g., cooking and catering in French. We have kids in this school who want to be chefs, but there are no facilities for them to train here, so they have to go elsewhere. If we had the facilities for the cooking side, we could work it in with French – and there would be some real interest. But we teach it in such an academic way, that it only attracts some of the boys. I know we can do it in a different way! We're getting a lot of kids from primary schools who have had some really good experience of languages being taught in very different ways: French rap, for example, drawing the kids in, building on what they're interested in and good at.
>
> (T.M.)

A female teacher in the same school also talked energetically about the need to make classes interesting and interactive, to use the target language as much as possible for genuine interaction and to allow the students to be 'noisy' – which she sees as a prerequisite for effective language development. When talking about her own understanding of effective teaching she referred repeatedly to the kind of teaching which she sees happening in other classes and which she believes is contributing to boys' disinterest in continuing with languages:

> My classes are noisy places! I use the language as much as I can, and encourage the boys to do so too. Above all, I try to make it fun. I know teachers who just work with the textbook: they work their way through it, getting the kids to translate it page by page, write down the vocabulary and then learn it. And the kids hate it. I start from the minute they come into my room – I greet them and talk to them in Italian, we say the prayer in Italian, then we move on to a warm-up game in Italian – and so it goes on. And I don't care if they're noisy – I WANT them to be noisy! They have to USE the language.
>
> (M.R.)

The same insistence on teaching communicatively and using the target language as much – and as authentically – as possible came through many teacher commentaries on what they see as effective language teaching, many of them either explicitly or implicitly juxtaposing such approaches with what they clearly think of as 'traditional' grammar-translation methodology. The Head of Languages in a large independent school described her teaching team in the following terms:

> On the whole we have a good team, and most of us are teaching as communicatively as possible, using technology and trying to incorporate tasks into our planning. We do have two teachers who are very traditional, and like to work with the textbook – they've been teaching for a long time, and that's what they know and what they believe works. And it DOES work in terms of the students getting their grammar! I try to get them to change their approach, try to force them to use technology for example, but it's hard. I often get kids coming through to work with me at senior who have worked with these teachers at junior level, and it's quite hard for them initially to adjust to my way. But they do – they readjust. And the interesting thing is that quite a lot of them have been very happy with the more traditional way – they're not necessarily put off! They're often some of our

best students in the long run. The girls particularly just want to please
and work hard . . .

(M.W.)

It was clear from teachers' commentaries about their teaching that while
most subscribed to current theories of task-based, communicatively oriented teaching and learning, there is still a lot of traditional grammar-
translation pedagogy happening, especially at more advanced levels.
The commitment to using language authentically often seems to crum-
ble in face of the 'programme': the content which teachers have to cover
in order for students to complete the assessment tasks required by senior
syllabuses. Considerable tension was evident in teachers' explanations
of why they're not using the target language as much as they 'should' or
as much as they would 'like to'.

The clear points of intersection between what the boys had to say
about languages and language learning and their teachers' commentaries makes it easy to identify key issues. The following chapter presents
a much briefer snapshot of girls' views on these same issues. In some
senses this represents a minor 'sub-text' to the narrative we are assem-
bling; but it is interesting and confirming complementary data.

7
Girls Talking About Boys

Given the insistence in both boys' and teachers' commentaries on binary accounts of gender – in school, in the language classroom and in broader social contexts – it seemed important to collect comments from the other side of the divide, to talk to girls working alongside boys in language classrooms.

Socially framed accounts of the early years of high school suggest a culture characterised by what could be described as less than cordial relationships between girls and boys (Frosh, Phoenix and Pattman, 2002). Fairly determined voluntary gender segregation characterises a lot of what happens both in and out of class, these early years seeming to engender a degree of mutual antipathy which is evident in a disinclination to communicate, work or socialise together, to enjoy each other or indeed to take each other seriously. Comments from younger boys in Chapter 4 suggest a degree of annoyance and irritation where girls are concerned, as well as genuine perplexity about the ways girls *are*. These comments suggest 'species separate' attitudes: girls being perceived by boys as inferior or defective versions of themselves, unable or unwilling to participate in the real business of life, bizarrely interested in studying, predisposed to engaging in unhealthy amounts of talking, inexplicably focused on the future rather than living enjoyably in the here and now; biologically wired to be better at linguistic skills and in-school learning.

As boys get older, the relationships change, as do the opinions. Girls become more interesting; but remain markedly 'other'. Some of the boys in Chapter 5 described themselves as having minimal contact with girls, attending all-boys' schools, and sometimes having no sisters. These boys talked more dispassionately about girls, less negatively, but usually in a similarly bemused fashion. Overall, there were few positive or enthusiastic comments about girls in this data set, the general tone of gender relations being one of diffidence – if not of outright antipathy. The divide between the gender territories feels well established and continuously reinforced. It seems to lose much of its sharpness in the later years of high school, with easing of 'tribal' tensions, more interaction and communication, more investment in connection with each other; but there remains a clear sense of difference and demarcation. Conversations with boys proved them to have strong and often un-negotiable opinions about girls; girls, it seems, have even more elaborated opinions about boys.

The girls we interviewed had all studied/were studying languages alongside boys. We talked around the same issues: about attitudes to and reasons for studying languages; about teachers and classrooms; about interaction patterns, connections between language learning and real life and other areas of the curriculum. When they understood that our main focus was the boys–languages relationship, girls had plenty to say; but their views on boys as language learners invariably progressed into wider discussions about how boys 'are': how they 'perform' themselves in school; how they behave around girls, around each other, around teachers; how they communicate – or don't.

Most of these conversations happened in all-girl groups, proceeding very easily, comfortably and enjoyably. Girls had a *lot* to say, and their opinions were interspersed with a lot of attendant joking and laughing. They were less constrained than many of the boys had been, not seeming to care too much about what others in the group might think, happy to put their opinions on record. Talk space was often vigorously competed for, with girls talking over each other, alongside each other, running out of time, lamenting the fact that we couldn't talk on further. A smaller number of girls were interviewed in mixed-gender groups. Perhaps not surprisingly, data collected in these contexts were different in predictable ways. Girls' commentaries on boys when boys were listening were predictably more guarded and circumspect. This made for less interesting data for the purposes of this study, but was interesting in different ways, providing additional evidence of the relational dimension of gender performance, the influence of the 'gaze' of the 'other' (boys) clearly affecting the girls' performance of 'girl'. But it is the commentaries from the all-girl groups which provide most of the data for this chapter.

Girls' talk

The first difference to be noted about the conversations with the girls has to do with the sheer volume of ready opinion referred to above. Where boys often seemed to have to think quite hard about what they thought about girls, and about how their comments might sit in relation to their collective 'boy' identity, and girls in mixed groups clearly edited their comments in strategic and socially prescribed ways, girls in the safety of a boy-free zone talked freely, expansively and enthusiastically. Talking about boys is clearly something they do a lot of; something they enjoy, something they're good at. In this sense the data align with research evidence about women's speech communities, women's and girls' facility in constructing collaborative accounts, women's enjoyment of shared talk, the social construction of shared identities and values through these kinds of conversations (Coates, 2003; Romaine, 1994). Girls had no difficulty whatsoever in marshalling opinions about boys: elaborated, seemingly well-rehearsed opinions, mostly presented as general consensus, although there were certainly disagreements about detail. Boys are clearly a regular and enjoyable topic of these girls' conversations.

They talked about what it's like to study alongside boys, about boys' attitudes and behaviours, about how they see teachers interacting with boys. Their accounts do two things: they provide a solidly 'other' or outsider perspective on boys, and they provide insights to the resources girls themselves draw upon in their own identity construction as girls and as students in school. And like most of the boys' self-narratives and performances of gender, they tend to work from the binary model of cultural explanations.

The problem of the boys

The most dominant motif to emerge from these conversations was that of boys as 'problem'. Girls talk repeatedly about them as less mature, less serious, troublesome in the classroom, undisciplined, unfocused. This is detailed in specific terms of what happens in language classrooms, but also, more broadly, in every other area of in and out of school life. The data triangulate quite neatly: boys' versions of boys aligning closely with girls' versions of boys, both matching teachers' versions of boys. There appears to be general consensus about what is being played out and in all these narratives the binary frame is constantly in service, girls talking continuously about boys in comparative, oppositional terms:

- Boys are seen as unco-operative with each other and resistant to teachers; girls talk about themselves as co-operative and collaborative, working closely with teachers and with each other.
- Boys are described as having a short attention span; girls as being able to focus, concentrate and stay on task.

- Boys are seen to be (over) active; girls talk about themselves as being more passive.
- Boys are criticised for being over-concerned with image, for needing to be seen to be cool, of conforming to peer-group behaviour to the cost of their individual outcomes; girls describe themselves as having more individuality and being prepared to do what they want regardless of what other girls might think.
- Boys are criticised as being more concerned with the project of 'being a boy' than with academic or long-term outcomes; girls see themselves as having longer term views and more interest in shaping their futures.
- Boys are un-negotiably positioned by girls as less mature.

The words 'mature' and 'immature' are peppered throughout girls' commentaries, the difference in perceived maturity levels seeming to be the dominant distinguishing point of difference:

We're so much more mature . . . we want to work . . . even though they're bright, academic boys, and we all get high marks – they don't work like we do. They try to distract us, and want to drag everyone down, so we move away from them. They're immature.

(Sally, 15)

The boys don't ask the teacher stuff. We push so hard for work, want high marks, all 'A's. The boys sit back, and if you say something incorrectly, they mock us. But they don't try. They're immature.

(Michelle, 15)

They're less mature than we are. You have to put them in their place! Otherwise they get in the way of us learning. They're so much less mature than we are.

(Jan, 16)

It's boys who muck up – their friends get in on it, and they all follow. They're so immature!

(Tracey, 13)

The immaturity repeatedly referred to is seen to manifest in behaviour, attitudes and work habits. While the focus of our conversations was the language classroom, the immaturity is seen to spread right through boys' lives at this stage of their development and it was interesting to note how often girls referred to 'this stage' of boys' lives, with a kind resignation about the inevitability of it all:

They're SO immature at this stage: they do get better later . . .

(Susan, 13)

They're really immature at this age (Year 10). Boys in Year 12 get more serious. More like us.

(Jenny, 15)

At this level, we're at least two years more mature than boys of our age. They do get better eventually. It's a stage they go through.

(Clare, 13)

They won't be serious about anything because it's uncool, and the other boys give them a hard time. They're more immature than we are – if we want to work, we don't care what anyone else thinks, we work. But boys can't be like that.

(Alice, 16)

The belief that this is a 'stage' boys have to go through is similar to the account by the boy in Chapter 4 who identified the middle years of schooling as the danger zone that has to be negotiated, where risks of deviating from expected norms of boy-behaviour are so high that few boys survive as 'serious' students. While maturity was a main focus of girls' commentaries, there was a tightness of fit between many other points they made and comments from both boys and teachers. The solidity of the cultural account of gendered school behaviour is clear.

Different kinds of boys . . .

The girls' account of boys is not a totally straightforward binary account – a 'good girls' versus a 'bad boys' scenario. While this is the general shape of the narrative – repeatedly articulated, emphatic and agreed to in general terms – girls also talk about individual untypical boys (and girls), about boys who are prepared to take on different social roles; sometimes described as more 'girl-type boys'. And these different kinds of boys are often the ones who turn up in the post-compulsory language classrooms.

Girls pick up on the fact that individual boys can (and do) behave quite differently when away from other boys (cf. Kenway and Willis, 1998), a fact which appears to frustrate and annoy them – although it's also obviously a welcome relief on some levels. On their own, freed up from the collective performance of 'boy', quite a few of the most annoying kinds of behaviour disappear:

> I mean boys aren't that different – not on their own, they're not. On their own, they can be quite normal, like us really. But when they're with other boys . . . they just muck around. It's stupid. Why can't they behave normally all the time? It's such a waste of time! It's really annoying.
>
> (Leanne, 16)

When asked to talk more about this, girls usually ended up talking about peer pressure and boys' susceptibility in this respect – a deciding factor in their definition of them as immature. In senior language classrooms very small numbers of boys usually end up working with larger groups of girls – sometimes lone boys in groups of 10–12 students. In this situation, away from the surveillance of their peer culture, girls describe boys as being able to drop the expected norms of mainstream boy behaviour and to be a 'different kind' of boy; one who is in fact more like themselves. But they also comment that many of the boys who opt to continue with languages *are* 'different kinds of boys'.

This difference is explained in various ways. Some boys are described as 'braver', more daring, prepared to risk peer disapproval by defying the expected norms of boy behaviour:

> He's not like other boys – well, he IS, he's a boy! – but he doesn't seem to care what the others think. He's prepared to be called a girl, and paid out . . . I actually think he's really brave. Lots of boys wouldn't do that. And it's not that he's uncool . . .
>
> (Lisa, 16)

Boys like the one described here are seen by girls as more interesting, more genuine and stronger than other boys because they dare to reject the expected norm of boy-appropriate behaviour:

> Like Mark – I mean that's the sort of person he is. You should hear him talk! He really loves French – he's just that sort of person. He's always talking about what he thinks, and he even talks about what he feels sometimes – and that's really not what boys do. I think he just says stuff it, if I want to do French that's who I am! I think that's really good. Really brave.
>
> (Caroline, 15)

These 'more genuine' and 'braver' boys are also described as 'nicer' than other boys, less aggressive, less into showing off, more comfortable to be with. The absence of other boys in the class is seen to free them up, to allow them to be nicer than they can otherwise be, to show the softer side of their personalities; to behave more like the girls themselves. Girls see the absence of the 'policing' of boys by boys as having distinctly positive pay-offs:

> Like with Adrian . . . he's cute, and he's athletic and stuff – and there's no doubt that he IS a boy! . . . but he's really more like one of us. We forget about him being a boy. He just does what we do . . . NOT quite like we do . . . like we're out there and noisy . . . and he's quieter than we are . . . but he doesn't bother or annoy us. And he's actually really nice! But he wouldn't be able to be like that if there were lots of other boys in the class.
>
> (Marianne, 15)

These descriptions of a different, more likeable kind of boy occasionally discovered in senior-level language classes are similar to those collected by Frosh, Phoenix and Pattman in their reporting of girls' accounts of the masculinities being constructed in London schools. Girls in that study talked about what some boys are 'really like', in contrast to the hard, football-fixated disruptive version which is the sanctioned norm (2002:141). The 'really like' included being 'really sensitive', capable of listening, even capable of talking about personal issues – like Mark, described above. These softer versions of boy are similar to those of the 'different' boys in girl-dominated language classes described in our data.

It's clear from the girls' conversations that identity construction and performance is something that they are aware of and talk and think about a lot. The points they make are well supported by detailed evidence, examples and stories. They have a well-developed metalanguage for this kind of analysis, talking about 'stages', 'peer pressure', 'community attitudes', 'socialisation'. They note, too, the tensions and complexities in play, not only for the boys themselves, but also in their own reaction to them. The shifting masculinities they're commenting on provoke responses in them which are also at times shifting and ambiguous. Context plays a key role. Girls talk approvingly about boys who behave more like themselves in the language classroom – settling down, being prepared to work, dropping the disruptive, mocking behaviour. These are welcome boys. But when the same girls talk about masculinities in a broader, more socially orientated way, these 'nicer' boys are not usually the ones identified as 'cool', 'attractive' or interesting in the less academic economy of gender relations. There is a definite sense that while these 'nicer' boys are easier to work with, they are less interesting as potential objects of social or sexual interest. Running through discussions of these different kinds of boys are indications of the complicated interplay of girls' own (multiple) performances of gender: and how these intersect with the range of masculinities on offer on the other side of the gender divide.

One conversation took an interesting detour around this issue of masculinities, attractiveness and image, showing the way two quite different economies of gender relations often intersect. The girls had been talking in a very declarative way about how boys who study languages are not usually attractive; not the kind of cool boys that head up the league table of desirable males in the school. They had earlier been talking very dismissively about the kinds of 'cool' boys who don't study, before leading into this discussion of the less attractive profile of most boys who do – or who study languages. One girl took off on an elaborated account of what she considers to be the ultimate desirable version of boy:

> If you meet a boy who can speak another language, he's so much hotter! It depends on what language though . . .. Not if it's Japanese or Chinese. But if it's French . . .! It's because it's so unexpected! The stereotype of boys is that they're stupid . . . no, not stupid . . . but that they're really not interested in language, no good at communicating. They're interested in sport, girls, sex, cars . . . but you don't think about them as being good at communication or speaking another language. They kind of grunt! Now girls – we talk about everything. We talk about feelings and stuff. Guys can't do that. So if you meet a boy who speaks another language – the right kind of language, French, Italian or Spanish – it makes him special! Whoah! You think of it in your mind: tall, blond, hot, with a rugby shirt, who can speak French! Now that's my idea of special!
>
> (Angie, 15)

The other girls in the group were nodding enthusiastically throughout this account, obviously agreeing that cool, attractive, plus a girl-like ability to communicate – especially in one of the European languages seen by these girls as attractive – adds up to their ultimate ideal boy.

Girls talked a lot about the all-important issue of 'cool': in some instances employing it as a negative signifier, used critically and dismissively, but more often as the ultimate positive signifier in the school social economy. The most extended discussion of 'cool' came from a very confident, articulate group of 15-year-old girls in an independent school in which almost equal numbers of boys and girls study languages. They talked knowledgeably and confidently about what constitutes cool, identifying some interesting gender differences in how this is played out. The cool boys were confidently identified as the less-academic types:

> The cool boys, we all know this, they're not very bright. We all know that. They're the ones who do sport and stuff – they don't do languages. The ones who do languages aren't cool. They're the ones who want to work, they stay in the library, not the common room. They're the people who are bright, and striving to succeed – the cool – the popular – boys are doing sport and hanging out, not studying. It's a more masculine thing. They go out a lot, hang out with girls a lot, play sport all the time.
>
> (Meg, 15)

The context of this conversation was the first 'snapshot' school with a long tradition of strong language enrolments and with several students studying two languages at senior level. If we were to find one site where official support for other-language proficiency might triumph over the usual norms of masculine cool, this was it. But here too the girls sketched out declarative accounts of the power of normative masculine behaviour and its negative impact on language study. They identified the advantage of being a girl in this context, arguing that cool girls – unlike cool boys – can, and do, study languages, without risking their status:

> Cool girls can get away with anything! They can behave differently and still be cool. Cool girls DO study! The girls are supportive of each other. Within a group of cool girls there'll be smart people, sporty people, and those who are smart WILL work. And this isn't going to make them less popular – they'll still be cool.
>
> (Kylie, 15)

The challenges for boys who want to do well academically *and* be cool are considerable. They have to go to all sorts of lengths to *not* be seen to work – and so to preserve their cool. Girls are very aware of how this works:

> It's NOT cool to work for boys! The guys who do work . . . they're smart, and they do well . . . but they fit in with the group by not looking like they're working hard. They work at home or something.
>
> (Meg, 15)

It's like they don't want to seem too interested in working because their mates will pay out on them more . . . .. That's actually a real problem for boys. If a girl is interested in a subject, her friends won't say anything – it's OK like, to be interested in something! But the guys might pay out someone who seems interested . . . and lots of boys can't handle that. They have to do all sorts of things to not look like they're working!

(Anne, 16)

The final evidence offered in the 'cool' debate between these students was the fact that in this school the two female School Captains both study languages and the two boy School Captains do not.

A group of girls in a different context made a similar distinction between what girls 'can' do as opposed to what they see as the more limited options for boys, talking too about the challenges facing boys who opt for curriculum areas identified as girl-appropriate. These girls were from another independent school with a strong tradition of language study, strong parental and school administration support for students choosing to continue with languages, and the possibility of studying two languages up to the final year. And these girls had also described the boys in their language classes as 'untypical' boys, talking about the difficulty for them of choosing languages:

It's not just that boys prefer the technical subjects, I think it's also because it's harder for them: they have a harder chance . . . they're expected to do maths and science and stuff . . . but women are just beginning to come into the business world, and to be able to do the things that boys do, so now we can basically do anything we want. But it's harder for boys. They're still expected to do boys' stuff. We have more choices than they do.

(Lindy, 16)

Several girls in this group expressed similar views about boys' compara-tively narrower choices; of them being 'stuck', confined by narrower social expectations of what they ought to be doing. They described themselves as being in much stronger positions in this respect; interest-ing observations when placed beside the comments from boys about girls' comparatively restricted career choices (Chapter 5).

Girls on boys and communication
Girls' views on boys as communicators aligned closely with boys' own commentaries about their relationship with language and with

communication. When I reported that boys had described girls as being 'better' at talk, there were generally confirming signals that varied from nods of agreement to snorts of derisive laughter:

> Boys are hopeless communicators! They just don't know how!
>
> (Jen, 15)

> Boys' idea of conversation is to talk about football . . .
>
> (Alice, 16)

> You try to talk about something serious with a boy, and they just can't do it . . . they turn it into a joke, or a laugh . . . or they get so embarrassed!
>
> (Rachel, 14)

Girls clearly recognise talk as a key marker of gender difference and as an identifying component of their collective sense of self. They talk a lot about themselves as talkers, identifying talk as a crucial part of their lives:

> We'd go weird if we couldn't talk! Talking's what keeps us close – it's what we do! We talk about everything . . . boys, family stuff, movies . . . boys. . . . Bitch about each other . . . talk about teachers, yeah, we talk!
>
> (Jackie, 15)

They tell about endless phone conversations, gossip sessions, talking through problems related to homework and study, but also to everything else in their lives. Nearly all the girls interviewed identify themselves as 'good communicators', although some report problems with 'talking out' in class or in other more public situations, although language classrooms appear less problematic than other lessons such as English, maths or social sciences. While much of the literature on classroom interaction and gender suggests that girls tend to adopt a low-profile in the 'public' arena of the classroom, the language classroom interaction patterns suggest a different dynamic (Sunderland, 2004). The performance of talk in a different linguistic code appears to align comfortably with girls' understanding of what they 'do'; thought of more as social communication and conversation than as display of propositional knowledge or argument. It is as if it is regarded as an extension of the social or private arena – the kind of place that girls are used to talking in. Talking in

French or Japanese appears to be primarily associated with social conversation of the type that girls are comfortable with and proficient in. The confidence that shores up girls' sense of themselves as effective communicators apparently serves them well in the language classroom. Their view of boys as poor communicators similarly underscores their explanations of why boys perform so poorly in this context.

Some girls spoke about the 'acting' dimension of other-language learning – acting a different self – which some boys had also talked about. Girls see this as a greater challenge for boys than it is for girls:

> It's sort of like drama . . . You can act and be someone else when you're speaking a different language. That's sort of fun . . . but not for boys! They find that really embarrassing! You sort of feel like it's hard – it's harder to speak another language, you have to try harder – and you're not comfortable with it sometimes, because you have to sort of be like the person you're trying to speak like. Boys really hate that!
>
> (Andrea, 16)

And they made connections again in this context between 'untypical' boys and languages. Quite a few of the individual boys described by girls were in fact identified not only as 'unusual' and 'untypical', but as the kinds of boys more likely to do drama. The same kind of willingness to step out of their expected normative self into the exploratory realm of drama and creative arts is seen by the girls as encouraging boys into other-language experience.

Girls on learning styles

Girls too had a lot to say about what they see as gendered ways of learning and behaving in the classroom. Like teachers and like some of the boys themselves, they too describe themselves as working collaboratively and cooperatively, supporting each other when things get tricky; and they see this as a key difference between themselves and boys:

> Girls are more supportive. We help each other. If I have a problem, I ring a friend and say "Help!" In class, if we make a mistake, we . . . we still laugh at each other, but not in a nasty way. We don't take offence at it. Like . . . 'Yeah, I stuffed up and it was funny' . . . but you just sort of help each other and move on. You don't feel bad. But boys . . . they really pay each other out. There's no way they're going to help each other!
>
> (Josie, 15)

They also talk about boys' reluctance or 'inability' to make the kind of effort required to do well in languages:

> One of the reasons boys don't do languages is because they find it hard. It's hard. It involves a lot of commitment. Boys aren't prepared to work like girls are.
>
> (Maggie, 15)

> Girls definitely work harder than boys. SOME guys – really exceptional ones – work really hard. But girls are evenly spread out. There are a few really good guys, but then lots that aren't any good. There's a big gap.
>
> (Jenny, 15)

> Girls try harder, they concentrate more, they put in more effort. Some boys put in effort, but not many. A much higher percentage of girls put in effort.
>
> (Annie, 14)

When asked to think about why this might be, several girls talked about the pressure they put upon themselves; something they don't see operating so much with boys. This pressure is sometimes filtered through others' expectations – parents', teachers', peers'. One girl talked at length about what she saw as the influence of her father's expectations on her performance:

> If you've got a father who believes that study is really important, then you're going to want to study. My dad has always encouraged me to study; told me that I've got to do well and that sort of thing. If you have a father who didn't study, and he doesn't believe in that kind of thing, then he won't teach you how to do it. My dad always wanted me to do well, so I really want to.
>
> (Lisa, 15)

She talked repeatedly about different pressures to succeed; identifying some as coming from her father, but others from herself:

> I put a lot of pressure on myself. My mum, she doesn't care how well I do, as long as I try. She always says: 'Just do your best – that's all that matters!' But I put a LOT of pressure on myself! I think girls are more self-conscious . . ... We have to prove ourselves. Boys have more

opportunities to prove themselves – they do a lot of sport, for example. My parents push my brother to do well at sport. He's only 11, but he's playing at state level at soccer, and my parents push him to do well in that. But they push me to do well in school – well, my dad does. That's how it is for girls. Because we're not good at sport, we have to be good at school.

The distinction made by this girl between pressure from her father and pressure from herself is clearly something of a blurred distinction; but her comments about the self-consciousness of girls' sense of themselves as good students aligned with other comments from girls about how they push themselves to do well. The boys they work alongside are described as being for the most part lacking in this kind of self-generated pressure.

Overall, therefore, girls' accounts of boys have aligned pretty closely both with the versions offered by boys themselves and by their teachers. They are seemingly well-rehearsed accounts, in the sense that the girls had clearly talked about these issues many times and had very confident views. The fact that they had more of a language than boys did to talk about issues such as peer pressure, socialisation is unsurprising, but provides food for thought when it comes to thinking about how to improve the boys–languages relationship. This suggestion will be elaborated in the following chapter.

8
Reading Between the Lines

We have now heard from the people this project has been about – boys themselves; and also from teachers who work with these boys and from some girls, who, it turns out, have a lot to say about boys. Our focus on the boys–languages relationship made us wonder whether what we were identifying as a problem would impact on the nature of the data we would collect. As the previous chapters have shown, however, boys proved to be rich informants, willing to talk directly and thoughtfully about themselves, about language and languages, and about their experience in the classroom. Summarising their schools-based project into 'young masculinities', Frosh, Phoenix and Pattman talked about the relationship between pre-research assumptions and what actually happened when they sat down and talked at length with boys, about the contradiction between 'everyday assumptions about boys and the reality of their capacity to show psychological depth and sophistication' (2002:256). Drawing from Hollway and Jefferson (2000), they concluded that 'perhaps it is simply that most individuals – boys, in our case – have very limited encounters with people who really listen to them in an active, sympathetic and thoughtful way' (2002:256). There were moments in our interviews – especially those presented in Chapter 4 – when this sense of novelty was strong. The decision to go to the source to test our assembled theories was a good one. The boys had a lot to say.

What began as a story about gender and language learning has finished up as something more complicated; something which needs to be thought about from a few different angles, and considered through a few different frames. It *is* about gender; and this is certainly the most challenging issue when it comes to recommendations to come out of the project; but as we knew when we began, gender is never a free-floating variable and other intersecting variables critically affect how it is performed. 'Gendered' language learners are always situated in particular social spaces and communities of practice; these too are part of the story. We also knew that gender is not an object of research attention which sits still or offers itself for easy analysis. Like all social constructs and organising principles, it is fluid, on the move, always up for contestation and renegotiation, shaped by larger cultural, social and institutional processes. And we knew that both performance and discursive conditions which frame performance would be central to our analysis.

Reconnecting with theory

On one level, it feels as if the narratives presented in the previous chapters have analysed themselves, making the points that we would make more tellingly than we can do; but as collectors of these accounts, we need now to reconnect with our initial research questions and theoretical frame, before coming to the shaping of recommendations. The problem which brought us to the project, contextualised and historicised in Chapter 3, has assumed a more human face through the variously inflected accounts in the preceding chapters. In a sense, these accounts have operationalised the theory for us.

As detailed in Chapter 3, our theoretical frame is discourse-oriented, foregrounding language and communicative behaviour as social practice, emphasising the co-constitutive nature of language and culture, acknowledging the performativity of defining variables such as gender. Through this discourse lens, we went looking for gender and for identity performance as they impact upon the boys–languages relationship; and we found them everywhere we went: in teachers' commentaries, in students' narratives, in accounts of pedagogy and curriculum organisation; in the statistics and trends identified in Chapter 2. While we have insisted on the term 'gender', it is clear that in the minds of many of our informants 'gender' is in fact biology. This is a core component of the truth *régimes* our project has negotiated; and of the problem we have been investigating.

Performativity and gender

Butler's notion of performativity helps with the analysis. Many of the narratives we collected in group-interview contexts feel like well-orchestrated and rehearsed collectively designed productions; not in terms of the actual wording of comments – which are often hesitant and unrehearsed – but in the overall sense of confident and coherent performance of 'boy'. Gee's notion of identikits came to mind when listening to the boys, to their inflections and rhythms, watching them do what they do with their bodies – ways of sitting, swinging on chairs, shoving each other, avoiding eye contact, sidestepping embarrassment; noting what was sayable and what clearly wasn't. Notions of wardrobes, scripts and performances seemed relevant. Some of the group interview transcripts read like exercises in collective identity confirmation, with boys 'talking the talk', 'walking the walk', policing and nudging each other into collective order, keeping in line in the doing of gender. This is *serious* gender work. But, as the data collected across different contexts show, not all boys perform the expected scripts. There are examples of alternative and resistant performances, hesitations, less sanctioned boy-like shapes, which draw from different discourses and come from differently angled perspectives. These provide the evidence of the 'cracks and fissures' discussed earlier in the book.

While different contexts, situations and relationships produced variations in performance, the point all performances had in common seemed to be the fact that they were – in Bakhtin's terms – relational and dialogic. While they were constituted through different discourses, all operated via an implicit sense of relationship with the 'other'; showing how identity performance always involves what Holquist calls 'the differential relation between a center and all that is not center' (2002:18). This relational sense varies. Sometimes it seems to confirm a shared sense of collective 'recognised' self, where the 'other' is reflected reassuringly back from the *'this is how boys are'* position. At other times – and these appear to be defining moments in terms of boys' relationships with language(s) – it is an oppositional, differentiated and defensive self; the *'that's how girls are, not how we are'* position; less frequently, it is an individually resistant and assertive self, the *'I refuse to be stereotyped'* position. Most of the individual commentaries presented in Chapters 4 and 5, from the most declarative and assertive to the more conflicted and uncertain, resonate with Bakhtin's proposition that individual consciousness – and the performance of self – is a drama always involving more than one actor; an interaction and a struggle 'between one's own and another's words' (1981:354). Different boys struggle in different ways. For some of the younger boys in our study the struggle appears to be minimal. There is more a feeling of consensus, collective conviction and enjoyment about resistance to schooling, language study and anything that might be read as feminine behaviour. Other boys, however, talk openly and in detail about the pressure and conflict of transgressing expected masculine norms; of the tension between the self they want to perform and the self that is expected of them; of the need for strategies and saving graces; and of the price of disapproval. Paechter details the role of opposition in the negotiation of identity: 'In order to have a sense of who I am, I need to have some concomitant idea of who I am not' (1998:5); the individual subject being defined as much in opposition to and through the exclusion of the 'Other' as through association with the sanctioned self. The narratives collected in our project show how this oppositional dimension of identity performance works.

Truth *régimes*

Foucault's genealogical tracking of the multiple and interconnected ways in which discourses shape, rationalise and regulate both the social world and the individual subject also guides our analysis. Foucault argued the importance of not only theorising power, but of tracking and demonstrating the nature of its deployment: about paying attention to 'time and place', noting the genesis and subsequent development of power–knowledge–truth *régimes*, recording the detail of how they are constituted, how they circulate, play out in different contexts, reach the point of commonsensical 'sedimentation' (Pennycook, 2004). The data we have presented sit within such an explanatory frame. The differently situated accounts of the boys–languages relationship – those of boys in different contexts, those of teachers and those of girls – show the closeness of fit that comes from dominant discourse formation; from the power of truth *régimes* which circulate in different sites and directions but merge to shape cultural commonsense. Boys' talk about boys often has the collective self in the frame and the spectre of girls lurking in the background, the need to disassociate from all things feminine being a core component of hegemonic discourses of masculinity. Girls' talk about boys carries implicit – and often explicit – binary comparisons, echoing wider community narratives about how girls and boys 'are', as well as broader community social processes and practices which are complicit in the constitution of these gendered ways of being. Teacher talk about both boys and girls rarely escapes biologically framed comparative analysis and draws insistently from educational discourses about learning styles and gender (although the understandings which underpin these discourses are in fact about sex rather than gender). There is a strong sense throughout of 'things that have been said before'; of power/knowledge work, circulating via the commonsensical 'truths' which keep social worlds turning. Our data therefore sit well within the kind of analytical grid offered by Foucault as a strategy for responding critically to the cultural co-ordination of power-truth effects (1980:198–9). This kind of mapping makes visible how discursive formations do what they do: how they move intentionally between texts and contexts, connect investments and outcomes, nudge individual moves into directions forged by larger collective cultural projects. Our data contribute to this larger project of attending to 'how things are' and to the even more important project of tracking 'how it happens' (Foucault, 1988:104): collecting evidence, paying attention, listening and looking closely, and then asking the 'why?' and 'how?' questions; the critical project of problematising the unproblematic, interrogating the way things are; the 'critique of naturalization and common sense that is at the heart of critical pedagogies' (Luke, 2004:23).

Our exploration of the boys–languages relationship discovered an entrenched, solid sense of how these particular things are; the kind of solid sense which, left undisturbed, makes change or intervention difficult.

Our research questions

Boys and language(s)

We had wanted to get a sense of how boys think and talk about the languages option: its relevance, usefulness, whether or not they see it as an appropriate choice. A first question, however, sits before these questions: how do boys think about themselves in relation to language more generally? This was clearly going to inform their views on themselves as learners of 'foreign' languages.

We went into the project armed with more than three decades of research evidence about gendered communicative practices, gendered speech communities, 'orders of discourse' and the kinds of communicative patterns commonly encouraged in classrooms (e.g., Cameron, 1992, 1998; Coates, 1993, 1996, 2003; Eckert and McConnell-Ginet, 2003; Romaine, 1994; Swann, 2003); and at first glance, both the experience of collecting the data and what the boys actually have to say confirm what we 'know'. As suggested above, the larger group interviews in particular were classically – or stereotypically – 'masculine' in tone and tenor, characterised by 'typical' boy behaviour: serious comments cushioned by jokes, too-personal individual contributions defused by laughter; the need to present a collective, coherent version of 'boy' evident in constant sideways glancing and policing of the collective self. And the collective, official account is clear: language – both talk and the in-school business of literacy – is not something boys need or want to see themselves as good at; it is not something which interests them, not something they *do*. ('Girls talk, boys *do*'.)

Our data indicate that this account continues to be understood by both boys and many of the adults in their world as biologically determined.

Surprisingly few teachers – and perhaps less surprisingly fewer boys – challenge essentialised biological accounts of what girls/boys 'can' do. Traditional narratives of innate predispositions and brain differentiation (e.g. Kimura, 1992), while expressed in more contemporary terms, continue to frame commentaries about schooling, in spite of progressively assembled evidence that this continuing separation of the physical and the social is problematic. Having reviewed the evidence in support of biological explanations for psychological phenomena in recent years, Halpern, for example, concludes: 'When it comes to biological explanations for cognitive processes, we still have more questions than answers' (1992, in Arnot et al., 1998:56); and it is now widely acknowledged that biological accounts of gender differences in academic performance are problematic. Paechter (1998), for example, reports that different life experiences can account for even the small differences that have been found in brain structures; and Sacks (1993) that neural connections are selectively strengthened as a result of experience. Patterns of sex differences are often unstable across cultures, across time within cultures, and through time in individual development (Arnot et al., 1998). Cultural support for this scientific evidence isn't hard to find. In many Eastern European countries, for example, far more women work as physicists, neurologists, engineers or scientific researchers than do women in the countries which are the focus of our study. This fact should disturb the other 'fact' – that women's brains are differently organised to the point where such activities are incompatible with their capabilities. What's 'in your brain' should now be a shakier proposition.

We have also shown that not all boys or teachers subscribe to the biological account. And there are certainly differences in degree in relation to this position. Some more academically oriented boys take a less officially anti-language stand, and occasional individual boys disassociate themselves from dominant discourse accounts; but overall, our data provide additional evidence of the cultural weight of dominant discourses about how men, women, boys and girls 'are' communicatively and linguistically. Commentaries slot easily into an explanatory frame of discourse constitution and regulation which constructs boys in uneasy relationship with language – and with languages.

Kenway (1995) reminds us of the time–place–gender connection; and, as we argued earlier, what it 'means' to be a boy or girl depends very much on where and when. The 'where' which has been our focus – different schools in current times – is shaped by the broader 'where' of wider community and culture; however, as Kenway argues, schools are crucial sites in terms of discourse formation, centrally involved in constituting discourses of masculinity which offer 'a range of ways of being male, but separately and together privilege some as superior' (1995:449). This works through both official and unofficial curriculum processes and practices as well as the discourses teachers speak through when talking to and about students (Mac an Ghaill, 1994). Mahony details the complicity of schools in the construction of the very masculinities now identified as educationally problematic (1998). There are in effect different options on offer, different versions of 'boy' available; but accounts provided in our data show in detail how the privileging of some masculinities over others works through mockery and marginalisation, through the naming of boys who behave in 'un-boylike' ways as 'girls', through the construction of them as defective and subordinate (Salisbury and Jackson, 1996).

However, the cracks and fissures in discourse performance discussed in Chapter 3 are also visible in our data. They usually constitute quieter, more tentative performances; at times bemused, defensive or resentful; occasionally confident and comfortable, but more often suggesting the tension associated with gender performances which deviate from expected cultural norms; reminding us that gender is both discursively shaped and differently impacted by school experience. The evidence emerges from moments which show boys interrogating offered roles, imagining alternative options, refusing commonsensical classifications: the boys in the single-sex Catholic College who argue that they *can* and *do* talk; the 13-year-old who lives in the 'all-girl' household, and who describes talk as 'what we do' in his family, speculating that maybe that is why he's good at Chinese; the 17-year-old who talks about parents 'installing' stereotypical gender behaviours in their children's frames of reference; the girls' accounts of boys who *can* shed their boy-like behaviour in the right conditions. These moments support the proposition that gender is indeed a 'verb'; and help in the unstitching of essentialist governing frameworks of 'knowledge' about gender, sex and language.

The evidence we collected relating to boys' relationship with foreign language learning aligns closely with boys' more general attitudes to language; but this was where the variable of social worlds comes into play. There is a shared sub-text across the data sets relating to biology and innate dispositions – from the *'it's in yer brain'* to the *'girls are better communicators'* position – differently articulated, but commonly subscribed to across the different contexts; but there were clear differences in relation to how the languages option aligned with social worlds.

Relevance – and social worlds

Most boys whose lives include access to positive other cultural experience need little convincing of the usefulness or relevance of foreign language study in general personal development terms. They have first-hand experience of intercultural travel and communication, talk confidently about 'increased understanding', 'accessing different ways of knowing', 'understanding that there's more than one way of being'. They comment on the excitement and exhilaration of being 'almost French', of 'learning to think differently', and of 'venturing out of comfort zones'. For many boys from less privileged socioeconomic backgrounds, there are few such points of connection (apart from the alleged usefulness of being able to call out to invading Indonesians); no imaginable relevant spaces in their lives. It is important to emphasise that we are talking general patterns and trends. There were instances of boys in each data set who took different positions. The 12-year-old who commented that he wanted to learn as much as possible at school, and that maybe learning Chinese would be helpful to him, spoke from one of the least privileged positions. Overall, however, the shape of commentaries about the usefulness and relevance of foreign language study is qualitatively different in the different social worlds. The questions we raised in Chapter 3 concerning 'which boys' are the subject of current crisis accounts, are also good questions to ask of the boys–languages analysis. While interest in post-compulsory language learning among boys is generally weak, it is particularly so among boys whose social worlds do not include the privilege of intercultural access and positive experience of other-language benefits.

What comes through the data from the more languages-friendly social worlds, however, is a problem of a different kind. Many of these boys connect easily with the intercultural competence argument for languages education, liking the idea of increasing their repertoires of ways of being in the world, recognising the inherent interest and appeal of languages, but finding it more difficult to align them with their targeted educational and career objectives. Evidence from a research project by the Scottish Council for Research in Education and the Institute of Education at the University of Stirling in 1999 (J. McPake and R. Johnstone, 1999) found that while students rejected the view that learning languages was pointless because 'everybody speaks English' – in fact expressing a strong desire to learn other languages and know more about other people and other cultures – the continuing decline in enrolments in language courses at senior levels was mainly due to the fact that languages seem unhelpful in terms of achieving career goals (Low, 1999). Students in this study talked about the long-term benefits of learning languages, but saw these as being down the track, in the future, once they had embarked upon a degree course or a career. An earlier

Australian study which explored incentives and disincentives for continuing to learn a language beyond the compulsory stage (Zammit, 1992) found that more boys than girls expressed a dislike for learning languages and that they too linked this to the 'irrelevance' of the subject to their (future) lives. For example, boys tended to strongly agree with the statement 'LOTE (Language other than English) will not get me a better job', and with the statement, 'I will never have the opportunity to use a LOTE'.

The results from our study were less rigid, but similar comments about relevance come through our data. Boys who are positively inclined towards languages seem to be faced by an additional hurdle less likely to be faced by girls: for boys there is a strong implicit, if not explicit, 'hierarchy' of subject choices, based on the parameter of usefulness or instrumentality in post-school options. In this hierarchy, languages continue to rate lower than many other subjects (e.g. maths, sciences), leading boys to opt out of them (sometimes regretfully) in favour of subjects seen as more useful for post-school life: entrance into tertiary study and/or employment. The 17-year-old quoted in Chapter 4, who spoke regretfully of giving up French – which he both enjoyed and valued – in favour of more useful choices for a 'good' career is an example of this tension. Relevance is an issue across contexts. Amongst more academically focused boys there is evidence of some internal struggles between enjoying and valuing languages and the dominant discourse of 'usefulness', but this tension is less evident among less academically oriented boys who on the whole see them as irrelevant to their social worlds and real-time interests.

Difficulty

Also emerging from comments and observations from the preceding chapters is the fact that many boys consider foreign languages to be a difficult option, suitable only for 'cleverer' girls. The comments we collected along these lines align closely with the data which came out of the British studies referred to in Chapter 3 (Clark, 1998a and 1998b; Jones and Jones, 2001) and the earlier Australian study by Zammit (1992). In fact the Australian study identified 'difficulty' as the most gendered of incentives/disincentives. In these studies and in our own project boys detail in very similar fashion the ways in which languages constitute a difficult option:

- **The fact that the language *is* the content.** Boys repeatedly complain about the fact that they're not 'learning about anything', but 'just doing language'; and that 'language' is 'hard'. The idea that language itself might be a valid focus of attention is not seen as a convincing proposition. For the majority of boys (possibly excluding boys who opt to study Latin), study of language as linguistic system – as grammar – is seen as difficult and boring; and the fact that the structures and systems of the new language don't work in the same way as English is seen as a major difficulty. Many of the boys in our study in fact have very little explicit knowledge of English as a grammatical system. Language and literacy education in Australian schools currently adopts a systemic functional approach to work with language, most teachers paying minimal explicit attention to grammar in either the functional or traditional sense. The kinds of linguistic and meta-linguistic knowledge encountered in foreign language programmes, therefore, are doubly foreign.

• **The separation out of the four skills** – reading, writing, speaking and listening – is identified by many boys as a major difficulty, as well as being seen as an 'unreal' way of doing language work. Each individual skill seems to present particular challenges, with reading and writing reported as especially difficult (see comments in Chapter 4), but listening too being seen as difficult (the comment by the 'good' language learner in Chapter 4 about the boys in his class who had great difficulty in listening activities is relevant here); and speaking poses very particular problems for many boys, requiring as it does for them to regress to a level of linguistic infancy at a stage in their lives when their sense of social self is at its most invested and precarious. Vocabulary learning is repeatedly cited as one of the most difficult and least enjoyable aspects of language lessons. Boys resent having to learn lists of discrete, unrelated language items ('hundreds of words!', 'all those verbs!') disparate parts of a whole which never seems to happen, never seems to 'arrive anywhere' (cf. Clark, 1998a:33). They see this kind of de-contextualised activity as 'too hard'; something more suited to girls' ways of learning.

• **The incremental and cumulative nature of language learning** is another element seen as being particularly difficult. The problem of sustaining concentration and levels of engagement is identified by many of the boys who are continuing with language study. As reported by one boy in our study, 'down time' in the language classroom can do irreparable damage. Another boy described a foreign language as being like a train: it never stops, usually goes too fast, and if you jump off for a while, it's impossible to get back on.

- **The amount of memorisation involved.** We collected many comments about having to learn things by heart, which is something boys identify as particularly difficult. Again, the explanations offered are usually 'brain' ones: boys report that the 'memory part of the brain' is less well developed in boys than in girls. There is a social account too, however, which is quite simply that learning by heart is boring and boys aren't prepared to be bored.

- **The teacher-centred nature of language classrooms.** This was commented upon in both the British and Australian data. The teacher is seen to hold all the power, being the only one who knows the language. Boys talked about feeling dependent and out of control; of being treated like 'kids', required to do what they describe as boring, simple (though difficult) tasks, such as copying from the board and filling in worksheets (worksheets figured significantly in terms of critical comments about teaching and learning). Boys compared language classes unfavourably with other curriculum areas, where they feel more autonomous and have opportunities to do 'real', relevant work, more appropriate for their age and interest levels. The fact that the teacher is the only one who 'has' the language – and therefore the power – is seen as a distinct problem.

The gendered curriculum

Our review of literature in Chapter 3 suggested we would find evidence of 'gendering' of the curriculum, and in our data curriculum areas emerge as clearly demarcated places. The territorial imperative appears to be particularly defined for younger students in mixed-sex schools, where subject choice continues to be a core signifying practice of socially inscribed gender performance. Gender is most publicly performed in physical spaces such as playgrounds and computer labs, but it is performed equally significantly in symbolic spaces such as curriculum areas. Riddell (1992) found that both girls and boys use each other as a negative reference group in the maintenance of gender boundaries, each actively reinforcing boundaries through perceptions of subjects as 'male' or 'female'; and that boys talk a lot about 'feminine' subjects, defending domains such as sport, science and technology as 'male' (explanations varying between mental ability and physical strength). Our data confirm this evidence. Across contexts, boys talk about 'suitable' curriculum choices; about subjects which boys/girls 'can' and 'ought' to do; about girl/boy appropriate lessons. Stables and Wikely (1996) found that gender patterning in subject choices indicate girls' preference for subjects which involve 'direct personal interaction' (ibid:8); our interviews contain many explanations about why language classes 'work' for girls and not for boys, and the 'personal interaction' dimension of this account is key. For many of the boys quoted in Chapter 4, the association between language classrooms, talk, physical inactivity and girls is too close to be comfortable for 'real boys'. Like English classrooms, language classrooms are regarded as feminine places, involving girl-appropriate activities such as conversation, writing, listening; all things that girls are 'good' at, and which – in the big scheme of things – don't fit into boys' more 'active' lives. Content of this talk and writing is also described as feminine, boys talking dismissively about topics and activities typically included in language programmes – families, food, pets – as unrelated to their lives or to their interests; as girl-appropriate.

While these territorial understandings are in evidence across most contexts, appearing to be particularly important in mixed-sex schools (cf, Stables, 1990), the variable of social worlds again comes into play. Some private-school boys studying in languages-friendly school environments talked approvingly about slowly shifting boundaries: about girls now playing soccer, about boys playing in the orchestra (though still thin on the ground in the flute section); about increased choices and changing life trajectories; and about boys out-performing girls in their language classrooms. These were positive – if slightly triumphal – comments, qualitatively different to the many dismissive ones about boys/girls who crossed acceptable gender boundaries. As commented earlier, (Chapter 5) there's also a discernible classed dimension to their tone, which emphasises again the interconnectedness of social variables such as gender and class. These particular boys live in Victoria, in a major metropolitan area, and clearly enjoyed constructing an oppositional 'sophisticated south versus uncultured north' account of 'how boys are'; enjoying it all the more as they knew that I live and work in Queensland. They spoke disparagingly and pityingly about 'Queensland boys', living in a 'man's state', where everyone plays football and few boys do languages; and proudly about their own good fortune to be living in a state which 'is doing quite well' in terms of breaking down traditional gender boundaries. This was an encouraging if privileged account, again shaped by the collective project of performing an approved version of 'boy', but showing evidence of movement in terms of discourse possibilities; an awareness of the social component of gender performance which is relatively uncommon through our data. Interestingly, however, nearly all the conversations along these lines concluded that girls are enjoying more expanded choices than boys. It is seen to be easier for girls to front up for soccer training than it is for boys to turn up to dance or choir practice. As the 16-year-old girl quoted in Chapter 5 commented: *'We can basically do anything we want. But it's harder for boys. They're still expected to do boys' stuff.'* The connections between broader societal change and in-school curriculum economies continue to affect both the status of languages and the range of available performance options.

The 'value' of language study

Our study has also confirmed the gendered dimension of the 'value' of language programmes in curriculum stakes. As argued earlier (see Chapter 2), this gendering has not always been the case. Languages continued to be a core component of the education offered to boys in the eighteenth and nineteenth centuries, and when education became more widely offered to women, science was considered to be particularly suited to female students, while classical studies continued to be regarded as a male preserve (Delamont, 1994). Paechter (1998) comments on the historical fact that middle-class white males have tended to appropriate whichever curriculum areas currently enjoy high status; our data suggest that this is still the case, with languages having slipped in status value with boys, now commonly regarded as a soft option more relevant to the kinds of careers girls are likely to choose. This correlates with broader cultural attitudes (sometimes explicitly, but more often implicitly endorsed by government discourses and actions) which transmit the message that English – as the global language – is all we need. We commented earlier that in Australia until quite recently languages were valued as indicators of academic ability and included as prerequisites for university entrance, seen as perfectly appropriate options for boys. Changing priorities have relegated them to lower-leagues status, and boys' attitudes mirror this change. We collected only occasional comments from boys about the 'cognitive challenge' or 'inherent interest' of languages (e.g., the comment by the 17-year-old studying Mandarin, who claimed it to be every bit as challenging and rigorous as physics).

What counts in the economy of schooling, then, is seen to be as variable and context responsive as gender itself; and value is increasingly imagined in material, economic and career-oriented terms. The report on the Scottish project referred to earlier (McPake et al., 1999) makes disheartening reading in bottom-line terms of retention figures, but shows how these reflect broader cultural shifts. Students surveyed indicated that – contrary to expectations, given the low retention rates at senior level which were the focus of the research project – there was surprisingly high value attached to the learning of languages. The majority of students expressed positive attitudes to other-language/culture experience, talking about their desire to learn more about other cultures and lives through learning languages. There was minimal evidence of the 'English is enough' attitude that came through in some of the Australian data. Students appeared to understand the personal benefits of other-language experience, even though their understanding of what would best serve their future educational and career aspirations meant that most of them chose to drop their languages. Value is increasingly understood in pragmatic, strategic, economically driven terms.

Boys' thoughts on the teaching and learning of languages

We have concentrated so far on the two main players in the relationship. We have looked at 'boys', as physically embodied, discursively constructed solo and collective performers; externally producing internally crafted performances of masculinities; navigating their in-school 'selves'; negotiating more or less successfully different discourses which tell them who they 'are' and what they should 'do'; and we have noted the points of collision and connection not only with discourses of schooling and broader community discourses and cultural knowledge, but most specifically with the languages option. And we have looked at foreign languages as an offered experience: a 'commodity'; a curriculum player with shifting value and status; a social space involving new 'grammars of the self'. There is, however, a third player in the relationship, which connects with the other two: pedagogy. It may be difficult to separate out what we mean by pedagogy from what we've referred to as 'foreign languages education', but it was clear from commentaries we collected that boys themselves do just that, drawing a dividing line between the two which has implications for our thinking at this point.

There appear to be different levels of resistance by boys to the languages option. Some appear more entrenched and intractable, shored up by solid commonsensical knowledge about what's possible, appropriate and desirable, by racist and xenophobic attitudes, or by the monolingual mindset of speakers of the global language who see no need to learn other languages. But other levels of resistance appear to be more provisional, more open to consideration and to influence from variables which are themselves more fluid.

The McPake and colleagues' report (1999) referred to earlier suggests this distinction. The students in that study were not for the most part opposed to the notion of foreign language study. Their reasons for dropping out were pragmatically framed, having to do with study pathways, career options, and the perceived value of languages to future employers. Evidence of similarly mixed response and motivation came out of the 1998 UK study by Clark, this time drawing attention less to the imperatives of broader community and work-related values and more to students' evaluation of the quality of the offered experience. While many students in this study had stereotypically framed views about the relevance of language study, reflecting narrow, insular attitudes, a key factor in explaining their disinterest appears to have been the absence of any intrinsic satisfaction in their language learning experience rather than disinterest in the option itself. This brings us, therefore, to this third major component of the boys–languages relationship: to what actually happens in language classrooms, how programmes are designed, how resources and materials are selected, how teachers 'teach'. Evidence from our data – like the evidence from the UK data and from the earlier Australian study (Zammit, 1992) – suggest this to be a major focus of concern. Back in 1992, Zammit identified three main explanations offered by boys for not continuing with languages: difficulty, dislike and negative experiences; the negative experiences relating to their classroom experience. They spoke of not learning much, of being bored, of disliking the activities they were expected to engage in. Our study suggests that things have not improved to any significant degree. Students talk repeatedly about boredom, lack of progress, frustration; of learning the same things 'over and over'; of irrelevant and meaningless tasks. Learning languages, for many of the boys we spoke with, is clearly an unenjoyable experience.

This reads as harsh judgement; and these comments have to be put in context. The focus of our project was boys' relationship with languages, already established as poor. What we knew about levels of satisfaction and interest when we started out prepared us for discouraging evidence. Of course we were hoping to find good stories too. In among the students interviewed would be boys enjoying languages and doing well; and we found them. Alongside stories of dissatisfaction and disinterest, there were positive and enthusiastic reports of 'great' teachers, who made learning 'fun' and 'really interesting'; of the cognitive satisfactions of 'cracking codes' and the cultural enrichment of seeing inside different worlds. Some of the case study conversations presented in Chapter 5, for example, provide the kind of positive, insightful comments that read like successfully achieved foreign language programme objectives. Overall, however, a far higher proportion of commentaries – those detailing the difficulties and problems summarised above – indicate low levels of approval of what actually happens in language classrooms; and provide a significant part of the explanation for the mass migration by boys (and many girls too) from post-compulsory programmes.

From theory to practice and back again: teacher knowledge in practice

'Pedagogy' is almost as complex as 'boys'. It involves the operationalised ensemble of informing theories, teaching strategies, course design and resourcing; plus all those more idiosyncratic and less definable elements such as personality, communicative style and relational skills which, while not always addressed explicitly in teacher education, are rank-ordered highly by students when they talk about what makes a 'good' teacher. Part of our interest in this project had been to find out as much as we could about what teachers are doing in language classrooms, why they are doing what they are doing, and how they are doing it; because this has to be a large part of the boys–languages equation.

Clearly there are significant variations in what happens in different contexts. The boys we spoke with inhabited – or had inhabited – some very different kinds of classrooms, ranging from prescriptive, teacher-fronted, traditional text-based places to more innovative, experimental and communicatively focused ones. And, as indicated in Chapter 6, the teachers we spoke with varied significantly. One of the things that came through most clearly from these conversations was a sense of the complexity, ambiguity and variability of what teachers do in classrooms. Not only of what they *do*, but also of what they *think* they do, what they *say* they do, and – articulated less comfortably – what they say they know they *ought* to be doing but are not. This is not to impute teachers' honesty or professionalism, or to engage in 'teacher bashing'; but rather to acknowledge the inherent complexity and difficulty of managing the theory–practice relationship which challenges everyone involved in education.

The relationship is a complicated one. As argued earlier, what teachers 'know' about teaching and about their own practice involves both experiential and received knowledge (Wallace, 1991) as well as the complicating factors of self-perception and subjectivity. Work in the area of teacher knowledge, curriculum development and teacher change tracks how this works (Fullan and Hargreaves, 1992; Piper, 1997). Individual knowledge is initially – and profoundly – shaped by what we ourselves experience through the many years spent sitting in classrooms (at least 16 years for most teachers); and alongside and underneath this first-hand experience, we absorb all those culturally specific common-sense understandings about what teaching is and what teachers do – our cultural truth *régimes*. The fact that every kindergarten child can confidently 'do teacher' – voice, body language, questioning and answer routines – shows how effectively this kind of knowledge is internalised, seemingly by osmosis rather than conscious attention (Carr, 2000). When we enrol in teacher education programmes, we're presented with a sometimes conflicting array of new knowledges, some of which sit well together, others of which collide quite spectacularly. This new, 'received' knowledge (Wallace, 1991) has to be sorted into working relationship with existing schema. Depending on when and where we receive it, this is a more or less successful process.

Most received knowledge in teacher education is theoretically based: theories of cognitive and social development, theories of language acquisition – psychologically or socially framed – theories of learning, theories of culture; and these theories come out of paradigms which themselves are shaped by different intellectual traditions. In there too is a component of 'craft' knowledge, passed on by practitioners in the field who supervise practicum experiences. Navigating the relationship between these differently framed knowledges is one of the greatest challenges for preservice teachers. Students returning from teaching practice regularly report advice from supervising teachers to 'forget all that theory'; to watch, listen and learn the 'real' nature of teaching. Collaborative university–school based projects have made some progress in breaking down the theory–practice divide, but most teachers carry this tension into their own practice.

Managing the theory–practice relationship has been particularly challenging for language teachers. As well as keeping up with general developments in educational theory, language teachers have been additionally affected by continuing moves in second language acquisition research. Many teachers talk of feeling battle weary from what they describe as continuous changes in methods, curriculum design and language teaching policy and practice; of feeling continuously encouraged, exhorted or required to reconceptualise and redesign their practice. Foreign language teaching methodology has probably been subject to more pedagogical shifts than any other curriculum area in recent years, as debates between second language acquisition theorists and applied linguistics practitioners continue to progress differently theorised practice.

We now know a whole lot more about how languages are learned; so in theory we also know more about how to teach them. The argument is increasingly made (e.g., Kumeravadivelu, 2003) that we have reached a 'post-methods' moment: an acknowledgment that language teaching must always be context-responsive, student-specific and culturally attuned; that 'methods' is an anachronistic concept, which takes insufficient account of the agency of learners or the significance of context. But this is not how most teachers out in the field feel, nor what the teachers we spoke to appear to believe. Many of them report a sense of juggling methods; of trying to reconcile different approaches. There is an overall sense of anxiety about methods. Teachers talk about what they *want* to do, what they *have* to do, what they are *able* to do, and what situations require of them; and use of the target language in the classroom emerged as the focus of many of these tensions. Many have a strong sense of 'knowing what they know', of what works best for them and for their students; but some talk regretfully about the misalignment between the pedagogy they had imagined, from the optimistic space of pre-service preparation, and the reality of practice in the real world of systems and classrooms. Others talk with resentment about 'swings' in methods and curriculum design, imposed from above, requiring radical changes at too-regular intervals. As language learners themselves, as graduates of teacher education courses, and now as teachers living and working within the tangle of real-life constraints and possibilities, they know a whole lot of things which don't always settle into coherent or comfortable practice.

The teachers in our study are probably fairly representative of the wider language teaching communities in the countries in question. Some are confident in their practice, feel well theorised and well practised; others appear conflicted and concerned for the reasons suggested above. Given the radical shifts in methodological orientation over the last three decades, this is unsurprising. It appears to be the case that more language teachers currently working are nearer the end than the beginning of their teaching lives, and shifts in teaching approaches during their careers have been considerable.

Changing methodologies: from grammar translation to the task-based classroom

Those of us old enough to have learned our languages in school in the 1950s and 1960s studied via the grammar-translation model, which meant exactly what it said. We learned languages as grammar, fixed and knowable linguistic systems, which involved declensions, conjugations, patterns, rules (and exceptions to rules). We gradually assembled the system, starting with basic building blocks – typically the present tense of verbs such as 'to be' and 'to have' – moving progressively to more complex systems and constructions, hopefully mastering the subjunctive as we exited senior programmes. The 'translation' part of the approach involved encoding and decoding: learning how to translate, backwards and forwards, from first to target language and back again. Much class time was spent copying, writing, reading, learning vocabulary and tenses, memorising, manipulating and reproducing for testing purposes. Our tools consisted of a grammar book (at appropriately sequenced level), an exercise book and the all-important small vocabulary book in which we wrote our lists of words. The one distinguishing feature of our 'modern language' classrooms (as opposed to Latin or Ancient Greek) was the oral component. In all other ways, learning French or German proceeded identically to learning the 'dead' languages of Latin and Greek.

The four skills were individually targeted for attention. We spent most of our time writing and memorising, repeating out-loud modelled forms, although reading became more important as we progressed, the ultimate learning objective being the ability to read set literary texts which constituted the major part of senior-level programmes. Listening was also prioritised, from early exercises in listening to carefully enunciated short texts (dictations) to more extended 'comprehension' exercises, more authentically delivered than dictations, but still pedagogically processed samples of grammatically correct language. As indicated, the only difference between learning French and Latin was the 'oral' component: typically a short, pre-rehearsed exchange dialogue, the recitation of a memorised poem, or a reading-aloud exercise. The focus of assessment for oral proficiency was accuracy of grammatical forms and native-like pronunciation. (e.g., for English speakers learning French, mastering the 'r' sound, the 'u' sound, and banishing the English 'th' constituted the major oral challenges). Life in the grammar-translation classroom was predictable, ordered and suited some learners very well; but excluded many others who found this cognitively oriented learning experience either too difficult or too unappealing. Languages were typically described as suitable for 'more able' learners; and for those students who succeeded, it delivered what it promised: the ability to 'do' grammar and to read, write and to translate.

Many language teachers now nearing the end of their careers learned this way. If they had the opportunity to also spend time in-country, immersed in the target language – which some of them did as part of their tertiary level language study – the chances are they came out with good levels of oral language proficiency on top of their grammatical and literacy competence. Without the in-country experience, they tended to be proficient readers and writers, with good knowledge of the target grammar, but low levels of oral communicative proficiency. These are the teachers who feel most confident when teaching closely to a grammar-based set textbook, and who typically resist more communicative approaches. Fewer Australian than British teachers benefited from the in-country component of teacher education/language study programmes, the European model of exchange language assistants never having worked well in the Australian context, due to the tyranny of distance and its associated costs. Some teachers in our data reported being limited in terms of their practice by their own levels of language proficiency.

The grammar-translation approach was followed by a variety of approaches which collectively made the fundamental shift away from learning language as a grammatical system – giving access to literature and some cultural experience – towards learning language for communicative and cultural use; for real purposes, in real situations. This shift translated into a range of different techniques and methods, before settling into the general orthodoxy of CLT – communicative language teaching. The focus on grammatical structures was replaced by a focus first on language functions and notions, and then on genres and text functions. While these different moves all signalled a change in intention – and practice – they were still in a sense 'synthetic' (Carr, Commins and Crawford, 1998), in that they still reflected the view that language acquisition is a gradual accumulation of parts which can be taught and learned separately until the whole structure has been built, when language proficiency will 'happen'. In synthetic syllabuses, units of language and culture still remain 'objects to be studied or examined' (Stern, 1992:301) – often through the learner's first language; practised in decontextualised ways until 'ready for use' (Savignon, 1991). The traditional present–practise–perform teaching model – the PPP still so prevalent in both FL and TESOL classrooms – demonstrates how this understanding drives practice.

The latest moves in the language teaching/learning evolution have led to the task-based classroom, where effective language learning is understood to involve authentic tasks; tasks which in turn involve real purpose and cognitive as well as linguistic challenge. These are qualitatively different to traditional language classroom tasks, designed to practise discrete skills and language forms, and to display knowledge for testing purposes (Carr, 2005; Skehan, 1996). These 'real' tasks are seen to hold real promise in terms of achieving 'real' outcomes, which ideally involve more than language; and which are achieved through authentic interaction patterns and social processes. While there are variations in what is meant by 'tasks' ('soft' tasks, 'hard' tasks etc., Willis, 1996), the distinguishing feature of a 'task' is an activity which has meaning as its primary focus (Skehan, 1996); authentic meaning, as opposed to contrived, simulated 'practice' meaning. Underpinning this shift in approach is the belief that language learning is more likely to occur when learners are engaged in purposeful, authentic communicative tasks and are exposed to significant target language input, rather than when they are required to study discrete language items or skills in a decontextualised, free-standing context, (*'lists of words'*; *'all those verbs!'*) in an environment where most of the 'real' communication happens in the students' first language.

Recent graduates of school and university language classrooms – the younger teachers in our study – have been prepared for the kind of task-based, target-language-rich, communicative learning environments described above. Current syllabus guidelines and programme initiatives reflect this approach (e.g., QSCC, 2000) as do their targeted learning outcomes. The current emphasis on outcomes is itself a reflection of a shift in focus from teaching to learning; from first objectives of grammatical competence and traditional literacy proficiency to more socially and communicatively framed additional objectives of discourse and cultural competence. In some places – in Queensland, for example – the move has been mandated by the provision of new syllabus documents and resources which are designed to provide 'rich tasks', 'embedded' (in other areas of the curriculum) language experiences and high levels of target language input. Many recent graduates have worked closely with the new materials before going out into the field, and have good understanding of the theory which has shaped them. For teachers already in the field, however, especially those whose teacher education pre-dates communicative times, the required paradigm shift is significant.

In some instances, as in Queensland, teachers are provided with professional development support for new syllabuses and resources (QSCC, 2000); but early research into the implementation of the new Queensland syllabus (Carr and Crawford, unpublished data) confirm what literature on curriculum change suggests: radical changes in teaching approaches require significant, sustained and negotiated support if they are to succeed (Fullan, 1991; Piper, 1997). Teachers have to be convinced of the need for ('yet more') change; they need to be involved in the design and the implementation of the change; and they require appropriate support through whatever kind of transition is involved. The effect of change on teachers personally and professionally has been found to include a sense of challenge to values, to accumulated wisdom and to the sense of professional self (Carr, Commins and Crawford, 1998:72). Teachers report a sense of being 'buffeted' by continuous change. Some openly resist new directions;

others deliberately 'mix and match' new and old methods, taking what they see as the best from different approaches and materials; others pay lip service to new mandated changes and continue to teach as they have always done.

Most teachers I spoke with described their practice as communicatively based; yet as they talked about their planning and teaching and about their students, a sense of some quite traditional classrooms emerged. What also emerged was a sense of contradiction, between intention and practice – at least in terms of the practice as it is experienced by the students. Students' descriptions of what happens in classrooms were sometimes totally different to their teachers' descriptions.

The misalignment seems to relate mainly to the use of the target language in the classroom and to the design of learning tasks. The authentically communicative classrooms imagined above presuppose authentic and purposeful use of the target language and opportunities for active, task-based learning. Boys' negative comments – about lists of decontextualised words, of endless copying from the board, of repeating things in chorus, of doing 'unreal' and 'boring' things – are the antithesis of interactive, collaborative, problem-solving language experience. Our earlier discussion of second language acquisition theory identified the need for sufficient 'raw material' for language acquisition processes to work; and for sufficient 'output' opportunities – the chance to try things out, make discoveries, backtrack, shift, negotiate; all the things which make up authentic communicative experience. The kinds of activities described by many boys we interviewed fall far short of these kinds of opportunities. For much of the time they appear to have been doing lockstep, teacher-fronted work, with far more focus on writing and learning by heart than on speaking or problem-solving. And their exposure to the target language on the whole does not appear to be extensive. The occasional accounts of rich language experience are the exception rather than the norm. (e.g., *'Our teacher uses Indonesian nearly all the time!! It's great – if we don't get it, he does it again, and again, and he does it differently – gives us clues – acts it out – till we guess it – it's really good!'* (Jamie, 14)).

A surprising number of teachers report using only minimal target language in the classroom, and the language they do use seems to mainly be what Willis (1992) refers to as 'inner language': the target language forms and functions which are the selected focus of learning. 'Outer' language – language used in an unprepared way for authentic communicative purpose – seems less common in most classrooms. Many teachers report 'feeling bad' about this comparatively low level of authentic target language use, which they explain in various ways, including anxiety about behaviour management, (*'the younger ones won't understand what I'm saying and will go wild'*, (H.P.)), concern about their own levels of target language proficiency (*'If I stray too far from the text, they might ask me language I don't know'*, (P.T.)), and syllabus constraints. Ironically, quite a few commented that they actually use less target language with senior students, who would be better able to cope with higher levels of language, because senior programmes are so 'heavy', 'crowded' and 'tight for time' that using the target language would slow things down and disadvantage students. There's a circular kind of 'Catch 22' dimension to these arguments that is concerning, suggesting as it does an inherent contradiction between current pedagogical objectives and actual pedagogical practice. Teachers talked about 'resorting' to worksheets and written exercises in order to keep control of large classes of resistant (mainly boy) learners (*'It's the only way! If I let them do group work, or even work in pairs, it would be total chaos!'* (G.P.); *'I do try – I've often tried – to do group work. But it's hopeless – nothing gets done'* (S.A.)) In small senior-level classes, where there are no management problems as such, teachers talk about the impossibility of 'losing time' trying to communicate in the target language: *'There's so much to get through! There's no time – it wouldn't be fair to them'* (R.L.).

'Best practice' according to the boys

The above discussion of classroom practice, teacher formation and programme development suggests a complex and conflicted world of FL classrooms. Obviously this is a 'situated' account. A different research project would have yielded different evidence. If we had focused on successful programmes and engaged (female?) learners, then the evidence would certainly have been more encouraging – although there's no certainty that the theory–practice relationship would have been differently balanced. We are not mounting a global critique of pedagogy, nor advocating uniform alignment with current 'best practice'. Some of the best 'best practice' is precisely the kind of hybrid, pragmatically shaped flexible practice which may be pedagogically unorthodox but which works. But the tensions we encountered between policy, programme design and practice, and between teachers' differently operationalised 'knowledges', and, most importantly, between teachers' and students' viewpoints, have to be part of the boys–languages problem – and part of our thinking about how to improve the situation. The misalignment between what we now know about language learning and what is actually happening in some classrooms is telling.

The programmes which boys talked about most critically and dismissively appear to be very traditionally delivered, teacher-fronted programmes, characterised by lockstep teaching, minimal use of the target language, and unchallenging tasks. The programmes which boys in our study talked about enthusiastically were more interactive, socially oriented, task-based and cognitively as well as linguistically challenging. This is not, however, a simple equation. As we have argued earlier, classrooms are complex 'ecologies', inhabited by social players whose relationships, social roles and social needs constantly change. The same boys who argued for more interactive, socially oriented language programmes might, in different contexts – and even in different moments of their individual school careers – back off from interactive activities and prefer reading and writing tasks, due to the 'cool' factor and the attendant fear of being teased by their peers. But they would still presumably prefer more task-based, relevant, authentic experience.

The Seal Wife

One such success story was that of *The Seal Wife*. The teacher referred to in Chapter 4 who experimented with a Process Drama approach to her French programme had designed a PD unit around a traditional Celtic folk tale about a fisherman and a 'selkie', a part-seal, part-human creature (Marschke, 2005), caught between two worlds, yearning for her lost life in the ocean, caught in the tangle of human emotions (children and husband), eventually making the choice to return to the sea, abandoning her grieving human family. On the face of it, not the obvious 'hook' to engage the interest of 13-year-old boys: definitely 'girls' stuff'. Yet the unit was a resounding success with boys as well as with girls. The same boys who had talked about 'choosing their behaviour' and about the refinements of 'mucking up' – unmistakably boy-like boys in terms of both individual and collective performance – turned up at lunchtimes and before school, helped to transform the classroom into the various sets the drama required (sea shore, classroom, home), swapped roles – being the 'father', the 'son', 'villagers', even 'young children' – acted out imagined feelings and relationships; and, most significantly, used unexpectedly high levels of target language. Several of them also opted to continue with French the following year. They behaved, therefore, totally out of role in relation to usual boy performance.

Process drama allows students to take on and experience different viewpoints, social behaviours and emotions from the safer position of in-role characterisation. It's predicated upon the notion of play; not in a trivial or unstructured sense, but in a way designed to support cognitive, affective and social development (O'Toole, 1992). In the fictional world of process drama, this kind of play minimises the consequences of enacted experience, while providing a concrete (if fictional) social context for affective, social and intellectual exploration (Marschke, 2005). All this adds up to a context and an experience which approximates the 'real' far more effectively than the 'Let's pretend' activities commonly included in language programmes. Unlike these more traditional, prepared and scripted drama activities, process drama involves unpredictability, genuine information gaps, choices as to how characters and plots develop. Outcomes are unknown; meanings unfixed. And the fact that the teacher is also in role alleviates the 'power' relationship identified by boys as a major problem in language classes.

The impetus for Marschke's study had been the discouragingly low level of engagement by students in her school – particularly boys. As a first-year-out teacher, she had found herself in a particularly challenging context: in a school of 650 students, French is the only language offered, and its profile was low. Before her appointment, there had been a regular French teacher turnover, and retention figures were extremely low. She decided to make the connection between her drama training and her language classroom, thinking that process drama might create the kinds of authentic communicative opportunities which would be more intellectually and affectively engaging than what usually happens in language classrooms. And it worked. The number of students – including boys – opting to continue with French increased dramatically. The previous year only two students had opted to continue with French into Year 10. Within 18 months of her appointment, and after the process drama experiment, there were 21 students continuing to this level.

What Marschke found was that the power of building belief in a fictional (but life-like) situation and working in role dramatically increased students' interest, enjoyment levels and motivation. Their willingness to project imaginatively into the roles, and to follow the rule that all in-role communication had to happen in the TL, surprised her. These were students with low levels of language proficiency, so out-of-role discussions – language-focus phases – were interspersed when needed, allowing for the negotiation of relationships and plot development and generation and practice of language structures and vocabulary as needed. But then students went back into role, and back into the target language, showing great inventiveness when they didn't know a word or a phrase which they needed, confirming Willis's argument that 'if the need to communicate is strongly felt, learners will find a way of getting around words or forms they do not yet know or cannot remember' (1996:24, in Marschke, 2005). The success of this process drama experiment was remarkable. The opportunity to genuinely negotiate meaning, to play out semi-'real' relationships, to problem-solve communicatively with very limited linguistic resources and to have shared ownership of what was happening resulted in surprisingly high levels of enjoyment, engagement and language production. This was a good example of real language experience. The fact that the boys who talked enthusiastically about it, and who talked of carrying on with French the following year, were among the most languages-resistant boys before the experience is telling.

The Seal Wife makes the argument for us. It also sits convincingly alongside the comments collected from boys in Chapter 4 about how language classes could be made more appealing. They had talked about learning 'real' language; about 'doing things' with language which had meaning, relevance, were enjoyable, 'fun'. They wanted language to come at them in authentic ways, not in discrete, unconnected lists or as forms to be learned, practised and tested. They wanted more independence in relation to what they did with this language, and more opportunities to communicate with each other rather than taking everything through the teacher. *The Seal Wife* went a long way to meeting most of these requirements. While it's clearly beyond the constraints of most language classrooms, and of most teachers' range of interest or knowledge base to design and implement process drama units of work, there are lessons to be learned here.

Where to from here?

The hoped-for outcome of all educational research work is to make things better; or – to use more scholarly discourse – to contribute to transformative practice. There is always an expectation that research leads smoothly into easily formulated 'implications for practice'. In theory this should not be difficult. In this case, we have contextualised our study, theorised the issues framing the boys–languages relationship, presented and analysed the data we collected and brought ourselves to the point where recommendations can be made. In a sense, this should be the easy part. The description and analysis of what we found lead logically into certain suggestions in relation to pedagogy, gender work and curriculum initiatives. In another sense, however, everything we have been discussing sits inside a broader frame which is hard to transform, as it does more than provide a backdrop to issues that can easily be separated out. It does the kind of 'senior management' work which determines possibilities for everything else. It's an ideological, attitudinal, cultural frame, which does the power–knowledge work – which in turn shapes material practices. It's difficult to come up with identifiable strategies or recommended practices which can impact easily on what are complicated intersecting frames. Our earlier discussion of the complexity of the theory–practice relationship in terms of pedagogy is just as relevant at this point of 'recommendations'. The closing chapter offers some suggestions about ways of thinking and talking about this issue and about the interconnected frames referred to above; and about possible ways of moving forward.

9
Changing Thinking, Transforming Action

'Moving forward' in relation to what has been the focus of this book – boys' relationship with foreign language learning – involves some foundational rethinking as well as different ways of 'doing'. As we have argued, both theoretically and through the evidence of our research data, the relationship is a complex one, which lends itself to neither fail-safe prescriptions, state of the art solutions nor best-practice guidelines. Things aren't that easy. But the nature and shape of the relationship is of concern, and there *are* recommendations to be made; and they are as much to do with changing ways of thinking and engaging in dialogue as prescribing ways of doing. We have argued throughout that the relationship between theory and practice is relational and reciprocal. Theory doesn't take the lead and practice the advice. As Pennycook suggests, we need to be thinking in terms of 'praxis' (2001:172). The issue we've been exploring sits inside several interconnected frames; each of which is juggling its own theory–practice dynamic; each of which calls for explicit attention.

Although Australia has provided the principal research site for our exploration of this issue, our links to data, commentaries and literature from other major English-dominant contexts – particularly the United Kingdom – show that the attitudes and participation levels of boys in foreign-language programmes are remarkably similar, despite differences in systems, policies and contexts. The 'frames' which are discussed below would almost certainly apply equally across these contexts.

Navigating new times in old style: the outer frame

The communities which are the contexts of the boys–languages relationship we've been examining share the massively significant experience of being speakers of the current dominant world language. How they live this fact constitutes the outer frame to the boys–languages issue. They have been used to seeing themselves as the core of the English-language world (Graddol, 1997; Kachru, 1996; Pennycook, 2001; Phillipson, 1992), and engagement with the linguistic aspects of globalisation has centred around debates about the nature, status, spread and evolution of English: as world language, as international language, as lingua franca, as plurally indexed 'Englishes'. The past decade has seen a phenomenal increase in academic scholarship and critical discussion around the changing shape, nature and politics of English in the world, and also of the possible consequences for the status and survival of other languages. There has been much less discussion, however, of the other side of the coin: of how the changing linguistic and world order impacts on monolingual English-dominant communities; of the implications of the increasing global order of bilingualism, multilingualism and plurality of cultural and communication systems; of the repositioning of monolingual players in the changing linguistic articulations of the new world order. This lack of explicit policy engagement with the learning of other languages in the global context does nothing to unsettle the 'English is enough' position which came strongly through the comments of many of the boys in our data.

Understanding of the interconnectedness of language and culture is not translating into changed practice. This is in sharp contrast to other regions of the world – whose populations are typically already multilingual – who are working seriously and systematically towards educational innovation and reform, taking account of changing world relationships and imperatives.

Nations such as Singapore, China, Malaysia and India are taking educational as well as economic steps to engage with the complexities of new global realities. Europe too is responding strategically to differently configured global relationships and economic orders, and bilingualism and multilingualism are core components of this response. Intersections between culture, language, identity and education – as well as between market economies – are being investigated and theorised (see, for example, Luke et al.'s analysis of Singapore's current educational and political response to changing global as well as local conditions, 2005). Regional debates and initiatives of the kind proceeding in Asia and Europe may not seem as relevant, urgent or contingent for the major English-speaking nations of the world, accustomed as they are to the security and privilege of being the 'keepers of the code'; and there are certainly differences in how and in what order changing global conditions impact on different contexts. But the new kinds of transcultural knowledge, skills and competencies which sit inside educational innovations in countries such as Singapore also sit inside the rhetoric, the intentions and the imagined reality of educational policy in the English-speaking world. The difference is precisely this: that they remain for the most part untransformed from rhetorical intent and narrative to practice.

In the study referred to above, Luke and colleagues (2005) talk about the complexity of moving from 'narrative educational policy goals' to 'practical classroom change' (ibid:24), of transforming the claims and propositions which drive policy narratives into real changes in relationship between teachers and students and between knowledge and curriculum (p. 14). They detail the policy initiatives and research-based analyses now progressing this move in the Singaporean context. This kind of concerted, theorised action understands that political will, intellectual and professional work and material resourcing have to work together, and that this is a complex process. In the contexts we are concerned with, policy is still for the most part at the propositional and narrative stage. It speaks enthusiastically about internationalisation, multiculturalism and global citizenship. Students are exhorted to think global; to imagine themselves as intercultural travellers; to take advantage of the flows of information, mass communication and globally distributed popular culture which characterise their out-of-school worlds. Diversity and difference are officially on the educational agenda and students are encouraged to study languages and to seek out other cultural experience. Yet, in spite of this propositional support, in the two places that have most influence – government policy and practice and school administration levels – little is being done to improve the likelihood of these kinds of outcomes.

Governments talk about intercultural and transnational competence and communication, and occasionally jump into red alert mode to appeal for increased interest in language study, as when the Bush administration sent out a 'Your country needs you!' call for recruits to language programmes. These imagined recruits were to think of themselves as frontline workers on the national security agenda. More recently, the Pentagon has provided an interactive video game to troops serving in Iraq – *Tactical Iraqui* – in an attempt to provide basic linguistic and cultural training; a first indication that maybe 'adequate equipment' for troops involved in overseas engagement might also include language proficiency (if only for the most militarily strategic reasons). A recent report on Australian Radio National's *AM* programme, commenting on the total lack of attention to linguistic skills at official government and Defence Force level, reported that 'small comments' are beginning to emerge from further down the systems. An officer with the Australian Defence Forces in Iraq, where

Australian troops are working alongside Japanese personnel, commented that the number of linguistically proficient ADF personnel can be 'counted on the fingers of one hand'. Given that Japanese is one of the most widely offered languages in Australian schools, this is a remarkable comment. Australian involvement in areas such as East Timor and Iraq is beginning to suggest – at least to a few individual commentators – that perhaps there is a need for attention to foreign language skills, at least in the constituent languages of the coalition (Radio National *AM* programme, 2/3/05). For now, however, governments and government agencies continue to be seen to conduct business in functionally monolingual mode wherever there is a choice. From the highest profile diplomatic and policy encounters to the smaller 'capillaries' of administrative and social practice, the major Anglophone government systems are characterised by their continuing confidence that everything that needs to be done can still be done in English. There is acknowledgement – and enactment – of community linguistic and cultural diversity in areas of social support (health, legal aid, housing and welfare); but there is a clear distinction between the 'distinction' (to borrow from Bourdieu, 1979) of operating multilingually in 'significant', elitist contexts and the 'necessity' and responsibility of providing translation services to the welfare and social service arm of ground-level community business. To the major English-dominant communities of the world, and to young people schooled within these communities, additional language proficiency is not seen as a particularly valuable or desirable cultural good. This message comes through loudly and clearly; and is certainly part of the story. Boys' comments in our data about the low status of languages in terms of good careers, about employers' lack of interest in language proficiency and the shape of the curriculum league show how the message filters down to school level; and how it contributes to boys' disinterest.

In terms of transforming this outer frame, it's difficult not to feel dispirited; and hard to think in terms of individual or even professionally collective agency; but as language professionals, parents, students, people who understand the need to respond to the intellectual and cultural requirements of changing global conditions, we have to do something. Maybe what we have to do in more concerted and more insistent fashion is what many of us already do in our various professional corners, which is to keep the argument out in the public arena; to insist more loudly and from an informed position about the need for change, about the nature of new global intersections and for more serious engagement with cultural literacy. There are wider conversations to be had, about identity and global change.

offers the kinds of engaging, relevant, language-rich and opportunity-broad programmes discussed earlier – making connections with young people's worlds, finding ways of accessing authentic cultural experience – then outcomes will change dramatically, and post-compulsory programmes throughout the English-dominant world will be filled with students of both sexes. This is an ideal, fictional scenario, complicated and contaminated by all the circumstances and constraints already examined. Teachers need to be convinced that change in practice is needed. They need to know how to do what they do differently. They need to be helped – resourced, supported, shown – and allowed to make changes. (More than one teacher interviewed commented that they would like to be using more authentic resources and materials, but that the school/parents had bought the set textbook, and insisted that it be used.) Materials have to be produced that fit new approaches; time has to be allocated, as well as opportunity for critical reflection. Parents, colleagues, employing authorities and students themselves have to be convinced that change is needed in order to achieve more productive learning outcomes; which will in turn promote languages as a more worthwhile and relevant investment. Most importantly, however, teachers need to have access to new knowledge about more effective ways of doing what they're doing.

Knowledge construction and dissemination

For practice to be transformed, knowledge has to be 'grown'. How this process happens is crucial. Research into professional development and curriculum reform identifies the need for bottom–up as well as top–down processes of knowledge construction. Knowledge which is theoretically based is typically the 'received', top–down kind referred to earlier in the book; delivered primarily in pre-service courses, and then on an occasional basis – like 'booster' injections – at conferences or professional development workshops. This is the theory–practice–theory knowledge loop which provides explanations as to why some things work in classrooms while others don't; why things happen in unplanned sequence; why different learners respond differently to input. Practice informed by this kind of knowledge has a good chance of being critical, reflective practice; this is necessary knowledge. But, as our data indicate, this kind of received knowledge slides all too easily sideways, and gets buried under the reality of practice, unless it is animated, sustained or retrieved via the 'bottom–up' kind of experiential knowledge of teachers' shared practice.

In Queensland, teachers involved in the trialling stage of the new languages syllabuses in 1998–9, argued long and loudly for fewer 'talking head' expert-delivered sessions, and more opportunities to show and tell each other what they were trying out, what worked, what didn't (Carr, Commins and Crawford, 1998). They wanted delivered expertise, but they also wanted opportunities to exchange strategies, resources, recipes; to 'nut it out' together. They wanted the kind of moral support as well as shared professional experience and collaborative energy which comes from this kind of exchange. They appreciated workshops delivered by designers and writers of the syllabus and experts in FL teaching methodology, but they appreciated more the time allocated to working with each other; the bottom–up, grassroots planning and design work. This point is often lost by those who control resources – curriculum planners, education authorities, school administration teams. A major recommendation to come out of this project, therefore, would be that teachers be given the space, opportunities and professional responsibility to develop their own changing practice – not only in relation to working with boys, but more generally; that the nature of 'teaching' be better understood to involve reflection, planning and design as well as delivery. All pre-service teachers are exhorted to be 'reflective practitioners', and are typically introduced to strategies such as action research to help develop this dimension of their work; but reflection requires time and space to notice as well as to reflect, to experiment as well as to implement. The ongoing theory–practice loop continues beyond initial training and needs space and support to happen.

This recommendation shifts the onus squarely where many teachers believe it to belong. Teachers' work is characterised by intensification at every level; and the change in practice which this study and others indicate is required to improve the appeal and the effectiveness of languages programmes represents significant additional demands on individual teacher resources. High-quality teaching is happening in language classrooms throughout the countries we're talking about; some of it comes to attention through projects such as this one, or through professional exchange networks such as conferences. There is, however, a significant amount of practice which needs support and new knowledge to improve; and what is lacking is a system which facilitates attention to good practice and provision of the kind of collaborative, principled, systematic and ongoing support for change of the type suggested above. Some years ago, in the UK context, Mahony (1998) made similar recommendations. Discussing the inherent contradictions between educational policy and management and what is recognised as 'best practice', she stressed the importance of utilising what she referred to as 'radical work' found in 'local spaces'. The major recommendation therefore, in terms of pedagogy, is not for teachers or students directly, but for those who have responsibility for developing, resourcing and managing language programmes and for supporting teachers' work: that they talk to teachers and students, listen to them and think about what they say and what they do, understand what is needed and deliver the required support; that they combine the 'radical work' from 'local spaces' with the ongoing development of the professional knowledge base. This is the kind of reciprocal action that's required for individual teachers to make the kinds of changes in practice that are needed. Language programmes need to be not only more attractive to prospective students, they also need to be more effective in terms of what they deliver. We collectively know a great deal more than we did about what constitutes effective foreign language teaching and learning – and our data show that students also have a good idea of what this might look like. As conditions change, knowledge changes; but at this point we know enough to do better than we're 'ordinarily' doing. While many conversations focus on 'teaching better for boys', this should be a purely strategic, short-term response to the most visible 'problem'. The reality is that we should be teaching better for *all* learners. Rather than thinking about pedagogical affirmative action for half the student population, we should be thinking about improved practice across the board.

The inner boys–languages frame: boy-friendly pedagogy?

Which brings us back to the final frame of this project, the boys–languages relationship itself. We came into this study wanting to find out more about what we recognised as a poor relationship; hoping to help improve it. We found several interrelated issues: what kinds of 'boys' come to the language classroom; what kinds of learning experiences are offered to them; what kinds of cultural environment frame their experience. We have talked about the implications of what we found: the constraints which frame normative performances of gender; the tensions which result when theory and practice aren't 'speaking to each other'; the need for transformative practice, professional – and dialogic – development support, for different kinds of programmes and materials, more supportive environments and changed cultural attitudes. But we have sidestepped an issue which sits at the heart of our data and which brings some theoretical tension back into the discussion: the 'boy-friendly' pedagogy debate.

What has emerged throughout our study is the solidity of the biological account of how boys/girls learn, what they're good at, what suits them, what is appropriate for them; and how to teach them. This account is far more popular than the more critically shaped, socially informed accounts of gender constitution reviewed in Chapter 3. The combined power of traditional power–truth *régimes,* popular *Men Are From Mars/Women Don't Read Maps* narratives, and scientifically and academically framed accounts of brain differentiation is daunting. Occasional oppositional voices are heard throughout our data, questioning the innate predisposition account; but overall nature wins hands-down over nurture. Both teachers and students detail in remarkably similar terms the 'shape' of boys in school – and in language classrooms.

This leads logically to thinking and talking about 'boy-friendly' pedagogy, about teaching strategies likely to engage boys' interest, to support their learning styles and innate predispositions. Teachers thinking about boys talk repeatedly about active and autonomous learning, about capitalising on boys' competitive nature, of accommodating their need for physical activity and their interest in technology; of offering variety in tasks, cognitive challenge, scaffolding for oral activities – and for anything else too closely associated with 'feminine' ways of learning or being (this last strategy suggests the seeds of a 'social' consideration). This way of thinking about boys as essentially different kinds of people, and innately different kinds of learners, leads easily to thinking about differentiated models of teaching. It keys comfortably into the wider boys-schooling debate discussed in Chapter 3, and the argument that schooling has to be more supportive of boys; that teaching and content be reconsidered in light of what we know about boys. The main response to the boys–languages misalignment is therefore to make language teaching and learning more attractive by crafting it into more 'boy-like' shape; adapting it to what are understood to be essentially differentiated cognitive systems. There is little evidence of moves in the opposite direction: to make boys more 'languages friendly', to craft them into shapes more compatible with the languages experience; little critical attention to the shape itself.

Maybe this doesn't matter. Strategically, in the short term, maybe it's even a good thing. Many of the identified features of 'masculine' learning styles are core components of 'good' learning styles. If we revisit the check-list of effective pedagogy – either the informally gathered version assembled by boys in our study or the formally defined version in L2 methodology courses – many of the items can be moved unproblematically from the 'masculine learning style' list to the 'effective teaching' list: active learning, cognitive challenges, authentic connections with real-life interests and experiences, learner autonomy, 'real' and holistic use of language, problem-solving. If these are characteristics of optimum learning conditions and experiences for boys, then shaping general practice around them can't be bad. Some of the items on the 'masculine' list, however, are more problematic: 'natural' competitiveness, for example, sits uncomfortably with collaborative and interactive learning; 'economical communicative style' doesn't promise the elaborated and experimental kind of self-expression and risk-taking which is part and parcel of developing language proficiency. There are some misalignments between the shapes of 'essential boy' and 'best practice' which make the fit less perfect; which support the argument we have developed throughout this project, that the reluctance to look both ways – and to think about transforming the shape of 'boy' as well as the shape of pedagogy – does actually matter.

The shadow of the binary

Problems associated with essentialist thinking about boys and learning have been discussed throughout this study; and the data we've presented provide examples of the damage done by global gender classification. Few of the teachers we talked with would officially – or consciously – subscribe to the biological, binary explanatory grid; yet so many of the comments collected suggest that thinking about boys/girls comes via a conceptual frame which has a line down the middle. Teachers talk about individual boys/girls who are different, implicitly confirming the normative binary model, and their repeated references to 'how boys are' indicate a significant disjunction between what they explicitly profess and what they discursively practise. We talked earlier about tension between theorised and practised belief systems in relation to methodology; the same tension is evident between the theorising and the practice of gender narratives. The binary model is alive and well, even though it does such a poor job of looking out for all constituents or planning for best practice. It not only 'counts boys out' of whole areas of experience, as schooling has always done in relation to girls and certain curriculum areas (Walkerdine, 1989); it also does serious damage to girls.

The compliant girl

Although boys have been the main focus of this study as we tracked the power of discursive and institutional *régimes* in the shaping of the boys–languages relationship, one of the most concerning issues to emerge from the data actually relates to girls; to the (oppositional) version of 'girl' which sits alongside that of 'boy'. This is a compliant and passive girl; the 'good student', willing to do boring worksheets because she wants to please; who works hard even when the work is neither easy nor enjoyable – because she wants to gain the approval of teachers, parents or herself; the girl who will be bored quietly. This girl is visible throughout our data. The memorable comment from a teacher that 'you can't expect boys to do boring work' suggests by implication that you can apparently count on girls to do just that. This is concerning, and needs to be factored into the many comments about making language classrooms more challenging and interesting for boys. These oppositional accounts not only reinforce mindsets – and restrictions – in terms of what boys/ girls can or can't do, they also shore up traditional gender politics and classroom power relations. Early gender studies into classroom interaction patterns (e.g., Spender, 1982; Walkerdine, 1989) documented how teachers typically accord significantly more time and attention to negative behaviour from boys than to positive (quiet) behaviour from girls. Talk about 'value added' pedagogy for boys suggests the power politics of gender are still close to the surface. Discussions around gender, performativity and classification schemes need also to include consideration of issues of equity, access and entitlement; and these are 'bi-directional' considerations: culturally-shaped 'boys' are typically 'counted out' (Walkerdine, 1989) of language-related experience; girls, it seems, may be 'under-sold' in terms of quality of experience.

Our data came from a limited number of contexts, and the 'compliant girl' might sit less well elsewhere. At first sight, it doesn't ring true for me, for example, when I think of my first-year undergraduate classes of students recently in school. Tutorials are often dominated by strong, articulate and assertive young women, who pull discussion into unsafe places and critical spaces. Typically, these strong female voices are matched by the (usually fewer in number) male voices in the group (usually drama students); but they are listened to by other women in the group who *do* more typically perform the 'quiet, compliant' model of girl. This digression to my own context reconnects with notions of discourse, truth *régimes* and gender as performativity which always intersect with variables other than gender. Like all groups, my first-year classes are never homogeneous. They have in common the fact that they are preparing to be high-school English teachers, but they all have different second teaching areas (all high school teachers in Queensland have to prepare to teach in two areas). There's usually a core group of drama students, others studying visual arts, music or dance; and a larger group studying languages, social sciences, legal studies, human movement, economics, science or maths. There are a few international students and a few mature-age students in each group. This brief description immediately activates schema: expectations about how these different students 'are', informed by what we 'know' about curriculum territories and people who inhabit them, about gender, generation and ethnicity; assumptions about 'out there' drama students and 'in there' accounting students; creative visual arts students and logical maths students. The performed identities never align totally with any of these classifications, although they draw from them to varying degrees. Butler's notion of performativity hijacks confidence in such explanatory schemes, but helps to notice them lurking in the background – sometimes in reasonably close proximity – and the effect they have on classroom interactions. Observing any group of students through a 'discourse/performativity' lens blows notions of generic characteristics right out of the water.

A recommendation in respect to 'boy-friendly pedagogy', therefore, must be that critical attention be focused on the essentialist principles which drive it; and on its apolitical and asocial character. Rather than thinking about 'boy-friendly' or 'girl-friendly' pedagogy, we need to be aiming for all-purpose effective practice; practice that is inherently interesting, challenging, relevant and productive, which will engage boys, but also value-add for girls, providing them with more productive learning experiences. (Repaying them for loyal service?) Boy-friendly teaching isn't good enough. This is not to dismiss teachers' observations about how differently boys/girls typically communicate, work and relate to each other. The accuracy of all these observations is self-evident – in our data as elsewhere. The coherence of so many differently sourced accounts shows the patterns to exist. This is how things are; but this is not how things necessarily have to be. There is sufficient evidence to counterbalance these truths, collected in the 'cracks and fissures' of different performances of both boys and girls; to unsettle the 'gender absolutism' (Jackson and Salisbury, 1996:82) referred to earlier in this book.

Gender and discourse

Which brings us back full-circle to where we began: with the interconnected concepts of gender, discourse and performativity. Again, any recommendation in relation to these key dimensions of the boys–languages issue will sound either deceptively simple or discouragingly difficult. Their relationship needs to be interrogated, explored, debated and 'discovered'. Identifying how things work – as Foucault advises – is the first step to changing how they work. The project then is one of critical analysis, involving the kinds of critical literacy and critical language awareness which now sit inside language and literacy programmes from early childhood to tertiary level. It's the project of looking explicitly at how discourse does its work in the ways theorised earlier in this book and at how gender is performed within the 'rigid regulatory frame' (Butler, 1990a:33) which serves no one well.

Changing practice in relation to gender requires knowledge about what gender is, and about the complicity of discourse in keeping it on track. Teachers won't change how they think about gender – about boys'/girls' language learning – if they don't see where their beliefs come from, how they are constituted and protected. They won't work towards different possibilities in their pedagogy, or support students in exploring alternative performances, if they don't see them as available. Students, for their part, won't step easily into different roles or perform alternative versions of themselves – as boys, as learners or as language learners – unless they understand the issue of agency. Lovell makes the comment that 'the performative self walks a knife-edged ridge' (2003:1), and that individual performance is always enacted alongside 'a large cast of others'. Getting the balance right, positioning the self appropriately in these ensemble performances, is the major challenge of 'self in culture'. A prerequisite for changing gender frames is, then, an understanding of gender as cultural construct, and of the role of cultural power–knowledge processes in shaping individual and collective identities. This means engaging explicitly in Butler's project of making 'gender trouble', of even engaging in what she names 'excitable speech' (1997): interrupting 'reiterative performance', the continuing reproduction of expected social norms; the way things are. This study has reconfirmed the solidity of how things are in terms of thinking about the boys–languages relationship. If this relationship is to be renegotiated, a first necessary step is to promote a more dynamic and relational view of gender.

This move doesn't have to involve advanced theoretical reading or analysis – close encounters with Foucault, Bakhtin or Butler. Critical literacy work in first-language literacy programmes in Australian schools has demonstrated how this kind of 'language–culture' knowledge can be developed from the earliest stages of literacy development (e.g. O'Brien, 2001). Exploring language as social and cultural practice is easy once a basic theoretical tool-kit has been assembled, because everyone has data to contribute, relevant experience to 'recognise' (Carr, 2003).

The 'truths' which frame the boys–languages relationship become much less truthful when gender is recognised as performativity and knowledge as culturally constituted; when discourse is recognised 'at work'. This recognition emerges directly from what has been the major theoretical project of the last several decades: the redefinition of the human subject, and acknowledgement of the central role of discourse in its constitution. It has served this project well. Understanding that if things are constructed, they can also be deconstructed is a crucial first stage of transformative action.

Final thoughts

In a recent contribution to a collection of papers on the work of the late French sociologist Pierre Bourdieu, Kramsch (2005) advocates a critical, reflexive, sociological approach to research work which, drawing from Bourdieu, 'combines the awareness of the theory with the empathy of the practice'. We have tried to manage this balance in this project. It's a model which can also apply to the next stage of dialogue and 'action'. Foucault's analysis of the power–truth relationship included his advice that wider societal patterns are constituted by 'smaller interactions' (1988); small, local processes and practices which merge both into and out of mainstream truths. If we engage in the 'noticing' work sketched out above in relation to smaller, local interactions – noting how they collectively do broader collective cultural business – then we can begin to change some shapes and directions.

Comments collected from both students and teachers during this project show many instances of 'smaller interactions'; but they also show moments of 'talking against the grain' of dominant discourses and normative accounts; of engaging in 'gender trouble'. We need more of this kind of trouble: radical and transforming, but also thoughtful and empathetic. Such a balance will help to recraft a gender–language order more suitable for changing world conditions.

Bibliography

Acker, S. (1994) *Gendered Education*. Buckingham: Open University Press.

Albright, J., and Luke, A. (2005) *Bourdieu and Literacy*. Malwah, NJ: Lawrence Erlbaum.

Ali, S., Benjamin, S., and Mauthner, M. L. (eds) (2004) *The Politics of Gender and Education*. Basingstoke: Palgrave Macmillan.

Alloway, N. (2002) *Boys, Literacy and Schooling: Expanding the Repertoires of Practice*. Carlton, Victoria: Curriculum Corporation.

Alloway, N., and Gilbert, P. (1997) *Boys and Literacy*. Carlton, Victoria: Curriculum Corporation.

Archer, J. (1992) 'Gender stereotyping of school subjects', *The Psychologist: Bulletin of the British Psychological Society*, 5: 66–9.

Archer, J., and Macrae, M. (1991) 'Gender perceptions of school subjects among 10–11 year olds', *British Journal of Educational Psychology*, 61: 99–103.

Arnot, M., David, M., and Weiner, G. (1996) *Educational Reform and Gender Equality in School*. Manchester: Equal Opportunities Commission.

Arnot, M., David, M., and Weiner, G. (1999) *Closing the Gender Gap: Postwar Education and Social Change*. Cambridge: Polity Press.

Arnot, M., Gray, J., James, M., and Ruddock, J. (1998) *Recent Research on Gender and Educational Performance*. London: Office for Standards in Education.

Bakhtin, M. M. (1981) *The Dialogic Imagination: Four Essays*. Trans. C. Emerson and M. Holquist. Austin: University of Texas Press.

Bakhtin, M. M. (1986) *Speech Genres and Other Late Essays*. Trans. V. McGee. Austin: University of Texas Press.

Baldauf, R. B., Jr, and Rainbow, P. (1995) *Gender Bias and Differentiated Motivation in LOTE Learning and Retention Rates: A Case Study of Problems and Materials Development*. Unpublished Report, Australian Second Language Learning Project (ASLLP), for Grant, Year 1991. Canberra, ACT: Department of Education and Training.

Berg, L. D., and Longhurst, R. (2003) 'Placing masculinities and geography'. *Gender, Place and Culture: A Journal of Feminist Geography*, 10, 4: 351–60.

Bettoni, C. (1981) *Italians in North Queensland*. Townsville: James Cook University.

Biddulph, S. (1997) *Raising Boys*. Sydney: Finch.

Biddulph, S. (1999) *Manhood: An Action Plan for Changing Men's Lives*. Stroud: Hawthorn Press.

Bleach, K. (1999) 'Why the Likely Lads lag behind', in K. Bleach (ed.), *Raising Boys' Achievement in Schools*. Stoke-on-Trent: Trentham.

Bly, R. (1992) *Iron John: A Book About Men*. New York: Vintage Books.

Bonvillain, N. (1995) *Women and Men: Cultural Constructs of Gender*. Englewood Cliffs, NJ: Prentice Hall.

Bourdieu, P. (1977) 'The economics of linguistic exchanges', *Social Science Information*, 16: 645–68.

Bourdieu, P. (1979) *Distinction: A Social Critique of the Judgement of Taste*. Trans. R. Nice. London: Routledge & Kegan Paul.

Bourdieu, P. (1991) *Language and Symbolic Power*. Cambridge, MA: Harvard University Press.

Bourdieu, P., Passeron, J.-C., and Saint Martin, M. (1994) *Academic Discourse, Linguistic Misunderstanding and Professional Power*. Stanford, CA: Stanford University Press.

Browne, R., and Fletcher, R. (eds) (1995) *Boys in Schools: Addressing the Real Issues – Behaviour, Values and Relationships*. Sydney: Finch.

Burke, P. J. (2002) *Accessing Education: Effectively Widening Participation*. Stoke-on-Trent: Trentam Books.

Butler, J. (1990a) *Gender Trouble: Feminism and the Subversion of Identity*. London: Routledge.

Butler, J. (1990b) 'Performative acts and gender constitution', in S. Case (ed.), *Performing Feminisms: Feminist Critical Theory and Theatre*. Baltimore, MD: John Hopkins University Press.

Butler, J. (1993) *Bodies that Matter: On the Discursive Limits of 'Sex'*. London: Routledge.

Butler, J. (1997) *Excitable Speech: A Politics of the Performative*. London: Routledge.

Butler, J. (1999) 'Performativity's social magic', in R. Shusterman (ed.), *Bourdieu: A Critical Reader*. Oxford: Blackwell Publishers.

Cameron, D. (1992) 'Not gender difference but the difference gender makes – explanation in research on sex and language', *International Journal of the Sociology of Language*, **94**: 13–26.

Cameron, D. (1995) 'Rethinking language and gender studies: some issues for the 1990s', in S. Mills (ed.), *Language and Gender: Interdisciplinary Perspectives*. London: Longman.

Cameron, D. (1998) 'Performing gender identity: Young men's talk and the construction of heterosexual masculinity', in S. Johnson and U. H. Meinhof (eds), *Language and Masculinity*. Oxford: Blackwell.

Canagarajah, S. (1993) 'Critical ethnography of a Sri Lankan classroom: Ambiguities in student opposition to reproduction in ESOL', *TESOL Quarterly*, **27**: 601–26.

Canagarajah, S. (1999) *Resisting Linguistic Imperialism in English Teaching*. Oxford: Oxford University Press.

Canagarajah, S. (2004) 'Subversive identities, pedagogical safe houses, and critical learning'. in B. Norton and K. Toohay (eds), *Critical Pedagogies and Language Learning*, Cambridge: Cambridge University Press.

Carr, J. (1999) 'From "sympathetic" to "dialogic" imagination: Cultural study in the foreign language classroom', in J. Lo Bianco, A. J. Liddicoat and C. Crozet (eds), *Striving for the Third Place: Intercultural Competence through Language Education*. Melbourne: Language Australia.

Carr, J. (2000) 'Action research and the language classroom', in S. McGinty (ed.), *The Politics and Machinations of Educational Research: International Case Studies*. New York: Peter Lang Publishers.

Carr, J. (2002) 'Why boys into LOTE will not go: The problematic of the gender agenda in LOTE education', *Babel, Journal of the Australian Federation of Modern Language Teachers' Association*, **37**, 2: 4–9.

Carr, J. (2003) 'Culture through the looking glass: An intercultural experiment in sociolinguistics', in A. J. Liddicoat, S. Eisenchlas and S. Trevaskes (eds), *Australian Perspectives on Internationalizing Education*. Melbourne: Language Australia.

Carr, J. (2005) *Listening to the Boys: Gender, Identity and Languages Education*. Paper presented at the International Society of Language Studies, Montreal.

Carr, J., and Crawford, J. (2005) *The Shifting Self: Negotiating the Constraints and Possibilities of Identity and Culture in the Language Classroom*. Conference Proceedings, New Humanities Conference, Prato, Italy, 2005.

Carr, J., and Frankom, C. (1997) 'Where do the boys go? The problematic LOTE gender agenda', *Australian Language Matters*.

Carr, J., Commins, L., and Crawford, J. (1998) *External Evaluation of the LOTE Curriculum Project (Years 4–10)*, Report 2. Queensland University of Technology, for the Queensland Government, QSCC.

Carroll, B. (1995) *Gender and Other Factors Influencing the Choice of Examination Subjects*, paper presented at the European Conference on Educational Research, Bath, September 1995.

Carvel, J. (1998) 'Help for boys lagging behind girls at school', *Guardian*, 7 January: 8.

Chavez, M. (2000) *Gender in the Language Classroom*. Boston, MA: McGraw Hill.

Chodorow, N. J. (1995) 'Gender as a personal and social construction', *Signs*, 20, 3: 516–44.

Clare, A. (2000) *On Men: Masculinity in Crisis*. London: Chatto & Windus.

Clark, A. (1998a) *Gender on the Agenda: Factors Motivating Boys and Girls in MFLs*. London: Centre for Information on Language Teaching and Research.

Clark, A. (1998b) 'Resistant boys and modern languages', in A. Clark and E. Millard (eds), *Gender in the Secondary Curriculum: Balancing the Books*. London: Routledge.

Clark, A., and Trafford, A. J. (1994) 'Boys into modern languages', *Gender and Education*, 7, 3.

Clyne, M. (1982) *Multilingual Australia*. Melbourne: River Seine Publications.

Clyne, M., Fernandez, S., and Grey, F. (2004) 'Languages taken at school and languages spoken in the community – a comparative perspective', *Australian Review of Applied Linguistics*, 27, 2: 1–17.

Coates, J. (1993) *Women, Men and Language: A Sociolinguistic Account of Gender Differences in Language*. 2nd edn, London: Longman.

Coates, J. (1996) *Women Talk*. Oxford: Blackwell.

Coates, J. (2003) *Men Talk: Stories in the Making of Masculinities*. Oxford: Blackwell.

Cohen, M. (1998) 'A habit of healthy idleness: Boys' underachievement in historical perspective', in D. Epstein, J. Elwood, V. Hey and J. Maw (eds), *Failing Boys? Issues in Gender and Achievement*. Buckingham: Open University Press.

Collins, C. W., Kenway, J., and McLeod, J. (2000) *Factors Influencing the Educational Performance of Males and Females in School and Their Initial Destinations after Leaving School*. Canberra: Department of Education, Training and Youth Affairs.

Connell, R. (1987) *Gender and Power: Society, the Person and Sexual Politics*. Stanford, CA: Stanford University Press.

Connell, R. (1989) 'Cool guys, swots and wimps: The interplay of masculinity and education'. *Oxford Review of Education*, 15: 291–303.

Connell, R. (1995) *Masculinities*. Berkeley: University of California Press.

Connell, R. (1996) 'Teaching the boys: New research on masculinity, and gender strategies for schools', *Teachers College Record*, 98: 206–35.

Cope, B., and Kalantzis, M. (2000) (eds) *Multiliteracies: Literacy, Learning and the Design of Social Futures*. South Yarra: Macmillan.

Danaher, G., Schirato, T., and Webb, J. (2000) *Understanding Foucault*. St Leonards, NSW: Allen & Unwin.

David, M. E. (2004) 'A feminist critique of public policy Discourse about educational effectiveness', in S. Ali, S. Benjamin and M. L. Mauthner (eds), *The Politics of Gender and Education: Critical Perspectives*. Basingstoke: Palgrave Macmillan.

Davison, K. G. (2000) 'Masculinities, sexualities and the student body: 'Sorting' gender identities in school', in C. James (ed.), *Experiencing Difference*, Halifax: Fernwood Press.

Davison, K. G., Lovell, T. A., Frank, B. W., and Vibert, A. B. (2004) 'Boys and underachievement in the Canadian context: No proof for panic', in S. Ali, S. Benjamin and M. L. Mauthner (eds), *The Politics of Gender and Education*. Basingstoke: Palgrave Macmillan.

Davy, V. (1995) 'Reaching for consensus on gender equity: The NSW experience'. *Proceedings of the Promoting Gender Equity Conference*, 22–24 February. Canberra: ACT Department of Education.

Day, E. M. (2002) *Identity and the Young English Language Learner*. Clevedon: Multilingual Matters.

Delamont, S. (1994) 'Accentuating the positive: Refocusing the research on girls and science', *Studies in Science Education*, 23: 59–74.

Dobie, M., and McDaid, P. (2001) *Gender Issues in Raising the Attainment of Boys and Girls*. Glasgow: Glasgow City Council.

Douglass, W. A. (1995) *From Italy to Ingham: Italian in North Queensland*. Queensland: St Lucia: Queensland University Press.

Eckert, P., and McConnelle-Ginet, S. (1998) 'Communities of practice: Where language, gender, and power all live', in J. Coates (ed.), *Language and Gender: A Reader*. Malden, MA, and Oxford: Blackwell.

Eckert, P., and McConnell-Ginet, S. (1999) 'New generalizations and explanations in language and gender research', *Language in Society*, 28: 185–201.

Eckert, P., and McConnell-Ginet, S. (2003) *Language and Gender*. Cambridge and New York: Cambridge University Press.

Education Queensland (2001) *New Basics Project*. Brisbane: Education Queensland.

Education Queensland (2002) *Education Queensland Submission to the Federal Inquiry into Boys' Education*. Brisbane: EQ Boys' Education Reference Group.

Ehrlich, S. (1999) 'Gender as social practice: Implications for second language acquisition'. *Studies in Second Language Acquisition*, 19: 421–46.

Epstein, D., Elwood, J., Hey, V., and Maw, J. (1998) *Failing Boys: Issues in Gender and Achievement*. Buckingham: Open University Press.

Epstein, D., Maw, J., Elwood, J., and Hey, V. (eds) (1998) *International Journal of Inclusive Education: Special Issue on Boys' 'Underachievement'*, 2, 2.

Eyre, L., Lovell, A., and Smith, C. A. (2004) 'Gender equity policy and education: Reporting on/from Canada', in S. Ali, S. Benjamin and M. L. Mauthner (eds), *The Politics of Gender and Education*. Basingstoke: Palgrave Macmillan.

Fairclough, N. (1989) *Language and Power*. Harlow: Longman Group.

Fairclough, N. (2003) *Analysing Discourse: Textual Analysis for Social Research*. New York: Routledge.

Faludi, S. (2000) *Stiffed: The Betrayal of Modern Man*. London: Random House.

Feldman, H., and Gardner, H. (2003) 'The creation of multiple intelligences theory: A study in high-level thinking', in K. Sawyer (ed.), *Creativity and Development*. Oxford and New York: Oxford University Press.

Fernandez, S., Pauwels, A., and Clyne, M. (1993) *Unlocking Australia's Language Potential: German*. Canberra: National Languages and Literacy Institute.

Foucault, M. (1972) 'The discourse on language', in *The Archaeology of Knowledge*. Trans. A. M. Sheridan Smith. New York: Pantheon. (Original work published in 1969).

Foucault, M. (1977) *Discipline and Punish: The Birth of the Prison*. Trans. A. M. Sheridan Smith. Harmondsworth: Penguin.

Foucault, M. (1979) *The History of Sexuality 1: An Introduction*. London: Allen Lane.

Foucault, M. (1980) *Power/Knowledge: Selected Interviews and Other Writings 1972–1977*. Hemel Hempstead: Harvester Press.

Foucault, M. (1982) 'The subject and power', *Critical Inquiry*, **8**, 4: 777–89.

Foucault, M. (1988) *Technologies of the Self: A Seminar with Michel Foucault*. Ed. L. H. Martin, H. Gutman and P. H. Hutton. Amherst: University of Massachusetts Press.

Frank, B. (1993) 'Straight/strait jackets for masculinity: Educating for "Real Men"', *Atlantis*, **18**, 1 and 2, Fall/Spring: 47–59.

Frank, B., and Davison, K. (eds) (2001) *Masculinities and Schooling: International Practices and Perspectives*. Halifax: Fernwood Press.

Frosh, S., Phoenix, A., and Pattman, R. (2002) *Young Masculinities: Understanding Boys in Contemporary Society*. Basingstoke: Palgrave – now Palgrave Macmillan.

Fullan, M. (ed.) (1997) *The Challenge of School Change: A Collection of Articles*. Cheltenham, Vic.: Hawker-Brownlow.

Fullan, M., and Hargreaves, A. (1992) *Teacher Development and Educational Change*. London: Falmer Press.

Gee, J. (1991) What is literacy? *Rewriting Literacy: Culture and the Discourse of the Other*. Westport, CT, and London: Bergin and Garvey.

Gilbert, R., and Gilbert, P. (1998) *Masculinity Goes to School*. St Leonards, NSW: Allen & Unwin.

Gorard, S., Rees, G., and Salisbury, J. (1999) 'Reappraising the apparent under-achievement of boys at school', *Gender and Education*, **11**, 4: 4411–54.

Gordon, T., and Lahelma, E. (1995) 'Being, having and doing gender in schools', in *Gender, Modernity, Postmodernity – New Perspectives on Development/Construction of Gender*. Universitetet I Oslo: Senter for Kvinneforskning. Arbeitsnotat, 2/95.

Gordon, T., Holland, J., and Lahelma, E. (2000) *Making Spaces: Citizenship and Difference in Schools*. Basingstoke: Palgrave Macmillan.

Graddol, D. (1997) *The Future of English? A Guide to Forecasting the Popularity of the English Language in the 21st Century*. London: The British Council.

Gray, J. (1992) *Men are from Mars, Women are from Venus*. New York: Harper Collins.

Grieshaber, S. (2004) *Rethinking Parent and Child Conflict*. New York and London: Routledge Falmer.

Griffin, C. (2000) 'Discourses of crisis and loss: Analysing the "boys" under-achievement debate', *Journal of Youth Studies*, **3**: 167–88.

Grosz, E. (1995) *Space, Time and Perversion*. New York: Routledge.

Halpern, D. F. (1992) *Sex Differences in Cognitive Abilities*. New Jersey: Hillsdale Publishers.

Hanson, K., Flansburg, S., and Castano, M. (2004) 'Genderspace: Learning online and the implications of gender', in S. Ali, S. Benjamin and M. L. Mauthner (eds), *The Politics of Gender and Education*. Basingstoke: Palgrave Macmillan.

Harris, S., Nixon, J., and Rudduck, J. (1993) 'Schoolwork, homework and gender', *Gender and Education*, **5**, 1.

Harris, V. (1998) 'Making boys make progress'. *Language Learning Journal*, **18**: 56–62.

Hedgecock, J. (2002) 'Towards a socioliterate approach to L2 teacher education', *Modern Language Journal*, **86**, 3.

Her Majesty's Stationery Office/Equal Opportunities Commission (HMSO/EOC) (1996) *The Gender Divide: Performance Differences between Boys and Girls at School*. London: HMSO.

Hodgkin, R. (1998) 'Partnership with pupils', *Children*. UK, Summer.

Holliday, A. (1994) *Appropriate Methodology and Social Context*. Cambridge: Cambridge University Press.

Hollway, W., and Jefferson, T. (2000) *Doing Qualitative Research Differently*. London: Sage.

Holquist, M. (2002) *Dialogism: Bakhtin and his World*. London and New York: Routledge.

Howe, C. (1997) *Gender and Classroom Interaction: A Research Review*. Edinburgh: Scottish Council for Research in Education (SCRE).

Jackson, D. (1998) 'Breaking out of the binary trap: Boys' underachievement, schooling and gender relations', in D. Epstein, J. Elwood, V. Hey and J. Maw (eds), *Failing Boys? Issues in Gender and Achievement*. Buckingham: Open University Press.

Jackson, D., and Salisbury, J. (1996) 'Why should secondary schools take working with boys seriously?', *Gender and Education*, **8**: 103–15.

Jackson, P., Stevenson, N., and Brooks, K. (2001) *Making Sense of Men's Magazines*. Cambridge: Polity Press.

Johnson, S. (1998) 'Theorizing language and masculinity: A feminist perspective', in S. Johnson and U. H. Meinhof (eds), *Language and Masculinity*. Oxford: Blackwell.

Johnson, S., and Meinhof, U. H. (1997) *Language and Masculinity*. Oxford: Blackwell.

Jones, B., and Jones, G. (2001) *Boys' Performance in Modern Foreign Languages: Listening to Learners*. Centre for Information on Language Teaching and Research, London.

Kachru, B. (1996) 'The paradigms of marginality', *World Englishes*, **15**, 1: 241–55.

Kebede, S. (1998) *The Relationship between Uptake and Questioning*. Centre for Research in Language Education (CRILE), Working Paper, 32, Lancaster: Department of Linguistics and Modern English Language, Lancaster University.

Kenway, J. (1995) 'Masculinities in schools: Under siege, on the defensive and under reconstruction', *Discourse: Studies in the Cultural Politics of Education*, **16**, 1: 59–79.

Kenway, J., and Willis, S. (1998) *Answering Back: Girls, Boys and Feminism in Schools*. London and New York: Routledge.

Kimura, D. (1992) 'Sex differences in the brain', *Scientific American*, September: 81–7.

Kramsch, C. (2002) 'Beyond the second vs foreign language dichotomy: The subjective dimensions of language learning', in K. Spelma and P. Thompson (eds), *Unity and Diversity in Language Use: Selected Papers from the Annual Meeting of the British Association of Applied Linguistics, University of Reading, September 2001*. London and New York: BAAL/Continuum.

Kramsch, C. (2004) 'Language, thought and culture', in A. Davies and C. Elder (eds), *The Handbook of Applied Linguistics*. Malden, MA, and Oxford: Blackwell.

Kramsch, C. (2005) 'Pierre Bourdieu: A biographical memoir', in Albright, J. and Luke, A. (eds), *Bourdieu and Literacy*. Malwah, NJ: Lawrence Erlbaum.

Kruse, A. M. (1996) 'Single-sex settings, pedagogies for girls and boys in Danish schools', in P. Murphy and C. Gipps (eds), *Equity in the Classroom: Towards Effective Pedagogy for Girls and Boys*. London: Falmer Press.

Kryger, N. (1998) 'Teachers' understanding and emotions in relation to the creation of boys' masculine identity', in Y. Katz and I. Menenzes (eds), *Affective Education: A Comparative View*. London: Cassell.

Kumaravadivelu, B. (2003) *Beyond Methods: Macrostrategies for Language Teaching*. New Haven, CT, and London: Yale University Press.

Lam, E. W. S. (2000) 'L2 literacy and the design of the self: A case study of a teenager writing on the internet', *TESOL Quarterly*, 34, 3: 457–82.

Lave, J., and Wenger, E. (1991) *Situated Learning: Legitimate Peripheral Participation*. New York: Cambridge University Press.

Lee, J., Buckland, D., and Shaw, G. (1998) *The Invisible Child*. London: Centre for Information on Language Teaching.

Lemke, J. (1995) *Textual Politics: Discourse and Social Dynamics*. London: Taylor & Francis.

Lightbody, P., Siann, G., Stocks, R., and Walsh, D. (1996) 'Motivation and attribution at secondary school: The role of gender', *Educational Studies*, 22, 1: 13–25.

Lin, A. (2004) 'Introducing a critical pedagogical curriculum: A feminist reflexive account', in B. Norton and K. Toohey (eds), *Critical Pedagogies and Language Learning*. New York: Cambridge University Press.

Lingard, B., and Douglas, P. (1999) *Men Engaging Feminisms: Pro-Feminism, Backlashes and Schooling*. Buckingham: Open University Press.

Lo Bianco, J. (1987) *National Policy on Languages*. Canberra: Commonwealth Department of Education.

Lo Bianco, J. (1995) 'Hard option, soft option, co-option', *Education Australia*, 31, 8–13.

Lo Bianco, J. (2001) 'One literacy or double power', *Babel*, 35, 3.

Lovell, T. (2003) Resisting with authority: Historical specificity, agency and the performative self. *Theory, Culture and Society*, 20, 1.

Low, L. (1999) 'Foreign languages in the upper secondary school: A study of the causes of decline', *Research in Education*, 64, Spring.

Luke, A. (2004) 'Two takes on the critical', in B. Norton and K. Toohey (eds), *Critical Pedagogies and Language Learning*. Cambridge: Cambridge University Press.

Luke, A., Freebody, P., Lau Shun., and Gopinathan, S. (2005) 'Towards research-based innovation and reform: Singapore schooling in transition', *Asia Pacific Journal of Education*, 25, 2: 7–29.

Mac an Ghaill, M. (1994) *The Making of Men: Masculinities, Sexualities and Schooling*. Buckingham: Open University Press.

Mac an Ghaill, M. (ed.) (1996) *Understanding Masculinities: Social Relations and Cultural Arenas*. Buckingham: Open University Press.

MacNaughton, G. (2000) *Rethinking Gender in Early Childhood Education*. St Leonards, NSW: Allen & Unwin.

Mahony, P. (1998) 'Girls will be girls and boys will be first', in D. Epstein, J. Elwood, V. Hey, and J. Maw (eds), *Failing Boys? Issues in Gender and Achievement*. Buckingham: Open University Press.

Mahony, P., and Frith, R. (1995) *Factors Influencing Girls' and Boys' Option Choices in Year 9*. Report to Essex Careers and Business Partnership. London: Roehampton Institute.

Marschke, R. (2005) *Creating Contexts, Characters and Communication: Process Drama and Foreign Language Teaching.* Unpublished MEd (Research) Thesis, Brisbane: Queensland University of Technology.

Martino, W. (1995) 'Deconstructing masculinity in the English classroom: A site for reconstituting gendered subjectivity', *Gender and Education,* 7, 2: 205–20.

Martino, W. (2000) 'Policing masculinities: Investigating the role of homophobia and heteronormativity in the lives of adolescent school boys', *The Journal of Men's Studies,* 8, 2: 213–36.

McDowall, L. (2002) 'Transitions to work: Masculine identities, youth inequality and labour market change', *Gender, Place and Culture,* 9, 1: 39–59.

McGroarty, M. (1998) 'Constructive and constructivist challenges for applied linguistics', *Language Learning,* 48: 591–622

McPake, J. (2003) 'Languages education in the UK', in J. Bourne and E. Reid (eds), *World Yearbook of Language Education 2003.* London: Kogan Page.

McPake, J., Johnstone, R., Low, L., and Lyall, L. (1999) *Foreign Languages in the Upper Secondary School: A Study of the Causes of Decline.* Edinburgh: Scottish Council for Research in Education.

Mercer, P. (1995) *White Australia Defied: Pacific Islander Settlement in North Queensland.* Townsville: James Cook University. Studies in North Queensland History No. 21.

Mills, M. (2000) 'Issues in implementing boys' programmes in school: Male teachers and empowerment', *Gender and Education,* 12, 2: 221–38.

Mills, M., and Lindgard, B. (1997) 'Masculinity politics, myths and boys' schooling', *British Journal of Educational Studies,* 45: 276–92.

Morgan, B. (2004) 'Teacher identity as pedagogy: towards a field-internal conceptualisation in bilingual and second language education', in J. Brutt-Griffler and M. Varghese (eds), *Bilingualism and Language Pedagogy.* Clevedon and Buffalo, OH: Multilingual Matters.

Murphy, P., and Elwood, J. (1997) *Gendered Experiences, Choices and Achievement – Exploring the Links.* Paper presented at Equity Issues in Gender and Assessment. 23rd Annual Conference of the International Association for Educational Assessment, Durban, South Africa, June 1997.

Noble, C., and Bradford, W. (2000) *Getting it Right for Boys . . . and Girls.* London: Routledge.

Norton, B. (2000) *Identity and Language Learning: Gender, Ethnicity, and Educational Change.* London: Pearson Education.

Norton, B., and Toohey, K. (2004) *Critical Pedagogies and Language Learning.* Cambridge: Cambridge University Press.

O'Brien, J. (2001) 'Children reading critically: A local history', in B. Comber and A. Simpson (eds), *Negotiating Critical Literacies in Classrooms.* Mahwah, NJ, London: Lawrence Erlbaum Associates.

O'Toole, J. (1992) *The Process of Drama: Negotiating Art and Meaning.* London: Routledge.

OFSTED, (1993) *Boys and English.* London: HMSO.

Ortner, S. B. (1996) *Making Gender: The Politics and Erotics of Culture.* Boston: Beacon Press.

Ozolins, U. (1993) *The Politics of Language in Australia.* Cambridge: Cambridge University Press.

Paechter, C. F. (1998) *Educating the Other: Gender, Power and Schooling.* London, Washington DC: The Falmer Press.

Pauwels, A. (1995) 'Linguistic practices and language maintenance among bilingual women and men in Australia', *Nordlyd*, **23**: 21–50.

Pauwels, A. (2004) 'Strengthening scholarship in language study in higher education', in G. Wigglesworth (ed.), *Marking Our Difference: Languages in Higher Education in Australia and New Zealand*. Melbourne: School of Languages and Linguistics, 9–21.

Pauwels, A. (2005) 'Maintaining a language other than English through higher education in Australia', in A. Pauwels (ed.), *Maintaining Minority languages in a Transnational Environment: Australian and European Perspectives*. Melbourne: CAE – Language Australia.

Pauwels, A. (1998) *Women Changing Language*. London: Longman.

Pavlenko, A. (2001) 'Bilingualism, gender and ideology', *International Journal of Bilingualism*, **5**, 2: 117–51.

Pavlenko, A. (2004) 'Gender and sexuality in foreign and second language education: Critical and feminist approaches', in B. Norton, and K. Toohey (eds), *Critical Pedagogies and Language Learning*. Cambridge: Cambridge University Press.

Pavlenko, A., and Blackledge, A. (eds) (2003) *Negotiation of Identities in Multilingual Contexts*. Clevedon and Buffalo, OH: Multilingual Matters.

Pavlenko, A., Blackledge, A., Piller. I., and Teutsch-Dwyer, M. (eds) (2001) *Multilingualism, L2 Learning and Gender*. Berlin: Mouton de Gruyter.

Pease, A., and Pease, B. (2003) *Why Men Don't Listen and Women Can't Read Maps*. 3rd edn, London: Orion Books.

Pennycook, A. (1998) 'Cultural alternatives and autonomy', in P. Benson and P. Voller (eds), *Autonomy and Independence in Language Learning*. London and New York: Longman.

Pennycook, A. (2001) *Critical Applied Linguistics: A (Critical) Introduction*. Mahwah, NJ: Lawrence Erlbaum Associates.

Pennycook, A. (2004) 'Performativity and language studies', *Critical Inquiry in Language Studies: An International Journal*, **1**, 1: 1–19.

Phillips, A. (1994) *The Trouble with Boys*. London: Pandora.

Phillipson, R. (1992) *Linguistic Imperialism*. Oxford and New York: Oxford University Press.

Piper, K. (1997) *Riders in the Chariot: Curriculum Reform and the National Interest, 1965–1995*. Melbourne: ACER Press.

Powell, B. (1986) *Boys, Girls and Language in School*. London: Centre for Information on Language Teaching.

Powell, R. C., and Batters, J. D. (1986) 'Sex of teacher and the image of foreign languages in schools', *Educational Studies*, **12**, 3: 245–54.

Power, S., Whitty, G., Edwards, T., and Wigfall, V. (1998) 'Schoolboys and schoolwork: Gender identification and academic achievement', *International Journal of Inclusive Education: Special Issue on Boys' 'Underachievement'*, **2**, 2: 135–53.

Price, S. (1999) 'Critical discourse analysis: Discourse acquisition and discourse practices', *TESOL Quarterly*, **33**, 3: 581–95.

Pyke, N. (1996) 'Boys "read less than girls" ', *Times Educational Supplement*, 15 March.

QSCC (2000) *Languages Other Than English (LOTE) Key learning Areas 4–10 Syllabus*. Brisbane: Queensland School Curriculum Council.

Quinn, J. (2004) 'The corporeality of learning: Women students and the body', in S. Ali, S. Benjamin and M. L. Mauthner (eds), *The Politics of Gender and Education*. Basingstoke: Palgrave Macmillan.

Ramanathan, V. (2002) *TESOL Education: Writing, Knowledge, Critical Pedagogy*. New York and London: Routledge & Falmer.

Rankin, J. L., Lane, D. J., Gibbons, F.-X., and Gerrard, M. (2004) 'Adolescent self-consciousness: Longitudinal age changes and gender differences in two cohorts', *Journal of Research on Adolescence*, **14**, 1: 1–21.

Raphael Reed, L. (1998) 'Troubling boys and disturbing discourses on masculinity and schooling: A feminist exploration of current debates and interventions concerning boys in school', *Gender and Education*, **11**, 1: 93–110.

Raphael Reed, L. (1999) ' "Zero tolerance": Gender performance and school failure', in S. Johnson, and U. H. Meinhof (eds), *Language and Masculinity*. Oxford: Blackwell.

Riddell, S. (1992) *Gender and the Politics of the Curriculum*. London: Routledge.

Romaine, S. (1994) *Language in Society*. Oxford: Oxford University Press.

Romaine, S. (1999) *Communicating Gender*. Mahwah, NJ: L. Erlbaum.

Ruddock, J. (1999) 'Teacher practice and the student voice', in M. Lang, J. Olson, H. Hansen and W. Bunder (eds), *Changing Schools/Changing Practices: Perspectives on Educational Reform and Teacher Professionalism*. Louvain: Graant.

Sacks, O. (1993) 'Making up the mind', *New York Review of Books*, 8 April: 42–7.

Sadker, M., and Sadker, D. (1985) 'Sexism in the schoolroom of the 80s', *Psychology Today*: 54–7.

Salisbury, J., and Jackson, D. (1996) *Challenging Macho Values: Practical Ways of Working with Adolescent Boys*. London: Falmer Press.

Savignon, S. J. (1991) 'Research on the role of communication in classroom-based foreign language acquisition: On the interpretation, expression and negotiation of meaning', in B. F. Freed (ed.), *Foreign Language Acquisition Research in the Classroom*. Lexington, MA: D. C. Heath.

Skehan, P. (1996) 'Second language acquisition research and task-based instruction', in J. Willis and D. Willis (eds), *Challenge and Change in Language Teaching*. London: Heinemann.

Skelton, C. (1998) 'Feminism and research into masculinities and schooling', *Gender and Education*, **10**: 217–27.

Slee, R., Weiner, G., and Tomlinson, S. (1998) *Challenges to the School Effectiveness and School Improvement Movements*. London: Falmer Press.

Smith, S., and Yamashiro, A. (1998) 'Gender issues in language teaching', *Language Teacher*, **22**, 5: 1–2.

Speed, E. (1998) *Gender Issues and Differential Achievement in Education and Vocational Training: A Research Review*. Manchester: Equal Opportunities Commission.

Spender, D. (1982) *Invisible Women: The Schooling Scandal*. London: The Women's Press.

Stables, A. (1990) 'Differences between pupils from mixed and single-sex schools in their enjoyment of school subjects and in their attitudes to science and to school', *Educational Review*, **42**, 3: 221–30.

Stables, A., and Wikeley, F. (1996) *Pupil Approaches to Subject Option Choices*. Paper presented at European Educational Research Association Conference, Seville, October.

Stern, H. H. (1992) *Issues and Options in Language Teaching*. Oxford: Oxford University Press.

Stobart, G., Elwood, J., and Quinlan, M. (1992) 'Gender bias in examinations: How equal are the opportunities?', *British Educational Research Journal*, **18**: 261–76.

Street, B. (1993) 'Culture is a verb: anthropological aspects of language and cultural process', in *Language and Culture*, British Studies in Applied Linguistics, vol. 7. Clevedon: Multilingual Matters, 23–43.

Sunderland, J. (2000) 'Issues of language and gender in second and FL education', *Language teaching*, 33, 4: 203–23.

Sunderland, J. (2004) 'Classroom interaction, gender, and foreign language learning', in B. Norton, and K. Toohey (eds), *Critical Pedagogies and Language Learning*. Cambridge: Cambridge University Press.

Swann, J. (1988) 'Talk control: An illustration from the classroom of problems in analysing male dominance of conversation', in J. Coates and D. Cameron (eds), *Women in their Speech Communities*. London: Longman.

Swann, J. (1992) *Girls, Boys and Language*. Cambridge, MA, and Oxford: Blackwell.

Talonen, T. (1998) ' "Everyone at school thinks I'm a nerd" – Schoolboys' fights and ambivalence about masculinities', *Young*, 6: 4–18.

Veit, W. F. (1997) 'Misunderstanding as condition of cultural understanding', in M. Lee and M. Hua (eds), *Cultural Dialogue and Misreading*. Broadway, NSW: Wild Peony.

Walkerdine, V. (1989) *Counting Girls Out*. London: Virago.

Walkerdine, V. (1997) 'Redefining the subject in situated cognition theory', in D. Kirshner and J. Whitson (eds), *Situated Cognition. Social, Semiotic and Psychological Perspectives*. Mahwah, NJ: Lawrence Erlbaum.

Wallace, M. (1991) *Training Foreign Language Teachers: A Reflective Approach*. Cambridge: Cambridge University Press.

Warrington, M., Younger, M., and Williams, J. (2000) 'Student attitudes, image and the gender gap', *British Educational Research Journal*, 26, 3: 393–407.

Weedon, C. (1997) *Feminist Practice and Poststructuralist Theory*. 2nd edn, Oxford: Blackwell.

Weiner, G., Arnot, M., and David, M. (1997) 'Is the future female? Female success, male disadvantage and changing gender patterns in education', in A. H. Halsey, P. Brown, H. Lauder and A. Stuart-Wells (eds), *Education, Culture, Economy, Society*. Oxford: Oxford University Press.

Wertheim, M. (1995) *Pythagoras' Trousers: God, Physics and the Gender Wars*. New York: Random House.

Wetherell, M., and Edley, N. (1998) 'Gender practices: Steps in the analysis of men and masculinities', in K. Henwood, C. Griffin and A. Phoenix (eds), *Standpoints and Differences: Essays in the Practice of Feminist Psychology*. London: Sage.

Wikely, F., and Stables, A. (1999) 'Changes in school students' approaches to subject option choices: A study of pupils in the West of England in 1984 and 1996', *Educational Research*, 41, 3: 287–99.

Willis, J. (1992) 'Inner and outer: Spoken discourse in the language classroom', in *Advances in Spoken Discourse Analysis*, M. Coulthard (ed.). London: Routledge.

Willis, J. (1996) *A Framework for Task-Based Learning*. London: Longman.

Yates, L. (1997) 'Gender equity and the boys debate: What sort of challenge is it?', *British Journal of Sociology of Education*, 18: 3337–47.

Zammit, S. (1992) *The Challenge: Choosing to Study a LOTE through High School*. Canberra: DEET and ASSLP.

Author Index

Subject Index

Printed in the United States
70302LV00001B/91-102

9 781403 939678